To Herb –

whose lucid writing I wish I could emulate!! Many thanks for your support.

Harry.

Freedom of Speech

Hellenberg

July 1, 1994

Freedom of Speech

WORDS
ARE NOT
DEEDS

Harry M. Bracken

PRAEGER

Westport, Connecticut
London

Library of Congress Cataloging-in-Publication Data

Bracken, Harry M.
    Freedom of speech : words are not deeds / Harry M. Bracken.
      p. cm.
    Includes bibliographical references and index.
    ISBN 0–275–94719–X
    1. Freedom of speech—United States. 2. Freedom of speech—
Canada. 3. Racism in language. I. Title.
    KF4772.B73 1994
    342.73'0853—dc20
    [347.302853]   93–5444

British Library Cataloguing in Publication Data is available.

Library of Congress Catalog Card Number: 93–5444
ISBN: 0–275–94719–X

First published in 1994

Praeger Publishers, 88 Post Road West, Westport, CT 06881
An imprint of Greenwood Publishing Group, Inc.

Printed in the United States of America

The paper used in this book complies with the
Permanent Paper Standard issued by the National
Information Standards Organization (Z39.48–1984).

10 9 8 7 6 5 4 3 2 1

Copyright Acknowledgments

The author and publisher gratefully acknowledge permission to quote from the
following sources:

Editorial, Lead, *The Globe and Mail* (Canada's National Newspaper), February 29,
1992.

Editorial, "The Right To Be Wrong," *The Globe and Mail* (Canada's National Newspaper), August 31, 1992.

Stanley Fish, "There's No Such Thing as Free Speech and It's a Good Thing Too,"
Boston Review, February 1992 and "Reply" in "Reader's Forum," *Boston Review*,
March/April 1992. Used by permission of Stanley Fish. "There's No Such Thing as
Free Speech and It's a Good Thing Too" first appeared in *Boston Review*.

Eugene D. Genovese, "Heresy, Yes—Sensitivity, No," *The New Republic*, April 15,
1991, p. 30.

In a democracy it is necessary
that people should learn to endure
having their sentiments outraged.
Bertrand Russell

Contents

Acknowledgments

The McCarthy period made me abstractly aware of the role of the First Amendment to the U.S. Constitution in American political life. In the 1960s, I began to encounter some practical problems generated by efforts to implement and defend First Amendment values on a university campus. Discussions at Arizona State University with such friends and former colleagues as Douglas Arner, Myron Caspar, Marvin Fisher, Donald Gieschen, John Livingston, the late Robert Rein'l, and the late Morris Starsky greatly quickened my sensitivity to free-speech issues, and I continue to owe them my profound thanks.

I have also benefited over the years from discussions with, and research material provided by, Paul Austin, Albert Hart, Frits van Holthoon, George Kaufer, Sonya Kaufer, Patrick H. Kelly, F.R.J. Knetsch, Elisabeth Labrousse, D. Terence Langendoen, Thomas Lennon, Richard H. Popkin, Jane Rein'l, Walter Rex, Jeroen van Rijen, Ralph Stephenson, and Richard A. Watson. I am particularly indebted to Noam Chomsky for discussions of this and related topics, for providing me with research material, and for extensive criticisms of earlier drafts; to Elly van Gelderen for assistance with research data and for invaluable critical advice; and to Arnie Herschorn for providing me with vast amounts of legal information and many philosophical queries, objections, and useful philosophical recommendations. With so much excellent assistance, this text ought to be entirely clear and error free. If it is not, it is not their fault.

I wish also to thank Joshua A. Fishman, Shirley Brice Heath, and Robert C. Post. Arjo Vanderjagt and Frits van Holthoon have generously helped make it easier for me to pursue my research the University of Groningen.

Thanks also go to Richard Sillett for his advice, assistance, and patience on editorial matters.

Small portions of this material were read at the 1988 Rotterdam Conference on 18th Century Philosophy and published in *Truth and Tolerance*, ed. E. J. Furcha (Montreal: ARC Supplement #4, Faculty of Religious Studies, McGill University, 1990).

Lake Oscawana, New York

Introduction

I have long been interested in the uses to which certain philosophical ideas and principles have been put in the service of one or another political or ideological doctrine. Some years ago my research was focused on the late seventeenth-century development of racist ideas and their roots in empiricist thought, as well as on the opposition to racism generated within rationalist/dualist thought. As I explored the ways in which empiricist and rationalist/dualist ideas interacted, I realized that many of the same factors were at work in articulating, defending, and attacking the free-speech principle. That realization prompted the research for this book.

In the last decade of the eighteenth century, the Bill of Rights, a series of ten amendments, was appended to the newly framed Constitution of the United States. The First Amendment specifies that "Congress shall make no law . . . abridging the freedom of speech." This radically absolutist formulation appears to have no historical antecedents in earlier declarations. It is, however, my contention that the philosophical foundations of this position can, in whole or in part, be found in the arguments that Pierre Bayle (1647–1706) advances favoring religious toleration. By *philosophical foundations* I have in mind the ontologically grounded mind/body dualism articulated by Descartes and the account of human nature consequent upon it, together with the placing of human speech on the side of mind. Although I am very sympathetic to the absolutist interpretation of the free-speech principle, my concerns in this book are more philosophical and historical than polemical. My second interest is to suggest how, in the light of the more empiricist doctrine of human nature that achieves priority in the nineteenth century, one can understand the shift from "freedom of speech" to "freedom of expression" in U.S. Supreme Court decisions in the twentieth century. Finally, I compare Canadian and American jurisprudence on this topic with particular attention to the erosion in the free-speech principle, often in the interest of so-called group rights, that we can observe today throughout democratic societies.

Freedom of Speech

1

Bayle and the Origins of the Doctrine

The absolutist doctrine of freedom of speech originates in the arguments and discussions of Pierre Bayle (1647–1706). Although Bayle has long been seen as a major figure in literary studies and the history of ideas, his contributions to philosophy have, until recently, largely been ignored in the English-speaking world. Philosophers have, however, become more knowledgeable about Bayle in some measure because of the writings of A. A. Luce and Richard Popkin, writings in which the profound impact of Bayle's thought on both Berkeley and Hume is made evident.[1] Bayle's most famous work, the *Dictionnaire historique et critique*, first published in 1697, is shot through with extended discussions of such topics as atomism, finite/infinite divisibility, sceptical argumentation, historical method, and the primary/secondary quality distinction, as well as a wide range of religious and theological topics, including fideism, atheism, and toleration.

Born into a French Calvinist family, Bayle was eventually obliged to flee France before the limited religious toleration accorded members of the "Églises Réformées de France " under the Edict of Nantes (1598) was, after a score of years of increasing governmental oppression, revoked in 1685.[2] Accurate estimates are difficult to make, but it seems that in excess of 200,000 Huguenots abandoned their worldly goods and often some of their family members and illegally fled France. Many, like Bayle and Pierre Jurieu, found refuge in the Netherlands. Until his death, Bayle remained in Rotterdam where he taught philosophy and history and later edited one of the most important journals of his day, *Les nouvelles de la république des lettres*.

Bayle's older brother remained in France, was sentenced to prison, and died there. There is biographical evidence that Pierre Bayle was deeply hurt and religiously shaken by this event. His monumental *Commentaire philosophique*[3] appears to be written as a response. Given the circumstances, it is a remarkable document. Published initially in 1686 and 1687, it is as close to being a complete defense of religious toleration as appears in the seventeenth or any other century. I believe it also contains the first articulation of a truly "absolutist" theory of freedom of speech.

The title of Bayle's work is *Commentaire philosophique sur ces paroles de Jesus-Christ, contrain les d'entrer*. His goal is to show that Luke 14:23 should not be taken as a biblical justification for coercion in matters of religion. He examines the text and shows that Augustine and other defenders of the persecution of heretics are acting contrary to the clear sense of the Scripture and of universal God-given moral principles. Bayle's use of the Cartesian language of clear and distinct ideas runs throughout his analysis of the words of Luke.

Bayle was well acquainted with Calvinist/Catholic debates over the interpretation of biblical texts, in particular over the Eucharist, that is, over the words *Hoc est corpus meum*. The Calvinists had already appealed to philosophical reasoning in order to circumvent a literal reading of that text. But the Philosopher of Rotterdam goes further: Philosophy is *not* the servant of theology. The theologians tacitly recognize this by their very use of arguments; thus, philosophy stands above theology.[4]

He seeks to establish in the opening portions of the *Commentaire*, as Walter Rex[5] puts it, "that the certitudes of natural light are a *criterium veritatis*" and that the literal interpretation of Luke 14 "is in direct contradiction with these certitudes and is, therefore, false."[6] Along the way, Bayle advances a range of what are often ad hominem arguments in order to strike down the pretensions of Catholic and Protestant supporters of the "compel them to enter" doctrine. Bayle sets out this first set of arguments in terms of certitudes revealed by the natural light—in terms, that is, of Cartesian and Malebranchian principles.

With the second theme in the *Commentaire*,[7] Bayle moves beyond the question of how to interpret the biblical text. He now emphasizes the special role of conscience. This time Bayle argues that we must take seriously the claims of conscience, even of an erring conscience. Hence, we are never entitled to persecute because to do so is to endanger the purity of conscience.[8] The state has no right to interfere with beliefs. Bayle holds that conscience is the voice of God and thus that no human authority can order us to go against our conscience. For Calvinists, conscience has a role connected with the "Way of Examination." One is obliged to examine a biblical text with all due care and deliberation. The judgment then made is sacrosanct. Admittedly, Bayle includes remarks on "obstinacy" and "relativity," but I believe Rex is right in holding that Bayle is *not* arguing from sceptical relativity to toleration: Bayle is *not* saying that because we cannot really prove that one religion is any more true than another, we should therefore be tolerant. Instead, Bayle is grounding toleration on the privileged position conscience holds within Calvinism.[9] The point Rex is making is extremely important. There is a widespread tendency to see toleration toward religious ideas as being the product of scepticism, a product of a realization that truth is a relative notion. Relativistic theories may develop long after Bayle—or Locke, for that matter—but there is no suggestion in the *Commentaire philosophique* that truth is relative. On the contrary, the argument Bayle advances to establish toleration employs an absolutistic doctrine of truth.

Bayle fully appreciates that Calvinism has at its core a doctrine about conscience that makes it impossible to adopt the Catholic thesis about an *informed* conscience. The logic of the Calvinist position leaves no room for an appeal to any sort of ecclesiastical authority that could *inform* us without thereby abandoning the Way of Examination in favor of the Way of Authority. Hence, conscientiously held judgments must be respected. That is the second foundation for Bayle's toleration theory.

A variety of philosophical positions and attitudes show themselves in Bayle's writings, but none is more important than Cartesianism. This is not surprising. Descartes quickly captured the attention of Calvinist theologians in such places as the Protestant Academy at Saumur. "In Descartes," writes Rex, "[the Protestants] acquired a whole philosophical system to reinforce their theory of the role of reason in matters of faith."[10] Moreover, the Oratorians had a Collège at Notre Dame des Ardilliers, and congenial intellectual relations developed with the Protestant academics at Saumur. The Oratorians were also philo-Cartesians, and the order produced one of the greatest Cartesians, Nicolas Malebranche. When Bayle went to study at Geneva in 1670, the young and brilliant Jean-Robert Chouet had recently left Saumur to join Louis Tronchin, his distinguished uncle. They were both expounding the philosophy of Descartes. Malebranche later becomes one of the most important philosophical influences on Bayle.[11]

I have already mentioned that Bayle appeals to the criterion of clear and distinct ideas at the very outset of his argument in the *Commentaire philosophique*. Of course, Bayle often advances Pyrrhonian and Stoic positions, and he enjoys recounting and modernizing the arguments of the atomists, but a range of Cartesian-type positions is apparent in his discussion of toleration. Bayle's remarks on universal moral principles reflect his rationalism, although of a more Malebranchian than a Cartesian sort. Moral knowledge is grounded on innate principles or their Malebranchian equivalents. Thus, more generally, and like most philosophers in the Cartesian tradition, Bayle rejects the empiricist thesis that principles can be abstracted from our sense experience. Second, the concepts innately accessed are, in a logically distinct move, said to be mental. The Cartesian ontology contains two very different substances: mind and body. The thesis that minds are separate and radically distinct substances is not a uniquely Cartesian contribution. It can be found in many scholastics. In any case, I take it that defenses of dualism— or for that matter, of monism—have always proved inconclusive in the sense that what is finally at stake are the several theories of human nature. Rationalism and dualism, although logically distinct, have tended to go together in opposition to the (monist) behaviorist-empiricist theory. Descartes had good reasons for introducing a second substance (e.g., that our creative use of speech cannot be understood in terms of the mechanics available to him).[12] A further contribution to an aspect of Descartes's dualism is his view that all conscious experience is irreducibly dual in the sense of having a subject and an object; one always thinks, and one thinks *about* something.

Third, Descartes, and later Malebranche, subscribe to strict will/intellect and essence/existence distinctions. We can, with perseverance, know the essence of material things but not their existence. We can know the existence of the mind but not its essence. And we have absolutely free wills—a position that Descartes baldly asserts in his reply to Gassendi's objections to the *Meditationes*.

Fourth, one reason Cartesianism was attractive to many Protestants is that its dualist ontology seems to provide a useful way of thinking about mental privacy. The privacy of consciousness is frequently discussed by seventeenth-century Protestant theologians because, for example, if the voice of conscience is the voice of God, how can we tell whether someone is making an honest appeal to conscience? This is crucial not simply because someone might try to defend a criminal action on the ground that it had been done under the direction of conscience. Of much more practical concern was the matter of biblical readings and the purity of intellect essential to an honest textual interpretation. It is not as if dualism helped remove dissemblers and liars. The Protestants knew that there were liars about, and they often feared that Satan, the Prince of Liars, animated the spirits of their own heterodox theologians. But they were also looking for ways to buttress their defenses against Catholics, especially against Catholic efforts to coerce consciences. They knew better than most of us how effective torture techniques are. French Protestants suffered cruelly at the hands of their Catholic brethren in the decades prior to the Revocation of the Edict of Nantes (1685). While a dualist ontology may be no match for thumb screws, it does provide a framework that makes better sense of the Protestants' views about human nature than the empiricist alternative. They could say to their opponents that humans possess souls that are independent of their bodies and that the ontological independence and privacy of these souls ought to be respected. We know that in our own time drugs, sensory deprivation, and lie detectors are used to probe "minds" even by people who do not think there are such entities. And we also know that suspicious inquisitors are often never satisfied that they have probed the innermost corners of their victims' minds. However, what is at stake is espousing an ontology that (or so the Protestants hoped) would have the effect of encouraging people to have more respect for their fellow humans. Echoes of this view are still present in Amnesty International's designation of certain people as "Prisoners of Conscience." On the other hand, a theory of human nature that takes talk about the human spirit to be meaningless may make it more difficult to construct a conceptual framework within which an account of human dignity can be articulated.

Such suggestions about the power and influence of these ideas may seem false or, at least, naive. We do not lack for recent evidence of cruel and inhuman conduct by people who purport to be acting in accord with Christian, Jewish, Muslim, or Hindu religious ideas and values. Yet when we read Bayle's views on toleration, we should recall that he is perhaps the first person to separate the domains of religion and morality by arguing that there is no logical anomaly in conceiving of a highly moral society of atheists. One can be religious and immoral and also nonreligious and moral. His rationalist views on universal natural (moral) law, that is, independent of religion or culture, should be seen in that context.

In any event, the Church was, I suspect, correct in placing Descartes's writings on the *Index Librorum Prohibitorum*. Part of the point to a theory of innate ideas (evident already in Calvin) is that access to God is direct and unmediated by a human "teaching" institution such as the Church. Descartes's struggle with the demon can be understood as his effort to withstand the truth-corroding forces of "external" authority.[13] His rationalism and his dualism were both out of phase with the orthodoxy that the Church was imposing after the Council of Trent. It is not surprising that Bayle and his fellow Protestants find in Descartes positions that are useful to their causes.

I think that Descartes was attractive to a number of seventeenth-century thinkers not because they were convinced by the filigree details in his philosophical arguments. Descartes was attractive, illuminating, and influential because his ideas made sense to people and meshed with their own experience. Some contemporary philosophers seek to demonstrate that this or that argument in Descartes's *Discours* or *Meditationes* is invalid. However interesting such discussions may be, it is not the precise structure of his arguments that makes him such a dominating figure in the seventeenth century. Those philosophers who persist in trying to show that what Descartes says is false, confused, or trivial[14] are not employed by the publishers of the *Index*, but, as I mention below, they, too, have ideological axes to grind.[15]

At the center of Bayle's theory of the erring conscience, a theory essential to his account of toleration, is Cartesian dualism. Bayle distinguishes the mental as inner from the body as outer.[16] He discusses mind/body (non)interaction. In fact, Bayle moves much beyond Descartes. Descartes's domain of clear and distinct ideas purported to be objective. But the effect of according conscience such a preeminent role is that Bayle makes the mind totally private. He makes the basis for judgment rest on our innermost feelings (*sentiment intérieur*).[17] The thesis that truth is ultimately discerned in feeling, that it is in taste that our awareness of truth is revealed, is a doctrine also found in Jurieu. If it is true that the most basic difference between Catholicism and Calvinism is that Calvinism rejects the possibility of a natural theology,[18] it becomes easy to see why that radically anti-authoritarian notion should generate the doctrine of the erring conscience. However, as Calvin's execution of Servetus shows, theory does not always accord with practice.

In summary, for Bayle, minds are not physical, and they cannot be probed by the physical. We can coerce the body, but we should not try thereby to coerce the mind. Because the mind is seen as private and ontologically distinct, we can never tell from the actions of the body whether an expressed view is being conscientiously (i.e., in good faith) held. Since our conscientiously held religious views are about our relations to God, and because we have access only to our own conscience, it follows that we cannot know what anyone *really* thinks. This move is not based on doubts we may all entertain about the possibility of this sort of human knowledge. It is not a sceptical move. Bayle is making a positive claim about knowledge, namely, that because of ontological considerations, we *cannot* know other minds. This is another instance where Bayle's defense of toleration is not based on sceptical considerations. In brief, we should not try to coerce consciences, although we can force people to behave in certain ways and to say certain things. Christianity, Bayle maintains, obliges its members to respect consciences. Bayle, as I note above, sees in a whole cluster of Cartesian ideas a way of encouraging respect for the human spirit. Those who practice persecution should reflect on the fact that we have in principle no way to determine what effects our persecutions, our uses of torture, and the like, have on the conscience or spirit itself. Whether the various Cartesian constituents that form the basis for Bayle's theory of toleration can do the persuasive task he assigns them is of course debatable. But he is seeking to provide a moral argument, not a mathematical demonstration.

The theory of the erring conscience is accepted by many of Bayle's contemporaries. But he carries it further and finds himself faced with a profound difficulty. What do we do with the murderer who makes an appeal to conscience? More embarrassing, how can one deal with inquisitors, with persecutors, who justify their use of torture by appeals to conscientiously held beliefs?[19]

The direction Bayle is following in trying to arrive at a solution to the problem of the murderer who appeals to conscience seems, first, to be his retention of the distinction between words as physical and their mental counterparts ("meanings") that he mentions at the outset[20] and, second, his acceptance of the Cartesian radical distinction between talk and action exactly parallel to that between mind and body. It is clear from his text that what Bayle wants is absolute toleration of religious *talk*—not religious *action*—but Bayle never quite says that. He never quite says that the persecutor who appeals to conscience is entitled to freedom of speech but not freedom of action.[21] But that is what I take him to be getting at because he explicitly rules out a right to public displays of religiosity.[22] Bayle wants us to be able to think and talk, to study, learn, and pray, without any interference from the secular arm. He does not argue that freedom of thought or freedom of speech is a good thing to be justified on pragmatic or consequentialist grounds. The domain of the secular authority is simply action—not our thoughts *or* their verbal expression.[23]

Pierre Jurieu, ever alert for an opportunity to take Bayle to task, offers various arguments against toleration, although after the Revocation he defends a limited doctrine of group autonomy as a device for holding that a large group, that is, the French Protestant community, should be tolerated. But he vigorously opposed the doctrine of freedom of speech. As early as 1683 he denies that the tongue has any privileged status. Our tongue is linked to our spirit exactly as our hand is. Accordingly, since the magistrate is entitled to restrain the hand, he is entitled to constrain the tongue.[24] This technique of assimilating talk to action finds expression in the straightforwardly antidualist models of the nineteenth and twentieth centuries.

It is out of materials derived from his Calvinist theory of conscience, his interpretation of the Bible in terms of clarity and distinctness, his Cartesian theory of mind/body dualism, and his theory of mental privacy that Bayle constructs a philosophical framework within which absolute religious toleration and, I suggest, absolute freedom of speech are direct consequences. There is thus a close relationship between his Cartesian-style theory of human nature and freedom of speech. Moreover, there are still echoes of his doctrine within modern absolutist views.

I mention Descartes on language because the special status accorded speech was a common concern of philosophers. Sounds may be physical, but the primary role of language is to express our thoughts. When Bayle defends the rights of an erring conscience, it is my contention that he recognizes the primary issue to be whether one can give *verbal expression* to one's thoughts and religious beliefs. If one takes freedom of thought simply to mean that one is free to *think* what one will, rather than to be able to speak one's thoughts, it is difficult to understand what role such a "freedom" can play in a political system.[25] However, when a state insists on absolute conformity of thought and action, then oaths are often used to "externalize" the contents of minds.[26] It is because speech has a uniquely mental dimension as a bearer of human meanings that it falls on the side of mind. Indeed, for Descartes and the Cartesians it is not only evidence for the existence of human minds but also of our free wills. Seventeenth-century philosophers were also aware not only of God's capacity to communicate with us without the mediation of material things but also of the role of angels. Although there is an understandable tendency in a secular world not to take the remarkably extensive talk about angels seriously, perhaps we should think of angels as the thought-experiments of medieval and early modern philosophers and theologians to explore the problems posed by pure minds. Thus, medieval thinkers not only ask how such minds can be individuated or accorded spatial location, or given causal powers in the material world, but also how they can express their ideas and communicate among themselves and to us. In other words, such reflections tilt the scale toward the mental when deciding the ontological status of language. They are virtually omnipresent in discussions of minds versus bodies, their interaction, and the priority of mind in expressing and communicating thoughts.[27]

Chomsky[28] has reminded us how important language and speech are within the Cartesian system. It is the human capacity to speak and understand that constitutes that feature whereby we are distinguished from other animals. And it is because of our unique capacity to innovate linguistically, to speak free of stimulus control, to reply in discourse appropriately, in brief because of these characteristics (already specified by Descartes [*Discours*, 5] and which Chomsky discusses under the rubric "the creative aspect of language use") that Descartes introduces mind as a second substance. He introduces this second substance because the linguistic properties he observed could not be explained in terms of the mechanics he had available to him.

Cartesian dualism was thus formulated with a fairly clear account of "body" or material substance. Today we no longer employ that notion of matter. Instead, our accounts of the constituent "parts" of "matter" now increase in complexity with each extension of our physical theories. When we reject dualism today by denying the existence of mind, we are not left with Descartes's material substance, even if some rejections of dualism suggest exactly that. However scientific exploration of the mind and brain proceeds, there is no reason to let fear of dualism block study of the mind. The matter that makes up the *body* half of the traditional mind/body discussion is no longer intelligible, and we are still seeking to increase the adequacy of such explanations of the "mental" as we currently have.

I have discussed some of these questions elsewhere. I have argued that while Cartesian rationalism and dualism are logically independent notions, they can function in combination to support a doctrine of human nature.[29] That is, *rationalism* helps make sense of human autonomy and freedom in that humans are not seen as blank tablets ready to be molded at someone's will. Dualism, on the other hand, *helps* provide a moral context in which mental privacy is sustained ontologically and our minds are somewhat protected from scrutiny. Finally, Descartes's doctrine of human nature includes a commitment to unrestricted freedom of will. This bears on the role of speech as not being a form of action. We are completely free to act, or not to act, on the basis of what we hear or read. Language does not, as it were, coerce us. If we are persuaded by what we hear, that is *our own choice*. Descartes presents a form of this hard doctrine in *Meditationes*, 4, when he tries to establish that we cannot err if we refrain from judging as true that which is not clear and distinct.

Theories of human nature, for example, empiricism and rationalism, are compounds of accounts that are thought to be grounded in "facts" or scientific claims or various commonsensical opinions as well as social, political, ethical, or religious values. That is why debates over learning theories, how concepts are acquired, the teaching of languages, are generally so heated. I find that the rationalist argument from language acquisition possesses explanatory power that behaviorist and earlier empiricist efforts lack. And that provides the rationalist theory of human nature with a certain strength.[30] Defenders of the empiricist picture, like John Locke, in the end rely on Aristotle's dogma that there is "nothing in the intellect which is not first in the senses." The traditional proof of this dogma is that if we lack a sense channel, we lack the concepts appropriate to that channel. Whether the argument from blindness can establish the empiri*cist* thesis with respect to learning and concept acquisition has often been challenged. If one means that the blind can't see, that is merely true by definition; if one means the blind can't use the language of color, it is false. Thus, in neither case does it constitute an argument in support of the empiricist claim.[31] Theories of human nature bear directly on such things as our "worldview," our ideological commitments, our notions of what is a reasonable topic for research in the so-called social sciences. Obviously how we think about humans directly informs our beliefs about social and political structures. It is my thesis that the rationalist model provides the basis for Bayle's absolutist position with respect to religious toleration and freedom of speech.

The Cartesian theory also contains modest defenses against treating humans as malleable as well as against racism and sexism, since color and sex predicates do not apply to Cartesian minds. I do not doubt that with sufficient ingenuity a Cartesian racist theory could have been produced. Such an expenditure of effort was not required. With his attack on the notion of substance, and by radically revising the traditional doctrine of essence and accident, Locke advanced a theory in which not only could humans be treated as malleable, but their skin color could count as an essential property.[32] In this way, empiricist theories functioned historically to provide, for example, a basis for racism (Locke and Hume) and sexism (Aristotle and Thomas). The cluster of ideas that constitutes a given theory of human nature does not, for example, include (or exclude) racism as a matter of strict logical necessity. Nevertheless, theories of human nature are extremely useful because they can and do facilitate one or another political agenda. Thus, it is not logically contradictory to suppose that religious toleration or, more relevant to present purposes, freedom of speech, can be defended within a nondualist theory of human nature. However, it appears that as a matter of historical fact freedom of speech developed from within a Cartesian-type theory and was undermined from within an empiricist-type theory. I believe that such uses of doctrines of human nature are not historical accidents.

Bayle's *Commentaire philosophique* marks the high point in the development of religious toleration. Despite the suffering imposed on him by a

Catholic state, he is recommending total and absolute toleration of Catholics, Socinians, and so on. Bayle rejects the "reciprocity" argument, later given wide currency by Locke, that one should extend toleration only to groups that advocate toleration themselves. Locke, who is generally seen as the patron saint of religious toleration in the English-speaking world, remains a fanatical anti-Catholic in his writings on toleration.[33] He does not accord primacy to conscience.

Although it is sometimes said that John Locke is the philosopher of the American Revolution, the freedom of speech principle incorporated into the U.S. Constitution ("Congress shall make no law . . . abridging the freedom of speech") at the end of the eighteenth century is not Lockean. This First Amendment principle is totally unqualified. It is a Baylean absolutist move. I have found little said at the time either for or against freedom of speech, although the intentions of the American Founding Fathers have long been explored, discussed, and debated by legislators, judges, scholars, and presidential candidates, as has been the question of the judicial significance of such intentions even in instances where they can be discerned. The free-speech clause is a radical addition to the other, and at the time more familiar, constituents of the First Amendment.

Both Jefferson and Madison were acquainted with Bayle's *Dictionnaire*.[34] I cannot, however, present evidence that Madison got from Bayle that absolutist idea of freedom of speech which he incorporated into the First Amendment. Nor have I yet discovered whether Madison could have had access to the *Commentaire philosophique*.[35] The 1708 English translation was in Jefferson's library (which Madison used), but its accession date is apparently not known. My suggestion is that Madison, as a (the?) major influence in the drafting of the First Amendment, inserted the absolutist free-speech clause because he, and probably others, took it to be a self-evident principle, rooted in a Bayle-type philosophical framework. What is obvious, however, is that the framework soon became less acceptable and the principle did not long remain self-evident. Indeed, some of the very framers of the Constitution supported the Sedition Act of 1798, and it seems clear that a number of political figures thought there was no incompatibility between the free-speech clause and seditious libel. Seditious libel carried over via the common law and Blackstone's *Commentaries*. According to Blackstone (and common law) and even among many of the American lawyers, truth was *not* a defense in any sort of libel action.[36]

By the middle of the nineteenth century, what had been more or less clear to a number of so-called Enlightenment figures was in need of a defense. Although Bayle is a major influence on Voltaire, Voltaire, like many other eighteenth-century figures, is philosophically more under Locke's[37] influence than Descartes's. For Bayle, freedom of speech and religious toleration follow naturally from philosophical positions. Subsequent debate challenges these Cartesian philosophical foundations and hence gradually creates the need to defend freedom of speech and religious toleration in themselves and on new grounds.

The most significant English-language contribution to the discussion of freedom of speech between the U.S. Bill of Rights (1791) and World War I is John Stuart Mill's *On Liberty* (1859).[38] It remains the classical defense of freedom of opinion and expression. Because Mill gives a range of good reasons for supporting this freedom, primarily in terms of the advantages that should accrue to a society which thus encourages the quest for truth and the intellectual and moral growth of its individual members (cf. chap. 3), *On Liberty* has proven to be an extremely influential document. Mill is considering these issues in the context of his commitment to democracy and self-government, a commitment that it should be remembered he did not extend to, for example, Indians or the Irish.[39] He wants us to see freedom of expression as a value essential to democracy and self-government. Regardless of whether one accepts the philosophical account I give of the First Amendment's free-speech clause, the fact is that the clause comes to us without reasons or arguments of any sort. On the other hand, however flawed we may find Mill's arguments, they continue to serve as an eloquent, extended, and provocative defense of freedom of expression.

Mill makes clear that he is extremely apprehensive about the control over opinions exercised by tyrannical institutions, and he worries that majorities will encroach on the freedom of the individual. He believes that a great battle was successfully waged against the Catholic church on behalf of "freedom of conscience as an indefeasible right" (11). Mill's strongest, but immediately contradicted, claim is that the "appropriate region of human liberty . . . comprises, first, the inward domain of consciousness, demanding liberty of conscience in the most comprehensive sense, liberty of thought and feeling, *absolute freedom of opinion and sentiment on all subjects*, practical or speculative, scientific, moral, or theological" (16, emphasis added). Most of *On Liberty* is devoted to providing reasons that are intended to persuade us to accept the principle of liberty. Mill argues that we run the risk that any opinion we wish to suppress may be true. "All silencing of discussion is an assumption of infallibility" (21–22). Moreover, even when an opinion is deemed to be true, its clarity is enhanced by the conflict with dissenting opinions. An opinion preserved by authority from conflict with other views "will be in danger of being lost and enfeebled" (14). Mill also rejects the view that free expression should be limited by "the bounds of fair discussion" (64) because it is practically impossible in any given case to determine those bounds.

Nevertheless, there is a basic flaw in Mill's position, and it appears to be irremediable. However much Mill fears the power of various institutions and the oppression one may encounter from the tyranny of the majority, he is prepared to grant that "the only purpose for which power can be rightfully exercised over any member of a civilized community, against his will, is harm to others" (13). He thus breaks with the absolutist tradition while at the same time giving us no guidelines for calculating, no less scaling, harms. He does not say what time periods are relevant. At the outset of chapter 3, Mill writes:

Even opinions lose their immunity when the circumstances in which they are expressed are such as to constitute their expression a positive instigation to some mischievous act. An opinion that corn dealers are starvers of the poor, or that private property is robbery, ought to be unmolested when simply circulated through the press, but may justly incur punishment when delivered orally to an excited mob assembled before the house of a corn dealer, or when handed about among the same mob in the form of a placard. (67–68)

Can we hold that Marx's "incitement" to revolution has harmful consequences such that his text should be suppressed? Or the American Declaration of Independence? (Presumably, it is on some such consequentialist version of the harm principle that many European countries ban Hitler's *Mein Kampf*.) How are we to decide which, if any, psychological harms are to count, or even the number of people that must be involved before a harm truly matters?

"Absolute freedom" is mentioned only once. The fact that the harm principle occurs frequently indicates that it represents his considered view. He is fully prepared to penalize expression whenever there may be untoward overt acts consequent upon it (cf. 20, n. 1 [chap. 2]), but he is always silent on guidelines. And most startling: "The liberty of the individual must be thus far limited; he must not make himself a nuisance to other people" (68). We have come some distance from that absolute freedom he speaks of earlier. We are no longer dealing with an "excited mob" but with a single individual who is deemed a "nuisance." And yet Mill also says that "[t]here are many who consider as an injury to themselves any conduct which they have a distaste for, and resent it as an outrage to their feelings," as when a "religious bigot" is offended by the opinions of others (102 [chap. 3]). That is, Mill seems to want to allow "offensive speech" up to the point that it becomes a *nuisance* to someone, but one should be free to offend a religious bigot. Presumably, racist, pornographic, or libelous speech falls on the nuisance side. As he comments in the same chapter, "As soon as any part of a person's conduct affects prejudicially the interests of others, society has jurisdiction over it, and the question whether the general welfare will or will not be promoted by interfering with it becomes open to question" (92). I think it is correct to say that what Mill *wants* is a distinction between speech as "incitement" and speech as mere "advocacy." Given the examples Mill himself provides, his own distinction seems based on nothing beyond "whose ox is being gored." The history of American Supreme Court efforts to make, in effect, Mill's distinction by applying the *clear and present danger criterion* provides no reassurance.

In the end, he appears to consider all expression as action; and if action, then potentially harmful; and if potentially harmful, then legitimately suppressible. Even when Mill contrasts the "inward" with the "outward," his remarks are not part of a larger theory of human nature. The most that can be said for them is that they mark a transition from taking conscience and consciousness as inward to treating all talk and opinion as *action*. Thus, Mill may be acknowledging the evolution of mind from a time when it was ontologically distinct and the inaccessible bearer of conscience to a more nondualist version—a monist version with which he is philosophically more comfortable.

Beyond that I cannot explain why Mill ever talks about absolute freedom. It really has no place in his philosophical system, although it fits with the dualist model some of Mill's contemporary readers might have still accepted. Despite standing in opposition to the theses of *On Liberty*, Mill does not delete the expression. Instead, he eviscerates it in two ways: first, by giving "absolute freedom" only to unexpressed thoughts. That is, you can *think* nuisance thoughts; you cannot speak them. That is why I think Mill may use this notion of unexpressed thought to remind us of a tradition from which his own ideas evolved but that he no longer accepts. Second, as soon as thoughts are verbally expressed, they fall under restrictions and constraints. Finally, the absolute freedom passage is not only surrounded by passages in which restrictions on freedom are specified; the expression, as already noted, never again occurs.[40]

Quite apart from the difficulties of establishing the causal efficacy of words, of formally distinguishing nonoffensive from harmful speech, and of calculating consequences in both a short and an indefinitely long run once psychological harm is included, Mill never faces the fact that virtually all speech offends someone. As U.S. Supreme Court Justice Oliver Wendell Holmes, Jr., remarked in *Gitlow v. New York* (1925), "Every idea is an incitement."[41] Although Mill advances a range of extremely influential arguments on behalf of freedom of opinion and expression, for which we should be eternally grateful, in the end he undercuts his own arguments. In short, Mill is not an absolutist. There are unspecified and, within his framework, unspecifiable conditions under which the risks that may be generated by expression warrant their suppression. He thus denies the absolute freedom he affirms.

One may wish to say that Mill should have drawn a distinction between that speech which might be considered to be an immediate part of a criminal act versus speech that is only an expression of ideas and opinions, even the opinion that one should engage in criminal action. The speech whereby the Salvadoran Jesuits were ordered killed might count as the first sort of speech, and a plea for the creation of an armed force to eliminate members of group X might be of the second sort. But even this gloss on Mill is not without its difficulties. First of all, neither the members of Mill's "mob" nor the Salvadoran executioners are automata deprived of the responsibility for their actions. Second, it is one thing to argue that certain words are morally reprehensible and quite another to show they are genuine violations of some nation's existent law and not merely contrary to some ex post facto principles. Thus, the more spectacular cases of speech one would proscribe are likely to escape one's net. Third, if speech can (in terms of the first alternative) be considered an actual part of a criminal action, and if a country's criminal code counts certain expressions of opinion to be criminal actions, then it is hard to see how one can avoid saying that the distinction one hoped would defend, à la Mill, a restricted version of freedom of speech, appears to collapse. One seems to end up having to proscribe the very sorts of speech that one's revised Millian principle was intended to protect.

Once *speech* is translated as "expression" and is then taken to be action, it is deprived of the categorial distinctness it possesses within Bayle's account. Like other actions, it falls more readily under the power of the state. Although today we retain our concern with free speech as a democratic value, we now need to provide arguments for it, and we find it easy to set limits on it. One reason for this is that the philosophical framework has changed. I am not able to explain why it has changed. I want only to mention that the worldview that Bayle and Descartes articulated, and that a number of their contemporaries accepted, is no longer in force. The rejection of mind/body dualism and the rejection of mental privacy were generally followed—at least in the English-speaking world—with the acceptance of an empiricist-behaviorist doctrine of human nature, although, on occasion, dualism and empiricism-behaviorism were both rejected. This is how Quentin Skinner puts his rejection of the categorial distinction: "The idea that speech is also action, that to say something is always and *eo ipso* to do something, had of course been emphasized by many philosophers of language before [J. L.] Austin. The central insight is most economically conveyed by Wittgenstein's remark that 'words are also deeds.' "[42]

NOTES

1. A. A. Luce, *The Dialectic of Immaterialism* (London: Hodder and Stoughton, 1963), esp. chap. 4. See also Richard H. Popkin, "Berkeley and Pyrrhonism" in *The High Road to Pyrrhonism*, ed. Richard A. Watson and James E. Force (San Diego: Austin Hill, 1980). An especially important paper in this connection is Jean-Paul Pittion, "Hume's Reading of Bayle: An Inquiry into the Source and Role of the Memoranda," *Journal of the History of Philosophy* 15 (1977): 373–386. See also my "On Some Points in Bayle, Berkeley, and Hume," *History of Philosophy Quarterly* 4 (1987): 435-446; and my "Bayle, Berkeley, and Hume," *Eighteenth-Century Studies* 11 (1977–78): 227–245.

2. For a discussion of this tortured period, see the prize-winning study by Elisabeth Labrousse, *"Une foi, une loi, un roi?" La Révocation de l'édit de Nantes* (Geneva: Labor et Fides, 1985).

3. Pierre Bayle, *Oeuvres diverses*, 4 vols. (Den Haag: Husson et al., 1727–31), vol. 2.

4. Ibid., vol. 2, 368a.

5. The definitive study of Bayle's life and work is Elisabeth Labrousse, *Pierre Bayle*, 2 vols. (Den Haag: Nijhoff, 1963–64). See also Gianni Paganini, *Analisi della fede e critica della ragione nella filosofia di Pierre Bayle* (Firenze: La Nuova Italia, 1980); idem, *Scepsi moderna: Interpretazioni dello scetticismo da Charron a Hume* (Cosenza: Busento, 1991). As is obvious, I am very much indebted to the insightful work of Walter Rex, *Essays on Pierre Bayle and Religious Controversy* (Den Haag: Nijhoff, 1965). I also discuss Rex's study in my *Mind and Language: Essays on Descartes and Chomsky* (Dordrecht: Foris, 1984).

6. Rex, *Essays*, 163.

7. Cf. pt. 1, chap. 1, but see Bayle, *OD*, vol. 2, 533b.

8. For example, Bayle, *OD*, vol. 2, 395ab.

9. Although Catholics have a doctrine of conscience, one that has received consideration since Vatican II, it traditionally was always subject to Church authority, whereby it was said to be *informed*, rather than as an independent source of truth.

10. Rex, *Essays*, 124.

11. See my essay "The Malebranche–Arnauld Debate: Philosophical or Ideological?" in *Nicolas Malebranche: His Philosophical Critics and Successors*, ed. Stuart Brown (Assen/Maastricht: Van Gorcum, 1991), 35–48.

12. Cf. Noam Chomsky, *Language and Mind* (New York: Harcourt, Brace & World, 1968), 6.

13. See my "Descartes-Orwell-Chomsky: Three Philosophers of the Demonic," chap. 6, in my *Mind and Language*.

14. Discussions of Descartes on such things as dualism or privacy or scepticism invariably "perplex" contemporary philosophers. This perplexity is largely created by the later Wittgenstein's analysis of the so-called private-language-argument. A difficulty is generally said to arise from what is *said* to be Descartes's account of pains. Cartesian pains are said to be private, but if private sensations were the bearers of the meaning of language, language would be private, and each individual would have his or her own private language. And that, it is asserted, contradicts the "fact" that language is a social institution. Languages are social institutions, intended, it is again asserted, for communication, in which meaning is learned publicly. Whatever Wittgenstein may have meant by the private-language-argument, few features of his philosophy have generated so many differing interpretations. See Ludwig Wittgenstein, *Philosophical Investigations* (London: Macmillan, 1953). See also Anthony Kenny, "Cartesian Privacy," in his *The Anatomy of the Soul* (Oxford: Blackwell, 1973).

15. See the informative paper by Richard Rorty, "Wittgenstein, Privileged Access, and Incommunicability," *American Philosophical Quarterly* 7 (1970):192–205. Although several of what are said to be Descartes's central theses (or rather, "fallacies") are discussed (no citations), there are difficulties that would take me outside my present attempt to make some sense of Bayle's philosophical background. Very briefly, it is generally accepted by Wittgenstein and his followers that the point to language is communication. It is not obvious how one might set about proving that thesis. Moreover, it is a thesis Descartes rejects. Second, there is widespread agreement among philosophers (although less so today among psychologists) that behaviorism provides the most fruitful theory of learning—or more crudely, that imitation and repetition are the *essential* features of the child's

linguistic learning experience. Neither Descartes nor the modern rationalists make that claim. Third, there is a textual problem. In Descartes's own theory, knowledge claims are not about sensations; they are about *ideas,* and although ideas are innate, each of us has access to identical ones. Despite the large twentieth-century literature on Descartes on pains, pains do not receive much attention in Descartes. The role of sensory data in, for example, the *Meditationes* [2] gives no support to the "private language" reading, and I find no support for the privacy interpretation in the oft-cited passages at *Principia philosophiae,* pt. 1, § 43. See my *Mind and Language,* chap. 1. But my concern here is not to present a brief for Descartes. The features that I here ascribe to Descartes are those that are influential in seventeenth- and eighteenth- century thought.

16. Bayle, *OD,* pt. 1, chaps. 1 and 2.

17. Bayle, *OD,* vol. 2, 439a. See also 397a, 407b, and esp. 441a. On the question of taste and feeling as articulated by Pierre Jurieu, see my *Mind and Language,* chap. 5.

18. See my "Bayle's Attack on Natural Theology: The Case of Christian Pyrrhonism," in *Scepticism and Irreligion in the Seventeenth and Eighteenth Centuries,* eds. Richard H. Popkin and Arjo Vanderjagt (Dordrecht: Brill, 1993), 254–266.

19. Bayle, *OD,* vol. 2, 430a.

20. Ibid., 369ab, 371ab.

21. Indeed, at pt. 2, chaps. 10 and 11, Bayle even appears to reverse field. He says that God cares only that one's decisions accord with one's conscience (439a). Rex maintains that "although time after time Bayle seems ready to sacrifice examination in favor of fallible persuasion, and the relativity of conscience seems to obliterate everything else, Bayle reminds us that conscience, after all, must be based on examination, thereby sending us back again to the absolutes so forcefully expressed in the first volume" (Rex, *Essays,* 185). Bayle's argument at this point is tortured. His personal involvement with the issues of toleration and persecution drive these sections. Some of his stranger remarks suggest that what he is seeking to do is to present an elaborate *reductio* of the *contrain-les d'entrer* thesis by showing that if it is strictly pursued, the result can be that a True Church can properly be persecuted since a False Church can also claim to be conscience driven. For his usual insightful remarks on these bewildering chapters, see idem, 177–193.

22. Bayle, *OD,* vol. 2, 414a. In this connection, see Labrousse, *Pierre Bayle,* vol. 2, chaps. 18 and 19.

23. The failure to draw some such distinction creates difficulties for systems within which a guarantee to religious freedom is maintained. People then claim an exemption from the application of ordinary criminal statutes on the ground of religious freedom. Thus, a group may claim a religious right to use violence to discipline their children; to prevent women from being educated; or to discriminate in employment, education, or housing on racial, religious, or sexual grounds. John Locke, however, does not get into the problem because he does not base his theory of toleration on conscience. There are practical reasons, for example, enhancing peace within the society, for encouraging toleration. Power remains in the hands of the magistrate. Cf. John Locke, *Epistola de Tolerantia: A Letter on Toleration,* ed. with a Preface by Raymond Klibansky, trans., Introduction, and Notes by J. W. Gough (Oxford: Clarendon, 1968), 111. See also James Tully's introduction to his edition of Locke, *Letter Concerning Toleration* (Indianapolis: Hackett, 1983); and his

"Toleration, Scepticism and Rights: John Locke and Religious Toleration," in *Truth and Tolerance*, ed. E. J. Furcha (Montreal: ARC Supplement #4, Faculty of Religious Studies, McGill University, 1990), 13–27.

24. Pierre Jurieu, *Histoire du Calvinisme . . .*, vol. 2 (Rotterdam: Reinier Leers, 1683), 279. For a discussion of Jurieu's compilation and editing methods for the *Histoire*, see the various papers by F.R.J. Knetsch and his definitive study *Pierre Jurieu: Theoloog en Politikus der Refuge* (Kampen: J. H. Kok, 1967), esp. 164. On Bayle and Jurieu, see the balanced and careful analysis by Herbert Schlossberg, "Pierre Bayle and the Politics of the Huguenot Diaspora" (Ph.D. diss., University of Minnesota, 1965).

25. Spinoza, in his *Tractatus-Theologico-Politicus* (Amsterdam: Christ. Conrad, 1670) discusses "Freedom of thought and speech" in chap. 20. However, it is evident from his discussion of seditious speech that he does not subscribe to the sharp speech/action distinction I ascribe to Descartes and Bayle.

26. See "Minds and Oaths," chap. 4, in my *Mind and Language*.

27. Cf. Gerard de Cordemoy, *Six discours sur la distinction & l'union du corps & de l'ame*, Discours 5, pt. 1 (148), and 27, and *Un discours physique de la parole* (248), both in his *Oeuvres philosophiques*, ed. Pierre Clair and François Girbal (Paris: PUF, 1968). Cordemoy discusses the physical aspect of speech (i.e., sound) and the mental meaning we use speech to express. He also holds that angels, although pure spirits, can communicate with us *without* voices. (Cf. *Discours*, pt. 2, 250.) See also Desmond Connell, *The Vision in God: Malebranche's Scholastic Sources* (Louvain: Éditions Nauwelaerts, 1967). He shows that Malebranche is indebted to Suarez's account of angels. See Helen S. Lang, "Bodies and Angels: The Occupants of Place for Aristotle and Duns Scotus," *Viator* 14 (1983): 245–266: "The problem of locating mind in a body for Descartes and his followers perfectly parallels Duns's problem of putting angels in place" (266). See also Louis De La Forge, *Traité de l'esprit de l'homme*, esp. chap. 10 in his *Oeuvres philosophiques*, ed. Pierre Clair (Paris: PUF, 1974).

28. Cf. Chomsky's *Cartesian Linguistics* (New York: Harper & Row, 1966) and *Reflections on Language* (New York: Pantheon, 1975), esp. chap. 4.

29. See my *Mind and Language*, esp. chap. 1.

30. This and related themes have been discussed by Chomsky from his earliest writings to the present. See his *Knowledge of Language: Its Nature, Origin, and Use* (New York: Praeger, 1986). For an illuminating discussion of the empirical as well as the methodological sides of these issues, see, for example, Norbert Hornstein and David Lightfoot, eds., *Explanation in Linguistics: The Logical Problem of Language Acquisition* (London: Longman, 1981), esp. essays 1 and 2.

31. This is discussed in Peter Geach, *Mental Acts* (London: Routledge & Kegan Paul, s.d. [1958]).

32. In "Essence, Accident and Race" and "Philosophy and Racism," chaps. 2 and 3 in my *Mind and Language*, I show in detail how Locke's philosophy facilitated the articulation of racist theory. In a word, this is accomplished by means of his antiessentialism (while retaining the old terminology), his allowing us to tally what we will in the forming of (nominal) essences for all things including humans, his thereby permitting a species "spectrum" from higher to lower humans (at *An Essay Concerning Human Understanding* [1690], ed. Peter H. Nidditch [Oxford: Clarendon, 1975], bk. 3, vi, § 23, Locke mentions that "if History lie not, Women

have conceived by [man-] Drills"), and his appeal to the blank tablet account of minds. Hume's explicit white-supremacist views, added as a note (probably for the first time) to the 1753 edition of his essay "Of National Characters," are perhaps better known. See my aforementioned papers.

33. See my *Mind and Language*, chap. 5, and my "Toleration Theories: Bayle vs. Locke," in *The Notion of Tolerance and Human Rights: Essays in Honour of Raymond Klibansky*, ed. Ethel Groffier and Michel Paradis (Ottawa: Carleton University Press, 1991), 1-11.

34. The first edition appeared in 1697, the second, in 1701. Bayle died in Rotterdam in 1706. There were several posthumous editions in French in the eighteenth century as well as at least two English translations. The *Dictionnaire* is a mine of arguments and discussions of religious doctrines, arguments, and polemics (as well as historical and philosophical matters). Toleration themes frequently occur.

35. My thanks to J.C.A. Stagg, editor of the Madison papers; John Catanzariti, editor of the Jefferson papers; James N. Green of the Library Company of Philadelphia; and James Gilreath of the Library of Congress, for help on this question.

36. Two states, Pennsylvania and Vermont, had free-speech, free-press clauses in their constitutions prior to the Bill of Rights. But the opinions of the Founding Fathers were many and often contradictory. A more libertarian theory (but still circumscribed with respect to the enactment of seditious libel legislation by states) emerges only in the aftermath of the Sedition Act. For an extremely detailed as well as wide-ranging and historically informed analysis of the formulation of the Bill of Rights and the development in the understanding and interpretation of the First Amendment, including the views of Madison and Jefferson and such later figures as St. George Tucker and Tunis Wortman, see Leonard W. Levy, *Emergence of a Free Press* (New York: Oxford, 1985). Levy is concerned with the free-press clause of the First Amendment—hence, his interest in the English background. I am concerned with the free-speech clause—hence, my interest in Bayle and the struggle for free religious speech, neither of which play as significant a role in English thought prior to the American Revolution.

37. See, for example, H. Mason, *Bayle and Voltaire* (Oxford: UP, 1963). Voltaire, however, follows Bayle and not Locke in taking freedom of conscience seriously in his discussions of toleration.

38. John Stuart Mill, *On Liberty*, ed. Currin V. Shields (Indianapolis: Bobbs-Merrill, 1956). My parenthetical references are to this edition.

39. In *England and Ireland* (London: Longmans, 1865), Mill writes that the Irish have "yet to prove their possession" of the "qualities which fit a people for self-government" (35).

40. A sympathetic effort is made to clarify Mill in T. M. Scanlon, Jr., "A Theory of Freedom of Expression," *Philosophy and Public Affairs* 1 (1972): 204–226; and idem, "Freedom of Expression and Categories of Expression," *University of Pittsburgh Law Review* 40 (1979): 519-550. John Rawls, "The Basic Liberties and Their Priority," *Tanner Lectures on Human Values* 3 (1982): 1-87, is a good example of how far one can get from a Baylean (absolutist) position and still mount a very modest defense of freedom of speech. Rawls appears to be in the Lockean tradition, that is, of elegantly yielding supremacy to the magistrate.

41. Cited in Thomas I. Emerson, *The System of Freedom of Expression* (New York: Vintage, 1971), 105.

42. Quentin Skinner, "A Reply to My Critics," in *Meaning and Context: Quentin Skinner and his Critics*, ed. James Tully (Cambridge: Polity Press, 1988), 260. The Wittgenstein reference is to *Philosophical Investigations*, pt. 1, § 546. The motto of the Tully volume is "Words are deeds." It is attributed to Wittgenstein, *Culture and Value.*

2

State Intervention

The history of the First Amendment to the U.S. Constitution is the history of attempts to withdraw what had been promised. Even before the end of the eighteenth century, Congress passed a series of direct attacks on freedom of speech (and of the press) with the Alien and Sedition acts (1798), thereby beginning the long tradition of subversion paranoia that, from that day to this, has been a hallmark of American political discourse. Alexis de Tocqueville detected a source of the problem 160 years ago: "I know no country in which there is so little true independence of mind and freedom of discussion as in America. . . . The majority raises very formidable barriers to the liberty of opinion: within these barriers an author may write whatever he pleases, but he will repent it if he ever step beyond them."[1] Herman Melville[2] also calls attention to the destructive force of "subversion paranoia" in his nineteenth-century classic *Moby Dick*.

British common law inhibitions on freedom of speech (libel, obscenity, conspiracy, etc.) carried over into American practice. The Supreme Court, throughout the nineteenth century, seems to have gone out of its way not to apply the free-speech principle even when it seemed appropriate. In *Barron v. Baltimore* (1833), the Supreme Court ruled that "the prohibitions of the Bill of Rights did not limit the activities of state or local authorities, or of private individuals."[3] Hence, the Court did not interfere with laws introduced in most Southern states, prior to the Civil War, that penalized all abolitionist speech.[4] The First Amendment is invoked more positively with Espionage Act cases at the time of World War I. Remarkably, only in 1925 (*Gitlow v. New York*) did it become applicable, via the Fourteenth Amendment, to state laws and courts.[5]

Parenthetically, it should be acknowledged that there is one class of talk that has traditionally been taken to count as being action. There are bits of language that are circumscribed by legal formularies and other sorts of hocus-pocus so that what is said under such conditions is, by agreed definition, said to constitute action. Thus, perjury, for example, requires the agency of a duly sanctioned judicial figure or an officer of a court and a prescribed form of oath to guarantee truth telling. A duly authorized agent, plus assembled witnesses, plus a prescribed form, is also required for such cases as marriages and ordinations. I contend that it is precisely because a category distinction between talking and doing is recognized that such elaborate procedures were introduced in order to permit the articulation of certain select forms of words to count as acts. Reflections on these distinctions, which have been much discussed by philosophers since J. L. Austin first raised the topic in the 1950s,[6] have contributed to the general breakdown of that speech/action distinction which supports the absolutist free-speech principle.

In general, those who have wanted to limit speech have viewed speech as action. Speech, it is believed, can damage reputations, undermine the state, challenge religious truths, demean the members of so-called identifiable groups, threaten commercial activity, incite trouble, and promote immorality. In the early twentieth century, confronted with antisubversive legislation, the U.S. Supreme Court made clear that the First Amendment had no absolute force. It was but one of several competing values. Speech was a form of action capable of generating criminal acts and, while deserving (because of the First Amendment) of special consideration, not an absolute. The "clear and present danger" standard is advanced by U.S. Supreme Court Justice Holmes in *Schenck v. U.S.*(1919), a *unanimous* decision supporting a conviction under the Espionage Act. Holmes did not hold that Schenck's leaflet (opposing military conscription) created a clear and present danger, presumably because he could not. Instead, the traditional bad-tendency rule was used to justify the conviction.[7] The case of four-time Socialist party presidential candidate Eugene Victor Debs followed soon after. He, too, lost his appeal in a unanimous decision, although the Court did at least acknowledge the possible application of the First Amendment. It is in *Schenck* that Holmes declared: "The most stringent protection of free speech would not protect a man in falsely shouting fire in a theater, and causing a panic." The passage is often cited without the benefit of *falsely* (e.g., by the Ontario Court of Appeal in *Regina v. Zündel*). Alan Dershowitz notes: "A comedian once told his audience, during a stand-up routine, about the time he was standing around a fire with a crowd of people and got in trouble for yelling 'Theatre, theatre!' That, I think, is about as clever and productive a use as anyone has ever made of Holmes's flawed analogy."[8]

The opinions of Hugo Black (a U.S. Supreme Court justice from 1937 to 1971), and William O. Douglas (on the Court from 1939 to 1975) are exceptions. Both often advance an absolutist position.[9] Black opposes tampering with what he believes are the clear words of the First Amendment: When the U.S. Constitution says "no law," it means *no law*. Although he does not tell us much about the philosophical presuppositions of the text, he takes *speech* literally and understands freedom of speech to be the cornerstone of the American democratic system.[10] He says (in dissent) in *American Communication Association v. Douds* (1950): "The postulate of the First Amendment is that our free institutions can be maintained without proscribing or penalizing political belief, press [etc.]." He sharply distinguishes talk and advocacy from behavior and action. He opposes extending speech to cover various forms of behavior often described as "symbolic speech," as in draft-card burning [*United States v. O'Brien* (1968)], which are then said to be entitled to First Amendment protection. Black makes his position on this point patently clear in *Cox v. Louisiana* (1965) by distinguishing laws controlling marching and other forms of *conduct* from laws affecting speech. Alexander Meiklejohn,[11] writing while Black was on the Court, seeks to show that the intent of the Founding Fathers was to make *political* speech free. That, he claims, is the point to the constitutional free-speech guarantee. Black was sympathetic to Meiklejohn's views but points out that the Founding Fathers were also concerned with guaranteeing free *religious* speech. Moreover, Meiklejohn's formulation entails drawing lines between political and nonpolitical speech—something that the First Amendment text does not authorize.

In a somewhat similar vein, Thomas Emerson makes a powerful case for interpreting the First Amendment as providing protection for freedom of expression. The key to Emerson's analysis is the distinction between *expression* and *action*. Expression covers a wider range than speech, for example, so-called symbolic speech, flag desecration,[12] and gestures. Emerson does not give us a philosophical framework within which to base his distinction. Rather, he contends that the proper way to understand the First Amendment is in terms of this distinction. The Baylean distinction between *speech* and *action* only partially parallels the one Emerson draws between *expression* and *action*, because Bayle actually draws a category distinction between speech and action, one that he bases on ontological considerations. Although Emerson wants to retain a form/content distinction, a "fundamental distinction between belief, opinion, and communication of ideas on the one hand, and different forms of conduct on the other,"[13] he balks at Bayle's step because he believes it undermines the First Amendment."Virtually all expression contains some mixture of nonverbal 'conduct,' and the Court's formulation affords no *functional* basis for deciding what is 'pure speech' and what is other 'conduct.' "[14] I believe he finds the merging of one (for Bayle, ontological) category with the other unproblematic because he is, from the outset, philosophically disposed to treat all speech as expression—and as expression, conduct. That is, Emerson rejects the category distinction of Bayle and the Cartesians—and of Madison. His inclusion of functional suggests that unless the distinction shows itself in behavior, that is, has practical consequences, it doesn't count. Such a rigorous meaning criterion is not self-evident; it needs a defense. None is provided. But in all fairness, I think there is a constitutional (i.e., legal) reason that lures Emerson into his rejection of a distinction between speech and conduct. And that is because he does not find it plausible to separate the free-speech clause[15] from what he calls the "right of assembly" clause. (That First Amendment clause reads: "the right of the people *peaceably* to assemble" [emphasis added]; thus, unlike the free-speech clause, the assembly clause includes a qualifying term.)

Cartesian ontological considerations only support a narrow reading of *speech* and thus work against a more general expression theory. Emerson, like most free-speech theorists, also holds that if a society is to be democratic, if the members of the society are to participate in an informed way in the deliberations of that society, freedom of expression is a primary desideratum. Emerson clearly wants to distinguish sharply between "belief, opinion, and communication of ideas on the one hand, and different forms of conduct on the other."[16] But his expression/action distinction is not absolute. There are many cases (as in Mill) where "speech is an integral feature of a course of action"[17] and hence may be suppressed to avoid the risk of violence in accordance with the harm principle. This sort of formulation is still with us: A *New York Times* editorial ("Mr. Bush and the Freedom to Hurt," 12 May 1991) asserts: "At some point, speech becomes action—and hateful speech becomes action that a community may protect itself against." Hitler's thesis that Jewish cultural "contributions" pollute the soul of the German nation can also be read as an application of the harm principle, thereby justifying the suppression of Jewish culture. Since the harm principle is prey to such uses, we should perhaps be somewhat less cavalier in surrendering the absolutist reading of the free-speech principle.

Thus far I have claimed that Bayle provides a clue to the absolutist form in which the First Amendment's free-speech clause is drafted and that a set of anti-Baylean and anti-Cartesian philosophical presuppositions help explain many of the U.S. Supreme Court's later free-speech decisions. By incorporating a free-speech principle into their Constitution, Americans guaranteed that there would be a continuing discussion of the subject and a concern with drawing lines between what is and what is not constitutionally protected. In spite of the role freedom of speech plays within American political life, the question of Madison's historical sources for the First Amendment has been largely ignored, and with it the possibility of appreciating a debt to Bayle's way of thinking. Thus, questions about the philosophical foundations for the free-speech doctrine as well as the philosophical presuppositions made by Courts applying the free-speech principle on later occasions have not received sufficient attention. This may have facilitated the demise of the absolutist interpretation.

Here is an example that illuminates how a different (and anti-Baylean, anti-Cartesian) doctrine of human nature may bear on freedom of speech.

In 1975, Conor Cruise O'Brien, in the course of defending censorship in a debate in the Irish Senate, had this to say about the matter:

Has the State the right to restrict freedom of expression? It is possible to hold that it is best not to do so at all: that the State should restrain, where necessary, overt and material actions, but should leave purely verbal utterances strictly alone.... [However,] words are in fact an integral part of many patterns of actions. If this is accepted that absolute distinction between words and actions is broken down, and words and actions together become part of a pattern of behavior which is and should be amenable to law.[18]

It is evident that O'Brien is *aware* of a freedom of speech tradition in which speech and action are radically distinguished, that he proposes to *reject* that tradition, and that his rejection is established by advancing a different philosophical claim: that speech simply *is* behavioral action.

NOTES

1. Alexis de Tocqueville, *Democracy in America*, trans. Henry Reeve (New York: Schocken Books, 1961). Vol. 1, 310; [pt. 1, chap. 15].

2. It is interesting that Melville was also a student of Bayle.

3. Cf. *Emerson, Haber and Dorsen's Political and Civil Rights in the United States*, 4th ed., ed. Norman Dorsen, Paul Bender, and Burt Neuborne (Boston: Little, Brown, 1976), pt. 1, 28.

4. Cf. *Political and Civil Rights*. . . 1, 30, where Nye, *Fettered Freedom* (1963) is cited.

5. For a detailed discussion, see David M. Rabban, "The First Amendment in Its Forgotten Years," *Yale Law Journal* 90 (1981): 514-595. He notes:

The overwhelming majority of prewar [World War I] decisions in all jurisdictions rejected free speech claims, often by ignoring their existence. No court was more unsympathetic to freedom of expression than the Supreme Court, which rarely produced even a dissenting opinion in a First Amendment case. Most decisions by lower federal courts and state courts were also restrictive, although there were some notable exceptions. Radicals fared particularly poorly, but the widespread judicial hostility to the value of free speech transcended any individual issue or litigant. (523)

Resistance to interfering with the rights of states in accordance with a federal system is evident when one realizes that as late as *Adamson v. California* (1947) the Court ruled (5–4) that the due process clause of the Fourteenth Amendment did not bring all the rights of the Bill of Rights under its purview. At issue was the Fifth Amendment guarantee against being obliged to incriminate oneself. *Malloy v. Hogan* (1964) extended the Fifth Amendment via the Fourteenth to state courts (5–4 decision). The issue may have been settled by *Murphy v. Waterfront Commission* (1964) (9–0).

6. See, for example, Kent Greenawalt, *Speech, Crime, and the Uses of Language* (New York: Oxford University Press, 1989), esp. chap. 3.

7. See Thomas I. Emerson, *The System of Freedom of Expression* (New York: Vintage, 1971), 65; Thomas L. Tedford, *Freedom of Speech in the United States* (Carbondale: Southern Illinois University Press, 1985), 71.

8. Alan Dershowitz, "The Analogy about Shouting 'Fire' Is Useless and Inapt," *Lawyers Weekly* (Canada), 27 October 1989, 1. Dershowitz is a Harvard Law School professor but is better known as the specialist in handling the appeals of such wealthy clients as Mike Tyson, Leona Helmsley, and Count von Bülow.

9. But not always. Franklyn S. Haiman sought to discover why Black and Douglas concurred in sustaining the conviction in *Chaplinsky v. New Hampshire* (1942). Black declined to explain. For Black's reply to the query, see Tedford, *Freedom of Speech*, 210n.

10. See Hugo Black, *One Man's Stand for Freedom*, ed. Irving Dilliard (New York: Knopf, 1963), for example, 478–479

11. Alexander Meiklejohn, *Political Freedom* (New York: Harper & Row, 1960).

12. Cf. John Hart Ely, "Flag Desecration: A Case Study in the Roles of Categorization and Balancing in First Amendment Analysis," *Harvard Law Review* 88 (1975): 1482–1508.

13. Emerson, *System*, 8.

14. Ibid., 295. Emphasis added.

15. For an excellent historical overview and analysis of the free-speech clause with particular attention to Court decisions bearing on the danger test and the balancing of individual versus government interests, see D. Terence Langendoen, "Freedom of Speech in America: How Free?" (City University of New York: CUNYForum No. 2, 1977). Langendoen examines each element in the clause, including the term *abridging*.

16. Emerson, *System*, 8. How this squares with his remarks at 295 where he objects (as noted above) to the Court's distinction between *speech* and *conduct* is not clear.

17. See ibid., 328, for a range of examples.

18. O'Brien, then a senator from Trinity College and minister in the Irish government, was moving the second stage of the Broadcasting Authority bill (1975) before the Irish Senate, 12 March 1975. (Senate report in *The Irish Times* [Dublin], 13 March 1975, 9.)

3

Bertrand Russell

Throughout much of the twentieth century the "subversion paranoia" I mentioned earlier has played a part in American life and has resulted in direct assaults on the free-speech principle. With the beginnings of labor unions at the end of the nineteenth century and the increased immigration from southern, central, and eastern Europe came talk of communist subversion. Concern was expressed about the loyalty of citizens. Ideas are the explicit targets of the Espionage Act of 1917, as amended in 1918, and especially of the Alien Registration Act of 1940 (the so-called Smith Act). This act makes it a crime to conspire to teach and advocate the overthrow and destruction of the government by force and violence. In reviewing the convictions of eleven leading members of the Communist party under the act, the U.S. Supreme Court (*Dennis v. United States* [1951]) found the dangers of the advocacy of certain ideas, and the use of "indoctrination," outweighed the force of the First Amendment's free-speech principle. Although no overt acts were alleged, only Hugo Black and William O. Douglas dissented. A variant of the clear and present danger test was also introduced. Chief Justice Frederick Vinson employed Appeals Court Chief Judge Learned Hand's formulation: "In each case [courts] must ask whether the gravity of the evil, discounted by its improbability, justifies such invasion of free speech as is necessary to avoid the danger."[1] Justice Felix Frankfurter's criterion was weaker; he proposed simply to "balance" the competing interests of the individual and the government.

The Internal Security Act (1950), also known as the McCarran Act, was the most stringent anticommunist legislation of the period, and elements of it still reverberate through the U.S. legal system. The attorney general sought, under the act, to compel the Communist party to register with the Subversive Activities Control Board. The Communist party lost on appeal, 5–4 (*Communist Party v. Subversive Activities Control Board* [1961]). Among the dissenters, only Black objected to the act's registration procedures on First Amendment grounds. He wrote: "The Founders drew a distinction in our Constitution which we would be wise to follow. They gave the Government the fullest power to prosecute overt actions in violation of valid laws but withheld any power to punish people for nothing more than advocacy of their views."[2]

With *Brandenburg v. Ohio* (1969), the Supreme Court (unanimous decision) imposed a stricter standard for justifying the suppression of advocacy. The case overturned an Ohio Criminal Syndicalism Act under which Brandenburg, a Ku Klux Klan leader, had been convicted. With this decision, suppressible advocacy must be "directed to inciting or producing imminent lawless action and [be] likely to incite or produce such action." While this is a stricter test than those that preceded it, the First Amendment free-speech clause is still constrained. Douglas, in his own concurrence (with which Black agreed) really rejected this incitement test when he held that "[t]he line between what is permissible and not subject to control and what may be made impermissible and subject to regulation is the line between ideas and overt acts."[3]

In drafting the Smith Act, the legislators were able to rely on a loophole provided by the common law tradition, that is, the crime of conspiracy. The English experience (especially in the sixteenth and seventeenth centuries) was, as the American experience continues to be, haunted by worries over what the natives are *really* thinking, particularly when it is feared that they may be thinking of challenging the power structure. The American system has increasingly found it expedient to draft conspiracy components in all sorts of criminal statutes, components that, on their face, seem clearly to violate the First Amendment's free-speech guarantee since the crime is, by definition, restricted to talk in the sense that the overt act it may precipitate may itself be further talk, for example, advocacy of certain ideas.

One of the more famous conspiracy cases involved Dr. Benjamin Spock, Rev. William Sloane Coffin, and others, protesting U.S. involvement in the Vietnam War. They were convicted of counseling Selective Service registrants to evade service in the armed forces. The First Circuit Court of Appeals dismissed the case but nevertheless held that some of the conspirators' conduct was not protected by the First Amendment. "The Court found that 'maintenance of an army in peacetime is a valid, in fact vital, government function,' and went on to say: 'If a registrant may be convicted for violation of the draft laws, surely "[a] man may be punished for encouraging the commission of [the] crime." ' ... The essence of the Court's view was that 'effective persuasion' is not protected by the First Amendment."[4]

On occasion, Americans have been charged with conspiracy even though the conspirators had never met with one another, as was apparently the case in the action taken against the leaders of demonstrations at the Democratic National Convention, Chicago, August 1968.[5] It was the first prosecution under the Federal Anti-Riot Act of 1968. That act

contemplates that no final action amounting to incitement, encouragement or participation in a riot is necessary. It is sufficient if the person travels [in interstate commerce or uses any facility of interstate commerce] with the requisite intent and then performs any "overt act to carry out that intent." . . . [N]othing in the statute requires that the overt act consist of action, much less action so substantial as to make the total conduct punished predominantly action. Consequently the conduct for which the accused is punished would include intent and expression, but no action whatever.[6]

Eight people were charged under the statute, including David Dellinger, Yippie founder Abbie Hoffman, Tom Hayden, and others. Black Panther Bobby Seale's case was severed from the others. They then became known as the "Chicago Seven."[7] The trial judge was Julius J. Hoffman. He imposed scores of contempt citations (reversed on appeal). The jury voted acquittals on the conspiracy charge but guilty on others. None of the seven, nor their attorneys, served time in prison, but the constitutionality of the act was upheld by the court of appeals in *National Mobilization Committee to End the War in Viet Nam v. Foran*.[8]

Given America's much-touted concern for freedom of speech and the values said to be expressed in the First Amendment, these cases may strike the non-American as surprising. And yet conspiracy was one crime that the Founding Fathers were very knowledgeable about. After all, they had been engaged in one. They had taught and advocated the overthrow of the government by force and violence. As a consequence, one conspiratorial crime is actually defined within the Constitution itself: treason (Art. III, § 3).

Returning to the vigorous antisubversive activities earlier in this century, and quite apart from the efforts of U.S. Attorney General A. Mitchell Palmer at the end of World War I, one finds that the New York State legislature began investigating communists in 1919, using procedures that investigation committees were later to emulate: issuing their own search warrants, ignoring legal safeguards, generating publicity, smearing witnesses, and so on. The fledgling American Civil Liberties Union (ACLU) was a particular target. It was in this period that duly elected socialists were not permitted to take up their seats in the New York State Assembly (lower house) (5) or the U.S. House of Representatives (1). In 1934, New York passed the Ives Loyalty Oath Law requiring all teachers to take an oath. (New York City teachers had been required to take an oath since World War I.) In 1939, New York State passed a law banning state employment to anyone who "by word of mouth or writing wilfully and deliberately advocates, advises or teaches" that the government should be overthrown "by force, violence or any unlawful means."[9]

The 1940 appointment of Bertrand Russell to teach such things as mathematical logic at the College of the City of New York (CCNY) marks a decisive step in the attacks on freedom of speech in America. Although a number of philosophers have always considered Russell the most distinguished philosopher and most original philosophical thinker of the century, he has generally had a somewhat ambiguous reputation. His English contemporaries never forgave him for his vigorous opposition to World War I—at which time his pacifist views cost him both his post at Cambridge University and time in prison. Subsequently, English academic philosophers, wherever and whenever possible, gave Gottlob Frege priority in matters of logic. By midcentury, Wittgenstein's "form of life" rhetoric displaced Russell's rigorous, tough-minded, and more historically knowledgeable approach to philosophical questions.

In any event, Russell gave up a position at the University of California–Los Angeles (UCLA) to accept an eighteen-month (by 1942 he would have reached the compulsory retirement age of seventy) post at CCNY (unanimous vote of the Board of Higher Education, 26 February 1940). Shortly after the appointment was announced, New York Episcopal bishop William T. Manning attacked both Russell and the board that appointed him. Half an hour after submitting his resignation to the president of UCLA, Russell, having just learned of the problems in New York, tried to withdraw his letter.[10] However, the UCLA president, hearing murmurings of California religious protests, refused. Manning said that Russell is a " 'recognized propagandist against religion and morality and who specifically defends adultery.' "[11]

A Mrs. Jean Kay of Brooklyn, represented by attorney Joseph Goldstein, brought an action against the board, claiming that she feared what might happen to her (young) daughter if Russell were allowed to teach. The case quickly became a cause célèbre. Justice John E. McGeehan issued a stinging rebuke to the board and a savage attack on Russell in his decision on 30 March 1940, a decision submitted only two days after the court hearing. At issue were said to be the views expressed in such writings as *Education and the Good Life, Marriage and Morals, Education and the Modern World,* and *What I Believe* and such conduct as Russell's adultery and divorces. The facts that CCNY was not open to women and was located in Manhattan and that Russell would be teaching such things as logic and the foundations of mathematics counted for little. The justice declared:

While this court would not interfere with any action of the board in so far as a pure question of "valid" academic freedom is concerned, it will not tolerate academic freedom being used as a cloak to promote the popularization in the minds of adolescents of acts forbidden by the Penal Law. This appointment affects the public health, safety, and morals of the community and it is the duty of the court to act. Academic freedom does not mean academic license. It is the freedom to do good and not to teach evil.[12]

Among other things, Russell was attacked for condoning homosexuality. (At that time the New York maximum prison sentence for homosexual acts was twenty years.) For various "moral" reasons (as well as two technical ones), the court voided the appointment, and the board was accused of establishing a "chair of indecency." The board was represented in the case by the New York City Corporation Counsel. He recommended against taking an appeal, fearing that Russell might win! Just to be on the safe side, Mayor Fiorello LaGuardia struck the funding for Russell's appointment from the CCNY budget. Nevertheless, the board, having been provided with free independent counsel, sought to appeal, but permission to change counsel was not granted, and appeals from *that* opinion were rejected by Judge McGeehan. An effort by Osmond K. Fraenkel of the ACLU to have Russell made party to the case (it was ruled to be solely between Mrs. Kay and the board) was rejected by Justice McGeehan. His decision was unanimously upheld (no written opinion) by the appellate division and later by the Court of Appeals (New York's highest court). Thus was Russell denounced by the court and deprived of his job without even having been given a hearing.

There is considerable literature on the Russell case, but the remarks by Arthur O. Lovejoy, professor of philosophy at The Johns Hopkins University and a founding member (1913) of the American Association of University Professors (AAUP), constitute a clear formulation of the issues.

The gravest feature of Justice McGeehan's decision consists in the assumption which he makes in order thus to bring the case within the scope of the criminal law. That assumption is that *the expression of an opinion that an existing legal prohibition is ill-advised and socially undesirable is to be judicially construed as an incitement to other persons to violate the law, and therefore as itself unlawful.* Thus Justice McGeehan declares Mr. Russell "not fit to teach in any of the schools of this land" on the ground that "he encourages the violation of the Penal Law of the State of New York"; and in his second opinion Justice McGeehan states, as the final and most decisive of the "ultimate facts" justifying the original decision, that Mr. Russell "does not deny that he has expressed opinions in conflict with existing penal laws which he characterizes in his proposed answer as 'antiquated' and 'in need of revision.'" No evidence is cited that Mr. Russell has in fact ever incited anyone to break any law of the State of New York or of the United States; it is simply assumed that criticism of the ethical premises underlying certain laws is *eo ipso* an incitement to break them. This principle, generally applied, would be destructive of liberty of speech and of the press; for it implies that any advocacy of alterations in, for example, the criminal law is an encouragement to crime, and consequently criminal.[13]

The board had taken the narrow but historically sound academic freedom position that appointments to academic posts should be made by people competent to render such judgments. Harvard, faced with objections to Russell giving the William James Lectures, took a similar tack; that is, neither institution appealed to freedom of speech. Russell received considerable support from across the United States, from the Philosophy Department at CCNY, from the American Philosophical Association, from the AAUP, but conspicuously not from the Harvard Department of Philosophy. Ernest Hocking's very unsupportive letter from Harvard (sharply criticized by John Dewey) is reprinted in Russell's *Autobiography*.[14] The *New York Times* editorialized against the board for making the appointment in the first place and against Russell for not having had "the wisdom to retire from the appointment as soon as its harmful effects became evident."[15] He was, however, supported in the *Herald Tribune* and the *Post*.

In his reply to the *New York Times*, Russell noted, "If I had retired . . . I should have . . . tacitly assented to the proposition that substantial groups shall be allowed to drive out of public office individuals whose opinions, race, or nationality they find repugnant. This to me would appear immoral." Russell went on to say, "It is an essential part of democracy that substantial groups, even majorities, should extend toleration to dissentient groups, however small and however much their sentiments may be outraged. *In a democracy it is necessary that people should learn to endure having their sentiments outraged*" [emphasis added].[16]

The dismissal of Russell marks a turning point in the history of freedom of speech in the United States. First of all, it meant that even an outstanding scholar could be successfully attacked *for his ideas*. Second, it meant that the Catholic church, with the able assistance of New York's Episcopal bishop, had more than enough power not only to banish Russell from the academic scene but also, through their influence within the New York judiciary, to deprive him of any means to defend his rights. Third, and most important, a connection with subversion was repeatedly made. City Councilman Charles Keegan called Russell an "'avowed Communist.'"[17] The Hearst papers (the *Journal* and the *American*) reportedly "branded Russell as an exponent of Communism."[18] They also found a connection between the Russell appointment and communist influence in the City Colleges, and Robert I. Gannon, the Jesuit president of Fordham University, argued (before a hearing of the Rapp-Coudert New York State legislative committee investigating subversive activities in the municipal colleges) that the investigations should extend to "subversive philosophical policies" in those same institutions.[19] The state legislature passed a resolution saying that Russell was unfit. An examination of academic freedom cases before the AAUP in the 1920s and 1930s shows how often religious views, or their lack, were a factor in academic dismissals. But no one of Russell's stature had ever before been dismissed. Mainstream organized religion saw with Russell a chance to galvanize popular sentiment in such a way that a defense of Christian values could be coupled to an already aroused fear of subversion. That they have proven to be successful beyond their wildest dreams would not have surprised Russell. In 1940, Russell already clearly saw the problem precisely in those terms. He writes (May 1940):

Academic freedom in this country is threatened from two sources: the plutocracy and the churches, which endeavor between them to establish an economic and a theological censorship. The two are easily combined by the accusation of Communism, which is recklessly hurled against anyone whose opinions are disliked. For example, I have observed with interest that, although I have criticized the Soviet Government severely ever since 1920, and although in recent years I have emphatically expressed the opinion that it is at least as bad as the government of the Nazis, my critics ignore all this and quote triumphantly the one or two sentences in which, in moments of hope, I have suggested the possibility of good ultimately coming out of Russia.[20]

Investigations of the Red menace in the schools increased in the intervening years, and in 1949, New York State passed the Feinberg law. It continued the Ives Oath but added that membership in any organization listed as subversive by the attorney general or the board of regents disqualified a teacher from employment. The law also specified that any schoolteacher or employee "shall be removed for the utterance of any treasonable or seditious word [sic] or words . . . while holding such position."[21]

New York was not the only state to set up legislative investigative committees, although it appears to have been more involved with the quest for subversives than any other. California's official concern with un-American activities began in 1940. From 1941 to 1949, its legislative committee was under the chairmanship of State Senator Jack Tenney. In 1949 and 1950, the Tenney committee's legislative recommendations (oaths, etc.) created great controversy. The board of regents, responsive to legislative pressures, imposed its own oath. Other states, for example, Washington, also had investigative committees dedicated in principle to exposing subversion. Actual practice was something else. The legislative proposals coming from these committees were taken to be of less importance than the publicity that hearings could generate. Washington State Representative Albert F. Canwell, chairman of his state legislature's investigative committee, is quoted (1948) as saying: " 'If someone insists there is discrimination against Negroes in this country, or that there is inequality of wealth, there is every reason to believe that person is a Communist.' "[22]

State activity did not occur in a vacuum. Anticommunism sold papers and got people elected (and others defeated).[23] In 1908, what was to become the Federal Bureau of Investigation (FBI) came into being. In 1919, J. Edgar Hoover (1895–1972) was named first head of the antiradical division. He became assistant chief of the bureau in 1921 and director in 1924, a post he held until he died in office in 1972.[24] Since his death, details about Hoover's power and personal life have slowly come to public attention. BBC-TV and PBS recently presented a program, "The Secret File on J. Edgar Hoover,"[25] reporting on Hoover's secret life of crime. Indeed, because of Hoover's gross misuse of government goods and services, John M. Doud, chief of the Organized Crime Task Force (1972–78), claims that had Hoover still been alive at the time of the probe, he would have been charged. It had long been noted that Hoover did his best to impede investigations into organized crime and the Mafia. He even denied there was any such thing as organized crime. But according to "The Secret File," it now seems that his "protection" of the Mafia was soundly based on self-interest. Hoover's own status as an "untouchable" in the Justice Department was based on his having, over the years, amassed material on the backgrounds and peccadillos of all important politicians, including President John F. Kennedy. Although Hoover and another of his close friends, McCarthy committee counsel Roy Cohn, were homophobes in word and official action, according to several interviewed sources, a chief of organized crime, Meyer Lansky, reportedly had photos of Hoover engaging in homosexual activity with his longtime friend and FBI number-two man Clyde Tolson. The program's thesis is that these photos guaranteed that organized crime was also accorded the status of "untouchable" for several decades. The program concludes: "It is now becoming clear that Hoover's personal corruption corrupted the very mission of the FBI, to fight crime."

Regardless of what now turns up about Hoover, the fact is that because of his incredibly long government service Hoover was directly involved with the suppression of certain ideas from the time of the raids on unions and communists by Attorney General Palmer (1919–20) through the McCarthyism period of the late 1940s and 1950s and the anti–Vietnam War protest movement.

With respect to this latter period, thanks to material retrieved via the Freedom of Information Act, Hoover's extensive and extended covert and illegal actions against the Socialist Workers party, and so-called New Left student groups, and the like, have become known. For instance, documents released under the Freedom of Information Act show that the FBI was already interested in activities at Arizona State University (ASU) in 1968. From the time of ASU's first teach-in against the Vietnam War in May 1965, antiwar activity was carefully monitored by members of the John Birch Society, Young Americans for Freedom, and Pulliam's *Arizona Republic* and *Phoenix American* newspapers. In any case, antiwar groups were open about their plans and activities since they were seeking to bring their message to as wide an audience as possible. Most also knew that their membership was bound to include informers. Moreover, the staffs of many university security forces included former FBI special agents. Thus, even John Duffy, the remarkably sane and fair-minded head of ASU campus security, was reported to have been a former FBI special agent.

What I continue to find inexplicable is that Hoover *personally* directed a campaign of phony letter-writing against the late Morris J. Starsky, an assistant professor of philosophy at ASU and a member of the Socialist Workers party. Anonymous letters signed "A concerned ASU alumnus" were directed to the members of the faculty committee for academic freedom and tenure. Despite incredible pressures, the committee voted unanimously in favor of Starsky.[26] He was later dismissed by the board of regents and, although an outstanding teacher, was never again able to obtain a regular academic post. Hoover may have miscalculated the amount of faculty and student support that Starsky would receive, but he knew that Arizona was a very conservative state and that the legislature and the regents would not tolerate Starsky. Starsky unsuccessfully fought his wrongful dismissal case in both state and federal courts. Arizona State was censured by the AAUP for its treatment of Starsky, and eventually the small amount a court had awarded Starsky (but that the state evaded paying by successfully appealing the award and thus making the cost of further litigation prohibitive) was met through private donations, and ASU was taken off the AAUP "black list." Presumably, Hoover knew that by destroying Starsky, nontenured staff throughout America would get the message that they had better keep their more radical ideas to themselves. Although Starsky's case was widely reported at the time, the full extent of Hoover's own activities only became known some years later with Freedom of Information Act disclosures about the FBI's COINTELPRO caper.[27]

Two congressional committees helped generate the atmosphere in which McCarthyism was to flourish. The House Un-American Activities Committee (HUAC) began in 1938 under Congressman Martin Dies. It was before this committee that admitted perjurer Whittaker Chambers accused Alger Hiss, former senior government official[28] and then president of the Carnegie Endowment for International Peace, of, among other things, having been, in the 1930s, a member of the Communist party and having passed documents to him. At that time, under another name, Chambers had been a dedicated communist agent. Like many other admirers of Joseph Stalin, he later had a religious conversion. He was a very good writer, a senior editor of *Time*, and the possessor of a lively imagination. With the fame and fortune he gained from the Hiss case, and in the spirit of those times, he seems to have taken sadistic pleasure in fabricating or misusing evidence that damaged or destroyed careers. So far as the Hiss case is concerned, it seems in retrospect that the most crucial evidence adduced to establish that Hiss had lied in his testimony before a federal grand jury was ultimately based on an old typewriter. It was on this machine that allegedly purloined government documents had been typed in the late 1930s. A prima facie case was made that the typewriter introduced into evidence by the FBI, and on which the allegedly incriminating documents were typed, had in fact been fabricated to establish Chambers's claims.[29]

It is now hard to believe that hysteria so gripped America that intelligent people could accept Chambers's incredible stories about himself, about Hiss, and about the papers. Chambers's account that he had hidden the microfilms of what he claimed was incriminating material in a pumpkin for safekeeping was so fantastic that he scored a media victory before the battle had even begun. Hiss came across as a legal quibbler, and although Chambers repeatedly perjured himself, he was forgiven because he had the essential virtue of being a marvelous storyteller. The Hiss case continues to generate polemics. Chambers's version of history remains a central article of faith for the neoconservatives. The courts were not moved by the new evidence about the typewriter and the documents to reopen the case, and so Hiss went to prison for perjury.[30] It was the Hiss case that enabled Richard Nixon to rise in politics. His tactics gained him a seat in the U.S. Senate in 1950. His career, from HUAC to Watergate, is well known.[31]

Although the pumpkin papers were hardly material that, on receipt, would excite a chief of espionage, that point was lost in the excitement of the Great Pumpkin. Hiss was the most senior (former) government person to be "uncovered" as a communist spy and agent. Worse, he was advertised as having whispered policy recommendations into President Franklin D. Roosevelt's ear at the Yalta Conference. And Yalta was important because it was at that conference, according to the gospel of the conservatives, that Eastern Europe had been "given" to Stalin. The fact that Stalin was able to triumph at Yalta must have been due to the subversive activities of Hiss. That perception of Yalta contributed significantly to the creation of the idea that the U.S. government was full of communists and that nothing short of elaborate security clearance procedures would help purge the government of spies. Indeed, nothing contributed so effectively to the escalation of the subversion paranoia that swept America in those years as the Hiss case. Although in October 1992[32] Russian president Boris Yeltsin's adviser Col. Gen. Dmitry Volkogonov declared that after an exhaustive search of KGB archives no evidence was found that Hiss had ever been an agent or provided confidential information to the Soviet Union,[33] those who (like Chambers boosters Allen Weinstein and Sam Tanenhaus) seem to consider the collapse of the Soviet Union to be part of a communist conspiracy reject the new information and even seem to be insisting on a Gödel-type "completeness proof" for archival searches. Hiss, on the other hand, sees in this report his vindication.

The attack on Hiss was handled with consummate skill by Chambers, J. Edgar Hoover, and Nixon. Although Nixon is still often referred to as "Tricky Dick" and is famous for his assertion "I am not a crook," he was much more effective with his smears than McCarthy was with his bludgeon. It is also interesting that Nixon's behavior was not tagged as "Nixonism." It is an indication of Nixon's ability to handle the media that the term that entered our political vocabulary to refer to techniques of character assassination is *McCarthyism*.

When Senator Joseph McCarthy made his famous 9 February 1950 speech in Wheeling, West Virginia, he claimed that the federal government was full of communists. He spoke without a prepared text, and there has always been a question of how many communists he actually claimed infested Washington. Pressed to name real communist agents in government, McCarthy named Owen Lattimore, a professor at The Johns Hopkins University. A Far East specialist, Lattimore was an occasional State Department consultant. He was charged with perjury in connection with his testimony before the Senate Internal Security Subcommittee. His case was later dismissed by a court[34]—but not before the foundation support, on which his institute depended, evaporated. The ease with which a scholar of Lattimore's learning and ability could be destroyed was not lost on the profession. Academic opportunists were only too happy to curry favor with the right-wing forces then in the ascendant and thereby to gain preferment. As for McCarthy himself, after the Republicans took power in the Senate in the 1952 elections, he got his own subcommittee and, with the aid of his counsel, the late Roy Cohn, waged war against "communists," the U.S. Army, President Dwight Eisenhower, and many others, until he was censured in December 1954. He died in May 1957.

The whole sorry history, from the attacks on unions and immigrants prior to World War I, through the Palmer raids and the rise of J. Edgar Hoover, then on to HUAC and McCarthy, and through Nixon's time in the 1970s as president, developed as de Tocqueville feared it might. It is a history permeated with two ideas: first, that certain beliefs are so "Un-American" that their advocacy must be suppressed; and second, that if a certain level of political paranoia can be created and maintained, the citizens will respond at the polls both by rewarding the crusaders and by being distracted from issues of real substance. Distraction devices are now a central part of election campaigns and may be a factor in the progressive decline in the participation of Americans in electoral politics.

NOTES

1. Quoted in Thomas I. Emerson, *The System of Freedom of Expression* (New York: Vintage, 1971), 114.

2. Ibid., 135.

3. Ibid., 156.

4. Ibid., 77. Emerson cites *U.S. v. Spock*, 416 F. 2nd 165 (1st Cir. 1969).

5. There is considerable literature on the convention as well as on the behavior of the police and Mayor Richard Daley. But a sense for the events can be gleaned from I. F. Stone's 9 September 1968 column in his *Polemics and Prophecies: 1967–1970* (Boston: Little, Brown, 1989), 44–49. His *I. F. Stone's Weekly* was, from the McCarthy period through the 1960s, one of the most informative and provocative journals in America.

6. Emerson, *System*, 408–409.

7. U.S. District Court, No. Dist. of Illinois. Emerson, *System*, 409n, gives the case as *United States v. Dellinger et al.* (No. 69 CR 180, N.D. Ill.).

8. Emerson cites 411 F. 2nd 934 (7th Cir. 1969). See ibid., 409n.

9. Quoted in Lawrence H. Chamberlain, *Loyalty and Legislative Action: A Survey of Activity by the New York State Legislature 1919–1949* (Ithaca: Cornell University Press, 1951), 65.

10. Bertrand Russell. *The Autobiography of Bertrand Russell: 1914–1944* (New York: Bantam, 1969), 319.

11. Quoted in John Dewey and Horace M. Kallen, eds., *The Bertrand Russell Case* (1941; reprint ed., New York: Da Capo Press, 1972), 19. (Chapter by Kallen.)

12. New York State Supreme Court Justice McGeehan's decision is printed as Appendix I, ibid. Quote appears at 222.

13. This statement to the Bertrand Russell Academic Freedom Committee was read before the board of higher education and is reprinted in ibid., 179. Observing the dismissal of a colleague at Stanford some years before he joined in the founding of the AAUP, Lovejoy took a most unusual step: He resigned his post in protest, although he did not have another position. His views on academic freedom resulted in his being unsympathetic to communists holding university teaching posts. He believed that the academic freedom of any scholar must be defended, provided he or she did not surrender their judgments to any other authority, be it party, church, or corporation.

14. Bertrand Russell, *The Autobiography of Bertrand Russell: 1914–1944* (New York: Bantam, 1969), 335–343, where the letters by both Hocking and Dewey are included.

15. *The Bertrand Russell Case,* 25.

16. Ibid., 29 and 183.

17. Quoted by Paul Edwards in his Appendix, "How Bertrand Russell Was Prevented From Teaching at the College of the City of New York," to Bertrand Russell, *Why I Am Not a Christian and Other Essays on Religion and Related Subjects,* ed. Paul Edwards (New York: Simon & Schuster, 1957), 250.

18. Edwards, in ibid., 211.

19. *New York Times,* 7 December 1940, quoted in Philip P. Wiener, reprinted in Russell's *Autobiography,* 348–349.

20. "Freedom and the Colleges," in Russell, *Why I Am Not a Christian,* 181.

21. Quoted in Chamberlain, *Loyalty and Legislative Action,* 192.

22. Quoted in Helen M. Lynd, "Truth at the University of Washington," *American Scholar,* 18 (1949): 346–354.

23. See the excellent study by Max Lowenthal, *The Federal Bureau of Investigation* (New York: Harcourt Brace Jovanovich, 1950).

24. According to tape transcripts released by the U.S. National Archives on 4 June 1991, "Nixon feared in 1971 that the FBI director, J. Edgar Hoover, might 'pull down the temple with him, including me.'. . . The transcripts shed additional light on Mr. Nixon's efforts to persuade Mr. Hoover to resign." *International Herald Tribune,* 5 June 1991, 2 (story by Associated Press). Knowing that Hoover kept the "goods" on all political figures, one wonders whether Nixon feared that Hoover would reveal what has long been suspected, namely, that he had conspired with Nixon to fabricate the typewriter that convicted Hiss. That would indeed have brought the temple down.

25. Aired on 24 February 1993, BBC 2 (with WGBH), on "Timewatch." A wide range of people are interviewed including former FBI agents (some still defenders of Hoover), including—among others—former Vice President Walter Mondale and President Kennedy's personal secretary, Evelyn Lincoln. Several provide information on Hoover's sex life, for example, Joseph Shimon (who reports that Hoover was once arrested by the New Orleans vice squad—records which were expunged), Seymour Pollock (close friend of mob boss Meyer Lansky), Luisa Stuart-Hyun, Gordon Novel, and Susan Rosensteil (widow of Lewis Solon Rosensteil, head of Schenley Distillers; he was an intimate friend of Hoover and Roy Cohn and a close associate of various mobsters). Rosensteil reported twice meeting

Hoover (he was in drag) while being present at sex orgies with, among others, Roy Cohn. Ralph Salerno, Hank Messick, and Anthony Summers are credited as historical consultants. Summers is the author of a recently published biography of Hoover: *Official and Confidential: The Secret Life of J. Edgar Hoover* (New York: Putnam, 1993). Extended excerpts appear in his "The Man Who Collected Dirt," *Independent on Sunday: The Sunday Review* (London), 28 February 1993, 2–8.

26. The Starsky case at Arizona State is sympathetically examined in Thomas Ford Hoult, *The March to the Right: A Case Study in Political Repression* (Cambridge, Mass.: Schenkman, 1972).

27. See Nelson Blackstock, *COINTELPRO: The FBI's Secret War on Political Freedom* (New York: Vintage, 1976). The Starsky case is discussed on 175–178, 184–187.

28. Hiss's long and distinguished career in government began, after his graduation from Harvard Law School, with a clerkship with Supreme Court Justice Oliver Wendell Holmes, Jr.

29. See Alger Hiss, *In the Court of Public Opinion* (New York: Knopf, 1957). Given what Americans now know about the FBI; about Nixon and Watergate; about the Nixon White House authorized break-ins in connection with efforts to discredit Daniel Ellsberg (because of his release of the *Pentagon Papers*; see the five-volume Senator [Mike] Gravel edition [Boston: Beacon, 1971, esp. the Critical Essays, edited by Noam Chomsky and Howard Zinn, that constitute vol. 5); about the Tonkin Gulf (Vietnam) congressional resolution; about the activities of Lt. Col. Oliver North, Assistant Secretary of State Elliott Abrams, and other White House officials (including George Bush) in the Iran-Contra scam; and finally, about the recent calls for an investigation to determine whether presidential-candidate Reagan had made a deal with Iran not to release the American hostages they held until after the elections of 1980, one does not need to be a conspiracy-theory buff to have reason to suspect that the Hiss case was a fabrication.

30. Hiss served forty-four months in Lewisburg Penitentiary in Pennsylvania. Unlike William Remington ("the little Hiss case"), he survived the ordeal, seems to have gotten on well with his fellow prisoners, and was readmitted to the Massachusetts bar in 1975. Remington was killed by fellow prisoners under suspicious circumstances. The case against Remington was the product of the fantasies of another professional ex-communist FBI informer, Elizabeth Bentley. Myles Lane, U.S. attorney for the Southern District of New York, claiming that he was angry and chagrined that a fellow Dartmouth College graduate was allegedly a spy, took the unusual step (for a U.S. attorney, rather than an assistant) of playing an active courtroom role in the prosecution. For the highlights of the Remington case, see Fred J. Cook, *The FBI Nobody Knows* (New York: Macmillan, 1964), esp. 327–345.

31. Nixon was still trying to get political mileage out of the Hiss case with an "Op-Ed" piece in the *New York Times*, 8 January 1986. See the letter(s) by Alger Hiss (and others) in the *New York Times*, 21 January 1986.

32. This was widely reported in the European press, by CNN, and in the *New York Times*, 29 October 1992.

33. General Volkogonov, who was responding to questions by historian John Lowenthal, two months later said that Lowenthal " 'pushed me hard to say things of which I was not fully convinced.' " The general, himself a historian, is also quoted as saying, " 'I was not properly understood. The Ministry of Defense also has an intelligence service, which is totally different, and many documents have

been destroyed. I only looked through what the K.G.B. had. All I said was that I saw no evidence.' " See *New York Times*, 17 December 1992. Given that the October interview was taped and broadcast by CNN, it would be illuminating to know who "pushed" the general this time. General Volkogonov's remarks are quoted in Tony Hiss, "My Father's Honor," *New Yorker*, 16 November 1992. See also Victor Navasky, "Nixon and Hiss," *Nation*, 4–11 January 1993. For the predictable *Commentary* view, see Sam Tanenhaus, "Hiss: Guilty as Charged," April 1993, 32–37.

34. See Owen Lattimore, *Ordeal by Slander* (New York: Bantam, 1951).

4

Loyalty Oaths

America's deeply rooted "subversion paranoia"[1] is most clearly exhibited in the loyalty oath. This, too, has a philosophical dimension. New York may have been the first, but many states introduced one or another form of loyalty oath[2] as a bulwark against the spread of such doctrines as communism and syndicoanarchism.[3] Anticommunist oaths were required of all sorts of people as conditions of employment. Union officials, schoolteachers, municipal, county, and state employees, physicians, and lawyers were often caught in this strange requirement.[4] Sometimes the prescribed oath was positive, that is, an oath to support the state and federal constitutions. Others were negative; that is, one was obliged to swear that one was not a member of any of a large number of groups declared subversive by one or another state or federal agency. The lists often ran into the hundreds and generally included, for example, members of groups that had supported the Loyalist cause against Franco and the fascists in the Spanish Civil War.

Some of those called to appear before a congressional (or state legislative) investigative committee avoided testifying by pleading their Fifth Amendment (one cannot be required to incriminate oneself) rights either because they had something to hide or because they wanted to frustrate the committee or, more often, because they did not wish to "name names." In the parlance of the day, they were often dubbed "Fifth Amendment communists." In order to "show" the extent of communist penetration of American institutions, committees were especially concerned to expand their "body count." Some witnesses were encouraged to think that the more names they could mention (as, e.g., being fellow members of some "dubious" organization), the less severely they would be treated by the committee. HUAC's investigation of Hollywood and the entertainment industry was successful in terrifying Hollywood writers, producers, actors and actresses, and so on. As the title of Lillian Hellman's book *Scoundrel Times* suggests, those called before the committee generally revealed weakness of character. As discovery procedures, the hearings were a total farce because it was later revealed that the Los Angeles police had had a direct pipeline into the local Communist party from 1936 through 1945.[5] A few targets of investigation, like the folk singer Pete Seeger, had the courage to refuse on principle to talk about their political beliefs and invoked the *First* Amendment. Seeger was convicted of contempt of Congress and served a year in prison. Other people, like Richard Nixon and Whittaker Chambers, used America's subversion paranoia successfully to promote themselves. Foreigners seeking entry to the United States must still be prepared to deny various political affiliations.

Legislators are generally either wise or cynical enough to appreciate that loyalty oaths do not guarantee that what people say is what they truly think and believe. Nevertheless, oaths play several useful functions. Thus, by means of an oath, one can hail a signer into court or before a committee, adduce evidence that he or she has lied, and have the person charged with perjury. In the 1950s, there was no shortage of professional (ex-communist) witnesses who would testify, wherever possible in their capacity as former officers in the party, that so-and-so was known to him or to her as a card-carrying member of the Communist party. People so accused would then be called before a committee and threatened with perjury charges if they disagreed with what the informer had testified to. In this way, the victims found it necessary to prove what in a normal court trial they would not have to prove, namely, that they were innocent—that is, *not* fellow travelers or communists, although paradoxically, for First Amendment reasons, the party itself was never formally outlawed. By the perjury route, it was easy to obtain convictions. Given the prevalent background assumptions that all communists lied, and that any evidence an accused might produce was ipso facto tainted, the witch trial character of these episodes was obvious. Nothing was deemed to count as evidence that might exculpate a person accused of being a communist. One's actions were not on trial, but one's thoughts and beliefs were, and these were accessible only by means of the FBI's trained troop of informers. It could even prove imprudent to bring forward impressive character witnesses on one's behalf. Thus, Supreme Court justices Felix Frankfurter and Stanley Reed and Illinois governor Adlai Stevenson appeared as character witnesses for Hiss at his trial. But given the antinomian attitudes then current, the fact that Hiss had such loyal and distinguished supporters was taken by some to prove his guilt. Who else, it was asked, but a communist could produce such witnesses? Whereas every time Chambers admitted that he had lied under oath, his credibility actually increased.[6] When, a few years later,

Owen Lattimore wrote about his own experiences, he titled his book *Ordeal by Slander*.

Oaths also intimidate and threaten those who are obliged to sign them. In the 1950s, teachers knew that it was easier to hurl a charge at someone than it was to mount a cogent defense. Academic research was constrained by justifiable fears. A generation of Far East experts was rooted out of the government and from universities on the ground that these experts had facilitated the rise of the Chinese communists and thereby contributed to America's "giving away of China."[7] American Asian policy still suffers from the damage done in this period. Congressional investigations turned up people who had been members of the Communist party, at least at earlier times, as well as fellow travelers. Real espionage agents were occasionally apprehended in that period, but they were, of course, not discovered by committees. Spies were not likely to use party membership as a cover, and in any case, the exposure of genuine spies was hardly the aim of the anticommunist movement. Often, as in the case of Lattimore, the methodology employed was to explore the theories and ideas of witnesses in order to determine where their views stood in relation to what the committee members (usually, the committee counsel) thought the Communist party position was. Thus, the goal was to anathematize a range of opinions.[8] The outsider, viewing American history in this period, may well wonder how, given the words of the First Amendment ("Congress shall make no law . . . abridging the freedom of speech"), legislative committees could ever be authorized to investigate in areas in which they were constitutionally precluded from legislating. But they were—and they are.

Hollywood, the professions, and especially teachers were prime subjects for investigation. State universities were often the objects of scrutiny by state legislative committees, but the American Association of University Professors was also obliged to declare itself for or against the appointment and retention of communist subversives on the university campus. To the extent that the association looked at the problem that way, its answer was clear. But in fact the AAUP struggled with the topic over many years.

One of those most active in the debate, and probably the most articulate in laying forth his argument, was the late New York University (NYU) philosophy professor Sidney Hook. (After his retirement, Hook joined Stanford's Hoover Institute for the Study of Communism, Revolution, and Peace.) His book *Heresy, Yes; Conspiracy, No*[9] seemed to draw a line between free speech of a sort that was deemed appropriate within the confines of a teaching environment and speech that it was felt would corrupt the youth and bring a university into disrepute. Unlike many of his contemporaries, Hook knew perfectly well that Socrates had been condemned to death for the crime of "corrupting the youth." Accordingly, he drew his distinction in homelier terms: Conspiracies were both wrong and illegal. But heresy, however disruptive and offensive, should be tolerated by a democratic society. Hook largely ignores the fact that in both the past and the present heresies are generally seen as conspiracies whenever religious authorities have sufficient political might to prosecute the claim. In whatever way Hook may wish to specify a distinction between religion and politics, we have no shortage of examples where the distinction is not drawn and of instances where heretics end up at the stake or are stoned to death or shot. By a heretic, Hook seems to mean a free-thinker dedicated to the honest pursuit of truth, unencumbered by any ideological blinders. Those criteria, however, are clearly grossly inadequate because no classical heretics or heretical movements measure up to them. There were people who supported Hook with regard to communists as teachers but who also believed that, for example, Catholics or fundamentalists disqualified themselves from teaching by virtue of their commitment to an authority that seemed to be outside the purview of the "logic of inquiry." Such a position might have won a few purist academic adherents in the 1950s, but given the overtly religious component to the cold war, it would not have meshed well with the larger anticommunist agenda. It was, after all, under President Eisenhower that the phrase "under God" was added in 1954 to the Pledge of Allegiance to the U.S. flag.

In any event, Hook holds that "the primary commitment of the teacher is to the ethics and logic of inquiry" (34) and applies that principle exclusively to communists because, he claims, they have pledged themselves to carry out "professional misconduct." They do not "teach"; they "indoctrinate" their students. Moreover, they "inculcate the Communist Party line that in case of war students should turn their arms against their own government" (35). Membership in the party is *"prima facie* evidence of professional unfitness to teach" (51). Hook makes it clear that he believes that no rights are absolute and that speech can often be a form of action. He approves of the Supreme Court's majority decision in *Dennis v. United States* (1951) upholding the Smith Act's prohibition against teaching and advocating the overthrow of the government by force and violence.

Hook is not an advocate of loyalty oaths, presumably on the ground that "true" communists would have no qualms about signing them, and although he favors, at least as a general rule, the dismissal of Communist party members and members of communist front organizations, he prefers that such decisions be in the hands of faculty, rather than legislative, committees. It is, he believes, a matter of enforcing "proper standards of professional conduct" (269). Some sense for what Hook meant by *professional* can be gleaned from the fact that in 1956 he successfully moved a resolution before the American Philosophical Association (APA) placing the APA on record as applauding and supporting the Hungarian Freedom Fighters. But after the APA had gone on record in 1970, in connection with the Indo-China War, urging with considerable specificity that universities cease to be "instruments of injustice," Hook mounted (together with nine other senior professors, including W.V.O. Quine and Harry Frankfurt) a much-publicized counterattack. Conveniently ignoring his 1956 resolution, he held that as a professional organization the APA had no business making "official political pronouncements." It was under such covers as "professional" and "university" that institutions, especially in the post–World War II area, eagerly welcomed the opportunity to be subverted by military, corporate, and intelligence agencies in return for handsome contracts.

Arthur O. Lovejoy had spoken eloquently in defense of Russell's academic freedom. With respect to communists, it was another story. Lovejoy largely follows Hook. In 1920, Lovejoy had already staked out his position with respect to academic freedom. Universities are "perverted from their proper function" if the teaching and research of their scholars do not reflect their own and their fellow specialists' research but rather the "opinions of other men—whether holders of public office or private persons from whom endowments are received." At that time, he was attacking an endowment for a special professorship "to be devoted to showing 'the fallacies of socialism and kindred theories and practices.' "[10] Lovejoy holds that "[f]reedom of inquiry, of opinion, and of teaching in universities is a prerequisite, if the academic scholar is to perform the function proper to his profession." Communists, on the other hand, are committed to subordinating their opinions to the dictates of the party. He adds, "No one, therefore, who desires to maintain academic freedom in America can consistently favor that movement, or give indirect assistance to it by accepting as fit members of the faculties of universities, persons who have voluntarily adhered to an organization one of whose aims is to abolish academic freedom."[11]

He rejects the argument that excluding communists would itself be a restriction on freedom of opinion, teaching, and research in universities. Speaking about that conception of freedom without which a university cannot pursue its proper function, he says that "it is not one which implies the legitimacy and inevitability of its own suicide. . . . [W]hat it implies is that there is *one* kind of freedom which is inadmissible—the freedom to destroy freedom."[12] Lovejoy would allow former communists to remain on faculties only if they give "evidence of loyalty to the principles of intellectual and political liberty" by displaying their genuine opposition to the "whole political system of the U.S.S.R." by a public denunciation of the suppression of freedom under communism, and by a rejection of the party's goal of a one-party dictatorship and of "the teaching of Lenin (still to be found in current Party publications) that a party member should, when it will serve the interest of the movement, resort to 'any ruse, cunning, unlawful method, evasion, and concealment of the truth.' "[13]

Lovejoy's view that academic freedom should not be accorded to those who would use it to deny it was certainly not at the time unusual. Indeed, it is but a variation on Locke's doctrine of not tolerating those who do not themselves respect religious toleration. What is unusual is the apparent consistency with which Lovejoy applied it. In 1913, he had been distressed by the restrictions on academic freedom imposed by religious institutions. A scholar who would surrender his judgment to an ecclesiastical authority has, ipso facto, surrendered his status as a scholar. Universities that accept "special" endowments (and most of them do), and professors who are awarded "special" chairs, are similarly yielding the core principle of academic freedom. Communists are similarly willing to undermine academic freedom by submitting their own judgments to an external and nonacademic authority. Although in the early years of the AAUP Lovejoy had ruffled many administrators' feathers by proposing to impose AAUP censure on those religious institutions that violated academic freedom principles, one wonders how he would have reacted to things like Stanford's Hoover Institute and Hook's acceptance of an appointment there. One knows how, given his principles, he *should* have reacted. As for communists, they are a menace because their party membership gives them an entitlement to lie. And that is a serious problem within the academy. Lovejoy's focus is largely restricted to education, and while he takes freedom of speech to be essential for a democratic society, he does not get into the question of loyalty oaths that so energized this period.

There is nothing new in America's employment of oaths. Already in the seventeenth century their efficacy and use took on a new urgency. With Calvinism came a new interest in the conscience as the private voice of God in each human. Reading the literature on oaths in the post-Reformation era one is struck by the real fear the Calvinist doctrine struck into the hearts of those Calvinists and others concerned with either acquiring or maintaining their power over their fellows. The problem is quite simple: If the doctrine of private conscience is taken too seriously, control of the individual is impossible. Thus, John Sharp,[14] archbishop of York, sees appeals to conscience as providing a "Shelter for Disobedience and Disorders." Calvin's notion that our relationship with God is unmediated through any human agency (such as the Church) was already a matter of concern to his contemporaries. But if minds are inaccessible—and that is what the Calvinist doctrine seems to say—then a philosophically grounded conceptual barrier to control of the minds of ordinary people has been put in place. That such an opinion might be internalized by large numbers of people was distressing to the philosophers (like John Locke) and theologians with an interest in the preservation of privilege. The English had already encountered problems with Protestants, thanks to Oliver Cromwell. Thus, William Fleetwood, bishop of St. Asaph, says:

An Oath is a most Religious thing; 'tis an acknowledgement of God's Omniscience . . . [and] that we believe he knows the very Secrets of our Hearts. . . . An Oath, is the solemn calling upon God, to bear witness, that what we utter with our Mouths, is what we believe in our Hearts to be exactly true; and it is also the solemn Calling upon God, to punish, and take vengeance on us, if we do not seriously intend what we say and promise. The Heart of Man lies secret to all the World; you want to know whether I speak the Truth; and whether I intend to do, as I say I will do. My bare Word is not sufficient in the Case; because all Men are, or may be Liars; and tho' their Words may be with you, yet their Hearts may be far from you.[15]

As I have explained in detail elsewhere,[16] a number of writers found it natural to think of the magistrate not just as God's representative but as his image on earth. After all, Paul had asserted: "The powers that be are ordained of God" (Rom. 13: 1). The trouble is that while we can find analogues between God's beneficence and omnipotence with that of the natural virtues of the magistrate, there is no analogue to God's *omniscience*. Happily for magistrates who worry about the loyalty of their underlings (and they always do!), the oath can fill that crucial gap. By making subjects swear an oath, one gains access to their otherwise inaccessible minds.

In order for oaths to externalize minds, in order for oaths to be politically effective, the oath takers must believe that God will wreak vengeance on those who lie under oath. Therefore, it is important to attack atheism and vigorously to preach the terrible torments of hell. Locke, for example, would exclude atheists from the state since their oaths have no such force or backing. There being no obvious way to turn back Calvinism, and perhaps no simple way quickly to defeat the Cartesian dualist model of human nature, theoreticians in the second half of the seventeenth century found the oath a means whereby the tongue and the heart could be threatened into agreeing one with another. In the seventeenth and early eighteenth centuries, England was profoundly troubled by the matter of loyalty. Quite apart from religious disputes and the constant fear of Catholic subversion, there was the problem of those who had taken the oath to the monarch "and his or her successors" prior to the Revolution of 1688. Could one, without violating one's previous oath, take an oath to William and Mary? This particular dispute occurred entirely within the confines of the Established church.

With the Test Act (1673) had come the sacramental test. This was conceived as a device to force underground Catholics either to expose themselves or to violate their religious beliefs. The test went beyond the mere oath, the sincerity of oaths being always open to question, by requiring that officeholders, university students, and so on, be seen to receive Communion within the Anglican church on a regular basis. Thus, a person, by walking to the Communion rail and receiving the sacrament, met the "behavioral" test of "outward conformity." This presupposed that at least sincere Catholics would not conform. Barriers to Catholics and dissenters lasted well into the nineteenth century. Russell's grandfather was instrumental in bringing about the repeal of the Test Act in 1828, but it did not alleviate Catholic hostility to the grandson!

Although probably quite unaware of why the Calvinists had troubled about oaths in the seventeenth century, or why the English employed the oath to detect Catholic "subversion," it was because the Americans also wanted to control minds, to control beliefs, that they went on their loyalty oath "binge" in the twentieth century. To some extent, anticommunists such as Harry Truman were intent on fashioning what was to become known as the cold war. And to some extent, a motley crowd, backed by considerable financial, media, and institutional support, managed to coalesce long enough to exert the necessary political influence to implement these thought-control measures once the wartime alliance with the Soviet Union was over.

Regardless of how one interprets the political/historical events, the interesting philosophical point about oaths is that they had for centuries been seen as a (the only?) means for peering into the human mind in order to detect impurities among one's beliefs. One could supplement oaths with such admittedly fallible means as lie detectors and so-called truth serum. Since all means, from torture to lie detectors, are said never to be "certain," those who employ them are implicitly acknowledging that they think about minds as being in principle inaccessible. Such uncertain means do, however, intimidate subjects.

The other option, often inconsistently employed together with the first, is to maintain that there really is no mind. Everything is already "external." This is very close to the line Henry Stebbing[17] takes in the early eighteenth century. Options of the first sort can be used to buttress the doctrine of oaths; the second enables one to dismiss worries about a deity and instead to invoke the fire and brimstone that the penal code applies to perjurers in *this* world. Since oaths are clearly directed at beliefs rather than actions, one might have expected the courts to ban them. After the McCarthy period, loyalty oaths were treated more severely by the courts,[18] but not before the damage had been done, not before a spirit of intimidation was abroad in the land. It remained at full strength for more than a decade and at half-strength for a decade after that.

There is nothing strange about subversion paranoia generating the machinery of thought control. What is paradoxical is that this has occurred within a legal system purporting to stand as a defense of freedom of speech and of freedom of religious belief. And so it generally seemed to Justice Black: "In my view, the First Amendment absolutely prohibits a State from penalizing a man because of his beliefs. . . . Here the State seeks to probe what an applicant's state of mind is to ascertain whether he is 'without any mental reservation, loyal to . . . the Constitution.' But asking about an applicant's mental attitude towards the Constitution simply probes his beliefs, and these are not the business of the State."[19] In *Lerner v. Casey* (1958), Black draws what I have been claiming from the outset is the philosophically relevant category distinction: "The realm of belief—as opposed to action—is one which the First Amendment places beyond the long arm of government."

NOTES

1. "When, in 1639, the first printing press in the English-speaking colonies began operation in Boston, the first item struck off was [a] loyalty oath." Harold M. Hyman, *To Try Men's Souls* (Berkeley: University of California Press, 1960), 15.

2. For a discussion of the seventeenth-century use of the oath as a device to probe, control, and "externalize" the mind, see my "Minds and Oaths," in *Mind and Language: Essays on Descartes and Chomsky* (Dordrecht: Foris, 1984), chap. 4.

3. Other pervading forms of oath have long been present: the "Pledge of Allegiance" to the flag, standing during the singing of the national anthem, and so on. These have sometimes been challenged on religious freedom grounds. In *West Virginia State Board of Education v. Barnette* (1943) the Supreme Court ruled against a compulsory flag salute requirement (in schools) on free-speech grounds: "We think the action of the local authorities in compelling the flag salute and pledge transcends constitutional limitations on their power and invades the sphere of intellect and spirit which it is the purpose of the First Amendment to our Constitution to reserve from all official control" (Justice Robert H. Jackson for the majority). Note that this was a wartime decision.

4. See Ralph S. Brown, *Loyalty and Security: Employment Tests in the United States* (New Haven: Yale, 1958).

5. For a detailed and judicious discussion of this grim period, see Victor S. Navasky, *Naming Names* (New York: Viking, 1980). Navasky has an informative discussion of the Remington case as well as of the trials and tribulations of the ACLU in those years. See also Lillian Hellman, *Scoundrel Times* (New York: Little, Brown, 1976).

6. Perhaps the best account of the role of the press in covering the Hiss trials is by *New Yorker* reporter A. J. Liebling, reprinted in his *The Press*, 2nd rev. ed. (New York: Ballantine, 1975), 197. Liebling also discusses why Hiss could not get a fair trial in New York and analyzes the reasons the courts gave for denying requests for a change of venue.

7. See, for example, Robert P. Newman, *Owen Lattimore and the "Loss" of China* (Berkeley: University of California Press, 1992).

8. See U.S. Congress, Senate, *Hearings before the Subcommittee to Investigate the Administration of the Internal Security Act and Other Internal Security Laws of the Committee on the Judiciary*, 82nd Cong., 1st and 2d sess. (1952), on the Institute of Pacific Relations. The extended investigation (and destruction) of the institute is a good case study in how committees actually handled ideas. The same subcommittee explored the anti–Vietnam War teach-in movement in 1965.

9. Sidney Hook, *Heresy, Yes; Conspiracy, No* (New York: John Day, 1953).

10. Arthur O. Lovejoy, "Communism *versus* Academic Freedom," *American Scholar* 18 (1949): 332. Lovejoy says that "the words 'holders of public office' " were not in the 1920 original.

11. Ibid.

12. Ibid.

13. Ibid.

14. John Sharp, *A Discourse of Conscience* . . . (London: Walter Kettilby, 1684), 2.

15. William Fleetwood, *A Sermon upon Swearing* (London: J. Roberts, 1721), 12–13.

16. See, for example, Thomas Comber's remarks (1682) discussed in my "Minds and Oaths," chap. 4 of my *Mind and Language*.

17. *Report of the Committee* . . . , 6th ed. (London: John Morphew, 1717), 4. The row was triggered by a sermon by Benjamin Hoadley, bishop of Bangor. The literature on the so-called Bangorian controversy is voluminous, and the discussion runs on for years. Stebbing, William Law, Hoadley, and others contribute.

18. The Supreme Court nibbled away at oath legislation, and although by the time of *Keyishian v. Board of Regents* (1967) the constraints imposed were severe, a few states still require oaths from certain employees.

19. Justice Black (with Justice Douglas) in dissent in *Law Students Civil Rights Research Council v. Wadmond* (1971), *Political and Civil Rights* . . . , 1, 186. *Lerner v. Casey* (1958) (Black and Douglas in dissent) is discussed by Thomas I. Emerson, *The System of Freedom of Expression* (New York: Vintage, 1971), 232.

5

Hate Literature and Related Problems: The Canadian Experience

The American doctrine of freedom of speech, as articulated in the Bill of Rights, is 200 years old. By contrast, Canada acquired its Charter of Rights and Freedoms only in 1982.[1] Although it grants the Supreme Court of Canada the right of judicial review, it also (in § 33) allows provinces that disagree with a decision (rendered under the Charter) to exempt themselves from its application for a five-year renewable period. This means that a Canadian's "rights and freedoms" may, and do, vary from province to province. Moreover, the Charter speaks of "freedom of expression," *not* freedom of speech. And this freedom is not accorded any special priority, it being but one of many values given a place in the Charter. Thus, one finds in a post-Charter recodification of criminal law that the crime of blasphemy[2] is retained. In addition, the multicultural nature of Canadian society is also specified in the Charter, and from this, as will be noted, certain legal consequences follow.

As Canada struggles with the continuing problem of satisfying Quebec's various demands, one finds three views about rights: (1) Each province should be master of its own affairs—including traditional rights. This looks, at least to Americans, like the familiar U.S. states' rights question. (2) The Quebec thesis: Rights are not individual. On the contrary, all rights inhere in the Quebec (linguistic) community. (3) In advancing the cause of the Charter of Rights and Freedoms, then–Prime Minister Pierre-Elliott Trudeau's vision was that the Charter rights inhere exclusively in each Canadian regardless of where he or she may live in Canada. Trudeau continues to argue that point, and it was a central factor in his powerful argument against the Charlottetown (so-called Meech II) agreement rejected in a national referendum in October 1992. Most other politicians now favor (1) or (2) and explicitly reject (3).

Over the last decade, a number of freedom of expression cases have come before the Canadian courts, for example, § 181 of the Criminal Code of Canada. It reads: "Everyone who wilfully publishes a statement, tale or news that he knows is false and that causes or is likely to cause injury or mischief to a public interest is guilty of an indictable offence and is liable to imprisonment for two years."

Ernst Zündel was convicted under this "falsification of history" statute for publishing so-called Holocaust revisionist literature.[3] Although § 181 was at that time ruled constitutional,[4] his fifteen-month sentence was quashed by the Ontario Court of Appeal in January 1987 and a new trial ordered. In the spring of 1988, Zündel was found guilty in his new trial and sentenced to nine months in prison. Initially, the courts refused to hear any further appeals.[5] Zündel's free-speech rights were defended by the Canadian Civil Liberties Association. Amnesty International, however, indicated that it did not propose to consider him a "prisoner of conscience" although he appeared to meet their standards.

Laws of this sort require that the court determine at least these three things: that the accused is wrong about some historical facts, thereby making the court the arbiter of history; that certain words can and do cause specific untoward consequences; and that the accused is saying things which that person *knows* to be false.

There is an obvious sense in which courts do settle matters of historical fact, as when they decide that an accused has committed a crime, say, the crime of burglary. What is of particular interest in falsification of history cases is that the court first specifies the historical facts (e.g., by taking "judicial notice" of them) and then applies criminal sanctions against those who speak "falsely" about those facts. That resembles the jurisprudence exhibited in the Stalin trials of the 1930s. Zündel's lawyer apparently agreed. In his November 1990 submission to the Supreme Court, he suggested that the law "enables special interest groups to seek judicial notice, or judicial imposition of an officially sanctioned view of matters of fact in history which should not be in the purview of courts in a free and democratic society."[6] The Supreme Court of Canada (with several new members) granted authorization for Zündel to appeal on this question, and in late August 1992 the Court struck down what is now § 181 [in *Regina v. Zündel* (1993) 95 DLR (4th), 202], the falsification of history statute by a 4–3 vote. The majority opinion by Justice Beverley McLachlin holds that

all communications which convey or attempt to convey meaning are protected by s. 2(b) [of the Canadian Charter of Rights and Freedoms]. . . . The content of the communication is irrelevant. The purpose of the guarantee is to permit free expression to the end of promoting truth, political or social participation, and self-fulfillment. That purpose extends to the protection of minority beliefs which the majority regards as wrong or false. Section 181 . . . has undeniably the effect of restricting freedom of expression and, therefore, imposes a limit on s. 2(b).

The dissenting justices opine that § 181 [in *Regina v. Zündel* (1993) 95 DLR (4th), 260] is aimed at restricting "not all lies, but only those that are wilfully published and that are likely to injure the public interest"(224). And "the harm caused by the wilful publication of injurious lies is sufficiently pressing and substantial to justify a limited restriction on freedom of expression" (239).

McLachlin begins her analysis by presenting a brief history of this remarkable statute. It dates from the 1275 Statute of Westminster: "It had as its primary aim the prevention of 'false statements which, in a society dominated by extremely powerful landowners, could threaten the security of the state' " (254). The offense of spreading false news was abolished in England in 1887. "It was enacted in Canada as part of the 1892 *Criminal Code*. The reason for the offence's retention in Canada is unknown" (256). She reports that F. R. Scott suggests its inclusion was an oversight, "no one in Canada being aware that the English provision had been repealed" [!]. In the 1892 Code, it was listed under "Seditious Offences" but later "as a species of 'Nuisance.' " Originally, it carried a one-year potential sentence. However, with parliament's 1955 transfer of the act from the "Seditious" to the "Nuisance" portion of the Code came an increase in the potential sentence to two years.

The Crown, to succeed, must establish beyond a reasonable doubt the following propositions:

1. That the accused published a false statement, tale or news;
2. That the accused knew the statement was false; and
3. That the statement causes or is likely to cause injury or mischief to a public interest. (256)

Justice McLachlin finds serious difficulties with all three points. First, the distinction between a statement of fact and an opinion was, "in a practical sense," settled by the trial judge and not the jury (257). "By applying the doctrine of judicial notice and telling the jury that the 'mass murder and extermination of Jews in Europe by the Nazi regime' was an (historical) fact 'no reasonable person' could dispute, the judge effectively settled the issue for them" (257-258). Second, as to the perhaps philosophically more interesting question of an accused's knowledge of the falsity of the claims he or she advanced, "the jury was instructed that it was entitled to infer from the judge's instruction that because the Holocaust must be regarded as proven, the accused must have known it to be proven and must be taken to have published his pamphlet deliberately for personal motives, knowing the falsity of his assertion to the contrary. . . . The logic is ineluctable: everyone knows this is false; therefore the defendant must have known it was false" (258). With respect to the third element in the offense, "the issue of whether a statement causes or is likely to cause injury or mischief to the public interest requires the identification of a public interest and a determination of whether it has been or is likely to be injured."

One is thus driven to conclude that this was not a criminal trial in the usual sense. The verdict flowed inevitably from the indisputable fact of the publication of the pamphlet, its contents' divergence from the accepted history of the Holocaust, and the public interest in maintaining racial and religious tolerance. There was little practical possibility of showing that the publication was an expression of opinion, nor of showing that the accused did not know it to be false, nor of showing that it would not cause injury or mischief to a public interest. The fault lies not with the trial judge or the jury, who doubtless did their best responsibly to inform the vague words of s. 181 with meaningful content. The fault lies rather in concepts as vague as fact versus opinion or truth versus falsity in the context of history, and the likelihood of "mischief" to the "public interest." (259)

The issue arises in many discussions of freedom of speech as to whether lies are protected. McLachlin maintains that even deliberate lies can, on occasion, "promote truth, political or social participation, or self-fulfillment," as when a "doctor, in order to persuade people to be inoculated against a burgeoning epidemic, may exaggerate the number or geographical location of persons potentially infected with the virus" (262). She also vigorously objects to the effort to reinterpret § 181 radically.

My colleagues say that it is a permissible shift in emphasis that the false news provision was originally focused on the "prevention of deliberate slanderous statements against the great nobles of the realm" and is now said to be concerned with "attacks on religious, racial or ethnic minorities." . . . But this is no shift in emphasis with regard to the purpose of the legislation—this is an outright redefinition not only of the purpose of the prohibition but also of the nature of the activity prohibited. To convert s. 181 into a provision directed at encouraging racial harmony is to go beyond any permissible shift in emphasis and effectively rewrite the section. (266)

It is the overbroad quality of § 181 that leads the majority on the Court to rule it in violation of the Canadian Charter.[7] This is largely the same Court that only a few years earlier found in *Regina v. Keegstra* that § 319, the "hate literature" statute, is not in conflict with the Canadian Charter of Rights and Freedoms. That law withstood challenge because it is much more specific with reference to the sorts of offensive speech it criminalizes and because it limits itself to statements intended to cause "hatred against any identifiable group," rather than the vague "mischief to a public interest" found in § 181. Thus, despite the Court majority's apparent commitment to the values of freedom of speech, in the end what are decisive in overruling the statute are legal considerations independent of the free-speech principle. *Keegstra* and the hate literature law stand unaffected by this decision, and presumably an action could still be taken against Zündel under that law, assuming he publishes new material.

The *Globe and Mail* (Toronto) editorialized that under this statute "no one need be demonstrably harmed by the 'false' speech, nor must it be shown that anyone has suffered a measurable injury."[8] In their news story on the decision, the paper quoted Justice Beverley McLachlin: " 'To permit the imprisonment of people, or even the threat of imprisonment, on the ground that they have made a statement which 12 of their co-citizens deem to be false and mischievous to some undefined public interest, is to stifle a whole range of speech, some of which has long been regarded as legitimate and even beneficial to our society.' "[9]

After toasting the death of the "false news" section of the Criminal Code last week, we return to some troubling questions. What does it say about the reasoning ability of the Supreme Court of Canada that a bare majority could be found to strike down so plainly ludicrous a statute? What does it say about the degree of absorption in government circles of the principles of a "free and democratic society" that the first reaction to the false news decision out of Ottawa and Queen's Park [seat of the Ontario government in Toronto][10] was not to reflect upon the quaintness of such attempts to criminalize ideas but to cast about for another law that will do the trick? . . .

It says that, ten years after the Charter of Rights and Freedoms, a century after John Stuart Mill, two centuries after the Bill of Rights, three centuries after Milton, the case for free speech still has yet to sink in. Certainly most people would say they believe in it, but when that belief is put to the test—when the speech to be defended is not what they find agreeable, but what they find abhorrent—even those schooled in law and legal philosophy seem to let their emotions overcome them. Perhaps they are especially prone, for they are best able to devise such pleasing bits of sophistry as might be needed to dress their illiberal urges in liberal drag.[11]

The editorial points out that only two years before, the Court had endorsed, unwisely according to the *Globe and Mail*, the ban on hate literature. "The Court's primary objection to the false news law, it emerges, is not one of principle, but of process: it is too broadly drawn."

To repeat: Not only does a falsification of history statute (1) make a court the arbiter of history, but antiadvocacy legislation in general (2) assumes without argument that words cause actions. Hence, advocating a crime becomes a crime. Within radical free-will systems such as Descartes's and Bayle's, each person is responsible for his or her actions. We may listen to someone urging us to reach for the rifles, but if we in fact *act*, that is, reach for the rifles, that is *our* decision. It is a decision each person makes on the basis of the reasons the speaker has presented. Only then should we (and *not* the speaker) be subject to criminal penalties. The thesis that speech does not of itself "cause" action follows, or so I have been suggesting, from speech/action dualism plus the freedom of our wills. On the other hand, antiadvocacy legislation presupposes that the category of talk can and should be assimilated to that of action. At the same time the United States was enforcing antiadvocacy laws, and insisting that people said to be under

Communist party "discipline" had to do what they were told, a strangely opposite view was applied by the Allies in the Nürnberg War Crimes trials and has become a standard that is not to be circumvented by claiming that one was only "following orders." The military personnel of all nations are now expected not to obey *illegal* orders, which is to say that even in contexts where commands are given, those who are commanded are not automata.[12] Even mere soldiers are free agents who must decide whether or not to obey the words they hear. The words do not "cause" them to act; they choose to act. No longer, at least in principle, does Tennyson's poetic reflection hold: "Their's not to reason why, Their's but to do and die." Traditionally, those who issue military commands are held to bear a "special" responsibility because their military commands are, by convention, said to be "performative utterances," and hence, like the words in marriage ceremonies, are formally counted as actions.

The context in which the causal efficacy of words upon actions is discussed usually includes incitement, propaganda, obscenity, pornography, and hate literature. That the discussion has persisted inconclusively over the centuries, despite a plethora of "scientific" studies, suggests that conflicting doctrines of human nature may be at stake in this dispute. In any event, the fact is that our knowledge of the causation of human behavior remains extremely limited.[13] Hence, the efficacy of legislation to suppress libels, hate literature, blasphemies, and the like, not being obvious, it is sometimes argued that since the empirical evidence may suggest that such legislation may have the effect of "fanning the flames," a freedom of speech policy may, for purely pragmatic reasons, be the path of prudence.

Descartes, among others, believes that humans have absolutely free wills and that they are responsible for their own actions. If that is the case, no science of human behavior, no psychological theory that purports to explain the causation of human behavior, is possible. The fact that by bashing people we can often affect their behavior is the core truth of (S)timulus-(R)esponse behaviorist theories. But such theories are unable to cast much light on how successfully to reduce sexist, racist, or anti-Semitic attitudes in our societies.

(3) The third legal point is one I have already discussed. It runs counter to the philosophical presuppositions in terms of which Bayle's doctrine of the erring conscience is cast and which I take to provide the foundation for his absolutist theory of freedom of speech. His thesis is, however, no longer taken to be intelligible. An appeal to a conscientiously held belief is not now easily sustained. As Bayle sees the problem, only God can scrutinize our inner beliefs,[14] and only God knows whether we mean what we say. The modern doctrine is very different. Although statutes may still require that the accused *know* that what they say is false, the knowledge requirement is easily waived. A 1936 British appeals court put the matter with elegant simplicity: "The best and often the only way of proving that a statement was known to be false by the person who made it is to prove that he had

the means of such knowledge."[15] It is a short step to the traditional Catholic doctrine that "error has no rights."

Probably the most important reason the Canadian parliament found it appropriate to pass legislation against hate literature is that in the aftermath of World War II it was obvious that steps should be taken to prevent another Holocaust. In the 1960s, a commission, under the chairmanship of McGill Law School dean Maxwell Cohen, studied the matter of hate literature and made a series of recommendations that were passed into law. The revulsion the members felt is understandable; the solution they proffered is not.

The same forces that prompted Canada to introduce hate literature statutes after World War II affected other countries as well and led to such international proposals as Article 20 of the *International Covenant on Civil and Political Rights*. It reads: "1. Any propaganda for war shall be prohibited by law. 2. Any advocacy of national, racial or religious hatred that constitutes incitement to discrimination, hostility or violence shall be prohibited by law."[16] It should not be forgotten that the Germany of the 1920s had laws banning anti-Semitic publications. Although there were notable exceptions, they were largely enforced.[17] The rise of Nazism was obviously not deterred.[18] Today some Canadians believe there is a risk that prosecutions under hate statutes may kindle rather than alleviate racist or discriminatory sentiment. If one really could establish that such a risk exists, then prosecutions would apparently themselves have to be proscribed as falling under the harm principle.

For example, Rose Wolfe, the present chancellor of the University of Toronto, was distressed by the possibility of a new trial of Zündel.[19] It would "permit the accused a renewed opportunity to stage-manage a circus" (9). Chancellor Wolfe is presumably not opposed to retrials ordered by appellate courts in all cases but only in those that would create a "circus." She attended the sessions of the first trial and was appalled by defense lawyer Douglas Christie's arguments and rigorous cross-examinations. She was pleased that in the second trial, Judge Ronald Thomas (Ontario District Court) "ordered [the jurors] to take 'judicial notice' that 'mass murder and extermination of Jews in Europe by the Nazi regime during the Second World War is a historical fact' " (11). Having, as a case worker with Toronto Jewish Family and Child Service, had to place children orphaned in World War II concentration camps, Wolfe was made deeply sensitive to the Holocaust. For most Jews as well as for many others, the Holocaust has a religious aura such that Holocaust denial is not merely offensive; it is an act of blasphemy, just as for believing Christians a claim that the historical Jesus never existed is blasphemous. Although blasphemy is a "speech crime" and is a criminal offense in some countries (e.g., Canada and the United Kingdom), it is seldom invoked precisely because it runs counter to the "freedom of expression" principle to which those same nations say they subscribe.

In any event, Wolfe's personal anguish over the Zündel affair is entirely understandable. Her stated reasons are more puzzling. "She and others felt Zundel had to be taken seriously. If they just dismissed him as a member of the lunatic fringe, his insidious theory might spread and become an accepted part of the history curriculum. The symptoms became apparent during the trial when some 'so-called historians and academics' supported Zundel's ideas" (9). Wolfe believes that " 'Holocaust denial is the worst form of anti-Semitism. . . . There have to be some limits on freedom of speech' " (9). She was pleased when a second guilty verdict came down. "Wolfe stressed [its] importance to all minority groups: 'It reaffirms the effectiveness of the Criminal Code in upholding social and racial harmony' " (11).

American Jewish communities have generally tended to accept the values of the First Amendment and to use education as the best means to try to keep anti-Semitism at bay rather than to take the Canadian "group libel" route. It is, however, difficult to compare Canada and the United States with respect to levels of anti-Semitism. It is also difficult to evaluate whether Canada's banning of offensive speech contributes to a reduction or an increase in "social harmony."

In addition to *Zündel*, a second Canadian case relevant to freedom of expression is that of James Keegstra. He was found guilty of the unlawful promotion of hatred against Jews (under § 319[20] of the Criminal Code, the so-called hate literature statute) while teaching his high school students in a small town in Alberta. His 1987 conviction was reversed on appeal to the Alberta Court of Appeal (1988) 43 CCC (2nd), 150,[21] but the original conviction was reinstated by the Supreme Court of Canada in 1990 and sent back to the Alberta Court of Appeal.[22] In March 1991 the Alberta Court of Appeal quashed Keegstra's reinstated conviction on the new ground that he had not been given the opportunity to challenge the impartiality of his jurors. In April 1991, the Alberta attorney general ordered a retrial on the hate promotion charge. The new trial began in March 1992. Keegstra conducted his own defense, Douglas Christie having withdrawn as his attorney. He was convicted in July 1992.

"In my view," wrote Justice Roger Kerans (for the Alberta court in unanimously overturning Keegstra's original conviction), "imprudent promotion of hatred falls within the definition of freedom of expression" (1988) 43 CCC (2nd), 162. Nevertheless, the court grants the possibility of imposing constraints on expression in its exploration of the so-called proportionality issue; that is, "if the injury is serious enough, a limit is justifiable." Kerans cautiously rejects the "absolutist" position: "[I] am not unmindful of the close connection of speech to matters of conscience and the possibility that somehow, if the expression of an opinion is limited, so also might be the right to hold that opinion" (172). In the course of a passage full of measured irony, Kerans writes: "Parliament has decided that Canadians will be better democrats for being taught, by the criminal sanction, that some speech is an abuse of the right to free expression" (175).

In reversing the Alberta court's acquittal and reinstating Keegstra's conviction, the Supreme Court of Canada ruled (1990) 3 SCR, 697 that "Parliament's objective of preventing the harm caused by hate propaganda is of sufficient importance to warrant overriding a constitutional freedom." Chief Justice Brian Dickson notes that the trial judge in *Keegstra* had already "observed that the wilful promotion of hatred against a section of the Canadian public distinguished by colour, race, religion or ethnic origin is antithetical to the dignity and worth of the members of an identifiable group. As such it negates their rights and freedoms, in particular denying them the right to the equal protection and benefit of the law without discrimination" (718). The purpose of the act (i.e., § 319(2)) is "to restrict the content of expression by singling out particular meanings that are not to be conveyed," that is, those intended to promote hatred against identifiable groups (730). In sum, Dickson holds that the hate literature statute constitutes a justifiable infringement on the constitutional guarantee of freedom of expression.

Chief Justice Dickson repeats what an earlier Canadian Supreme Court majority had held in *Slaight Communications Inc. v. Davidson* (1989) 1 SCR 1038, 1056: "The underlying values of a free and democratic society both guarantee the rights in the *Charter* [*of Rights & Freedoms*] and, in appropriate circumstances, justify limitations upon those rights." He cites his own opinion in *Oakes* (1986) 1 SCR, 103 in which he lists these cardinal values: "Respect for the inherent dignity of the human person, commitment to social justice and equality, accommodation of a wide variety of beliefs, respect for cultural and group identity, and faith in social and political institutions which enhance the participation of individuals and groups in society" (1990) 3 SCR, 736. He goes on to say that these underlying values are the "ultimate standard against which a limit on a right or freedom must be shown, despite its effect, to be reasonable and demonstrably justified."[23]

After discussing American jurisprudence (including its tendency to reject legislation controlling the content of speech), Dickson opines: "[T]he special role given equality and multiculturalism in the Canadian Constitution necessitate[s] a departure from the view, reasonably prevalent in America at present, that the suppression of hate propaganda is incompatible with the guarantee of free expression" (743).

The arguments, by both the majority and the dissenters, are by and large the traditional ones. Nevertheless, three interesting elements emerge. First, Canada is *officially* bilingual; the United States has no official language. And although all countries are multicultural (even Vatican City), Canada incorporates multiculturalism into the wording of its constitution.[24] The Court seems to be using multiculturalism to find a less problematic legal basis for group libel than, for example, the more "individualistic" U.S. model currently provides.

The Supreme Court of Canada not only is concerned with multiculturalism as a basis for group libel but also is concerned further to protect the legal basis for French/English bilingualism. To the extent that language is believed, correctly or incorrectly, to be a *communal* activity, the protection of the legal rights of the language per se means according priority to the group over the individual.[25] In the extreme, it means saying that all rights inhere in the group, a view often expressed in Quebec.[26]

Second, a state is entitled to defend itself against its enemies. Hence, all speech that might be thought to undermine, or have the potential for undermining, the state can be proscribed. This is reminiscent of Locke's account of religious toleration: Those only are entitled to toleration who themselves are tolerant of others. Thus, we seem to have a paradox: To utilize such Charter guaranteed rights as freedom of expression verbally to challenge democratic values, as articulated by the Court, is to risk criminal sanctions. Does that mean that a racist or an officially unicultural or unilingual state could not come to power by democratic means? Does that mean that democratic values can only be sustained by the use of criminal sanctions?

Third, these cases again remind us just how basic freedom of speech really is for a democratic system. If a democratic society is a self-governing one, then it seems incontestable that the governors should be free to say what they want. It is difficult to understand how informed judgments are otherwise to be arrived at. To assume that one is entitled to restrict the words and thoughts of others is, as Mill noted, to appoint *oneself* a member of the Elect. Such restrictive moves presuppose a doctrine of human nature—presumably, that the mind can be pressed into any desired shape by the appropriate application of verbal data and that one not only knows what is best for that community but also knows how humans are affected by words and ideas, as if human minds were blank tablets on which subversive, heretical, or other offensive ideas might be written. Without some such presupposition, boards of censors and the legislation authorizing them make no sense. But the historical record suggests that there is no better system for countering heretical, subversive, and defamatory speech than the encouragement of free and open discussion.

Nevertheless, societies are often unwilling to trust the capacity of individuals to form their own judgments. Hence, agencies charged with deciding what is and what is not fitting for us to see and hear and read are often incorporated into legal systems. In the age of Orwell, it becomes necessary to support censorship in order to preserve democracy.

Additional intellectual support for this notion of human nature is often contributed by theories about the nature of language. It is sometimes claimed that the conceptual structures of our minds are functions of language. Speakers of language X are thus said to think about the world differently than speakers of language Y. In its pristine form, this is known as the Sapir-Whorf hypothesis. Presumably because they can be used to support the belief that language, as a behaviorally controllable environmental factor, determines human identity, such theories often play a role in creating and supporting the more unpleasant aspects of some nationalist movements. Such linguistic-cognitive theories tend to merge with doctrines about the formation of human identity. Although *identity* has proven to be a rhetorically powerful term with a patina of scientific respectability disguising its current nationalist/racist employment,[27] its apparent constituent structure is open, for each of us, to an infinite range of defining elements, of which language is but one. The plausibility of official language acts (e.g., in Belgium, Canada, Quebec, and Switzerland) is sometimes enhanced by such ideas about language. For example, the Preamble to Quebec's *Charte de la langue française* includes this line: "langue distinctive d'un peuple majoritairement francophone, la langue française permet au people québécois d'exprimer son identité."[28] It is an interesting question whether such acts violate the free-speech principle. Can one be "free" to say anything under the restriction that one must say it exclusively in language X?

The United States has never had an "official" language. However, English has become the dominant language, and federal agencies (e.g., the Bureau of Indian Affairs), states, and localities have sometimes proscribed the use of other languages among government workers, schoolchildren, and so on. Historically most immigrant groups learned English and sought to assimilate, or at least to participate, in the majority culture. Nevertheless, as rights are increasingly seen as belonging fundamentally to groups instead of individuals, one can expect increased demands from linguistic communities for tax support for schools in their own languages and for a share of government jobs. Bilingual schooling was originally conceived as a means whereby a second language could be used to assist linguistic minority students and prepare them for full participation in the English educational stream. The experience in New York City, however, suggests that some such schools tend to become increasingly unilingual, and where the minority community is large enough, one can function without ever learning English, although one is denied access to higher education and good jobs.

Several states have recently made English their official language (and banned all others) either by statute or by (state) constitutional amendment, as in Arizona, California, and Florida. Hawaii has been officially bilingual since 1978. The Arizona amendment was struck down by U.S. District Judge Paul G. Rosenblatt as "unconstitutionally 'overbroad'—that is, as prohibiting speech protected under the First Amendment far beyond the means necessary to achieve a legitimate state purpose."[29] The Arizona amendment (1988) insists on the use of the English language in "all statutes, ordinances, rules, orders, programs, and policies . . . [and for] all government officials and employees during the performance of government business."[30] The Rosenblatt decision is now on appeal. Meanwhile, a group of state senators and state employees have taken an action in the Arizona state courts asking that the "Official English" state constitution amendment be declared unconstitutional because it violates "free speech and due process rights." Attorney Stephen Montoya claims: "Citizens have the right to communicate with elected officials in the language of their choice."[31]

The legislation in Arizona, California, and other states that makes English the official language of the state will presumably be challenged in the appeals courts. Perhaps, as in the Rosenblatt decision, these cases will also be resolved in terms of the free-speech principle. Although the issue has never been adjudicated, the U.S. Supreme Court, in *Meyer v. Nebraska* (1923), did rule (7–2) against a state law (Iowa had a similar law) prohibiting the teaching, in public or private schools, of any subject in any language other than English to anyone who had not passed grade eight. Meyer taught religion in a parochial school through the medium of German. The Court judged that the statute violated the Fourteenth Amendment's due process clause. No reference was made to the First Amendment. Holmes dissented.[32]

The larger question of whether a bi- or multilingual country is feasible is a complex issue far beyond my present concerns. I simply note (1) efforts to have formally multilingual states, even where the linguistic communities have some measure of geographical separation, have not met with much success, perhaps because they are often the consequence of earlier imperial policies or because one linguistic community feels itself to be culturally (and not just politically) inferior to the others; (2) Canadians and Americans, being colonials mainly from European lands, sometimes forget that all states have linguistic minorities and that all states must find ways to deal, equitably or inequitably, fairly or unfairly, with their polyglot fellow citizens. They also often seem to forget the extent of their efforts either to exterminate or, in a more benign mode, to make linguistically invisible the indigenous peoples of North America.

The Supreme Court of Canada has been obliged to rule on a large number of language rights cases in recent years. Canada is officially bilingual (French and English), but Quebec has introduced a number of laws prohibiting languages other than French on signs and has a language police (dubbed "tongue-troopers" by the minority groups). In December 1988 [*Ford v. Quebec* (1988)], "the court ruled unanimously that 'language is so intimately related to the form and content of expression that there cannot be true freedom of expression by means of language if one is prohibited from using the language of one's choice.' "[33] Although Canada's Charter of Rights and Freedoms guarantees freedom of expression, it also (§ 33) authorizes any province to opt out of any decision rendered under the Charter that it doesn't like. Quebec chose to do just that. Language legislation in Quebec is a complex topic, but the best brief and politically and historically informed English account of Quebec's language laws is the afore-cited *New Yorker* article by Mordecai Richler, one of Canada's (and Quebec's!) most noted writers and arguably the best political satirist writing in North America today.

Interviewed on CBC television about his new book,[34] an expanded version of his *New Yorker* article, Richler reportedly said that "in the Thirties [Montreal's] Le Devoir was 'interchangeable with Der Stürmer,' a weekly Nazi newspaper." In an editorial response, the publisher of *Le Devoir*, Lise Bissonnette, strongly condemned Richler and said that "many people are pressing Le Devoir to sue Mr. Richler, to silence 'such a liar.' She said the paper is hesitating because it respects freedom of expression and would not want to give him another platform. However, she did not rule out an eventual lawsuit, adding that with the editorial she wanted to respond immediately to such 'trash.' " She went on to describe the interview as a "Rhodesian scene." *Rhodesian* has been a term of art in Quebec politics ever since René Levesque used it to refer to Quebec Anglos. Several members of the Bloc Québécois party in the federal parliament, including MP [Member of Parliament] Pierrette Venne, demanded that the book be banned in Canada. Bissonnette disagrees because "[w]e should not turn him into another Rushdie." The leader of the Bloc, Lucien Bouchard, takes a softer line: " 'I'm fully against banning books. That's not the kind of Quebec we're trying to build.' "[35] In his new book, Richler not only provides more than enough data about *Le Devoir* to establish his claim; he also lays out the racism and the fierce anti-Semitism and misogyny of the Abbé Lionel-Adolphe Groulx (1878–1967), described as "the spiritual father of modern Quebec. Everything noteworthy, everything novel on the Quebec scene has carried the imprint of Groulx's thought."[36]

Richler's remarks prompted this comment from Pierre Péladeau, publisher of *Le Journal de Montréal*: " '[Richler] has the cheek to call himself a Quebecer,' he said recently, 'That's a bit as if I were to consider myself Chinese.' "[37] Howard Burshstein, a Jewish Montrealer now living in Toronto, is quoted as saying: "Once they started taking away language rights, our parents reminded us that that was how it started in Germany in the 1930s. They told us to leave."[38]

[In the Quebec national Assembly, Premier Robert Bourassa,] who three years earlier had pronounced the banning of English on public signs as "totally unacceptable," boasted that his government, showing its courage, had outdone the PQ [Parti Québécois] in putting it to *les autres*. "Never before in the history of Quebec," he said, "has a government suspended fundamental liberties to protect the French language and culture."[39]

Because provinces can choose to veto the application of any human rights guaranteed in the Charter to "all" Canadians, Premier Bourassa could ignore the Canadian Supreme Court's unanimous judgment, noted above, that "there cannot be true freedom of expression by means of language if one is prohibited from using the language of one's choice." This Canadian Court decision should be brought to the attention of the U.S. Supreme Court before it rules on the various English-only statutes that will eventually be before it. Although it may only be by virtue of historical accident that the United States has avoided making English the official language, the U.S. courts can now choose between adhering to the First Amendment's free-speech clause and an American version of the Bourassa principle.

Returning to American practices, seven months after his infamous *Schenck v. United States* (1919) opinion, U.S. Supreme Court Justice Holmes writes in *Abrams v. United States* (1919): "The ultimate good desired is better reached by free trade in ideas. . . . [T]he best test of truth is the power of the thought to get itself accepted in the competition of the market." It may seem from the sorts of difficulties often adduced when efforts to suppress speech are advanced that the ultimate argument for free speech is the futility of suppressing it. But the evidence does not sustain that interpretation. The tried and true method for suppressing ideas is to eliminate the people who hold them, for example, the Albigenses.

Pornography[40] is another area where strict adherence to the free-speech principle creates difficulties. In both the United States and Canada, attempts have been made to prohibit the manufacture and dissemination of pornographic literature, films, and the like. This is a huge topic, but very briefly the justification offered is that this material degrades women, it exploits the actual participants, and some people also believe that it encourages men to act violently toward women. University of Michigan law professor Catherine MacKinnon has sought to convince U.S. legal authorities that if the psychologically demeaning treatment of African-Americans was seen as a factor warranting state intervention to strike down school segregation,[41] that is, if the Court can act against *racial* discrimination, then it should act against material that discriminates against women. U.S. courts have not accepted her analogy and have tended to rely on the free-speech principle.

Against the feminist opponents of pornography, novelist and essayist Sallie Tisdale claims:

[These] censors [she mentions Catherine MacKinnon and Andrea Dworkin] are concerned with how men *act* and how women are portrayed. Women cannot make free sexual choices in that world; they are too oppressed to know that only oppression could lead them to sell sex. . . . What a misogynistic worldview this is, this claim that women who make such choices cannot be making free choices at all—are not free to make a choice. Feminists against pornography have done a sad and awful thing: *They* have made women into objects.[42]

In Canada, precisely because of the weaker status given freedom of expression in the Charter and hence the constitutionality of hate literature legislation, there is a more straightforward way to invoke government action in this connection. Although obscenity and antipornographic laws may appear to run counter to Canada's freedom of expression guarantees, the Supreme Court of Canada has, in a unanimous decision (27 February 1992), found that the current obscenity law does not conflict with the Canadian Charter. In its lead editorial, the *Globe and Mail* (Toronto) comments:

The courts will now be directed to judge pornography "on the basis of the degree of harm that may flow" from exposure to it. "Harm in this context," wrote Judge Sopinka, "means that it predisposes persons to act in an anti-social manner as, for example, the physical or mental mistreatment of women by men, or what is debatable, the reverse.". . . It establishes that the right to freedom of expression cannot be used as an excuse for spreading the most debasing forms of pornography—not when that right violates the right of women to equality, undermines their personal security or reduces them in a way that may leave them more exposed to violence. . . . "The objective [wrote Judge Sopinka] of avoiding the harm associated with the dissemination of pornography in this case is sufficiently pressing and substantial to warrant some restriction on the full exercise of the right of freedom of expression."[43]

A news report notes that "[a]ccording to a US legal expert [presumably MacKinnon], the court made Canada the first country in the world to recognize in its law a link between hard-core pornography and violence against women."[44] To those who doubt that there is a body of empirical evidence establishing such a link, this case will be another instance of a court establishing a "fact" and punishing deviation from it.

In both Canada and the United States, the difference between pornographic and erotic art has already proven difficult to characterize in law. And there are other complications: First, many U.S. and Canadian commentators favoring a ban on pornography consider pornography to be political. Assuming they do not mean to trivialize their thesis by saying that everything is political, a peculiar problem arises because even the less zealous defenders of the free-speech principle generally assert that at least political speech must be protected. Second, MacKinnon argues that the segregation-pornography analogue holds because both are *conduct*. She claims that segregation is conduct that expresses the idea that African-Americans are inferior; pornography is conduct that expresses the idea that women are inferior. Which is to say that by trying to bring pornography under the rubric of conduct, thereby collapsing both the speech/action and expression/action distinctions, she seeks to make it more readily subject to legal sanctions than when it falls under the category of *idea*.

I have said that Canada, by reason of its according civil rights to communities, and not just individuals, has little trouble with group libel legislation. One finds a ready acceptance in the recent hate literature decisions that if people can claim to be hurt by offensive speech, they are entitled to legal redress. As noted above, the Canadian Charter was drafted after World War II. Thus, the Cohen Committee, which was responsible for recommending to the Canadian parliament the first hate literature legislation, after explicitly rejecting the "simple faith of the Enlightenment" view that humans are rational said: "The successes of modern advertising, the triumphs of impudent propaganda such as Hitler's, have qualified our belief in the rationality of man. We know that under strain and pressure in time of irritation and frustration, the individual is swayed and even swept away by hysterical, emotional appeals. We act irresponsibly if we ignore the way in which emotion can drive reason from the field."[45]

Although Canadian and American jurisprudence seem to differ in several fundamental ways, there are forces at work in the United States that are driving them together, at least with respect to group libel. Admittedly, the contrast I have been drawing between the American individualistic tradition and the communitarian element in Canadian jurisprudence is a matter of emphasis rather than an absolute distinction. After all, the U.S. Constitution was drafted by and for white males. In calculating the number of congressional representatives to which a state was entitled, each (non-voting) slave counted as three fifths of a person (this changed with the post–Civil War Fourteenth Amendment [1868]). When Patrick Henry cried, "Give me liberty or give me death!" (1775) he was a slave owner. Moreover, several states had Established churches well into the nineteenth century. According rights and privileges to certain "identifiable groups" is not a doctrine of recent origin.

Commenting on the spring 1992 riots in Los Angeles, A. Lijphart, a professor at the University of California–San Diego, reportedly said that the United States "must distance itself from its 'political ethos in which the individual, not the group is central' and think more in the direction of group rights."[46] The paradox of this philosophical recommendation is that the racism, which it is assumed will be alleviated by group rights, is *itself* the product of an appeal to group rights. As just noted, group rights were incorporated into the U.S. Constitution when black slavery was authorized and women were excluded from the franchise. Racism, anti-Semitism, homophobia, sexism, and certain forms of nationalism are not products of individualism. They are affirmations of the political primacy of one *group* over another. The Politically Correct advocates of group rights and communitarian interests seem to ignore the fact that the racism, sexism, and the like, they would combat by "introducing" group or community rights are themselves rooted in a doctrine of group rights.

So we see that the Enlightenment doctrine of human nature, one that is readily compatible with making the individual the sole bearer of rights, has been shifting to a more communitarian model. The empiricist model in which the human is considered to be malleable and plastic and totally the product of external social forces is in the ascendant. Unlike the Enlightenment model, this one more readily provides a basis for the community to be seen as the primary bearer of rights. In the light of the twelve-year

German experiment with community rights, it is puzzling that democratic societies should once again find it so tempting to move in that direction.

NOTES

1. The opening portion of the Charter reads:

Canadian Charter of Rights and Freedoms.

Whereas Canada is founded upon principles that recognize the supremacy of God and the rule of law:

Guarantee of Rights and Freedoms

§ 1. The *Canadian Charter of Rights and Freedoms* guarantees the rights and freedoms set out in it subject only to such reasonable limits prescribed by law as can be demonstrably justified in a free and democratic society.

Fundamental Freedoms

§ 2. Everyone has the following fundamental freedoms:
   (a) freedom of conscience and religion;
   (b) freedom of thought, belief, opinion and expression, including freedom of the press and other media of communication;
   (c) freedom of peaceful assembly; and
   (d) freedom of association.

2. As late as 1971, blasphemy charges were brought under a Pennsylvania statute. See Robert C. Post, "Cultural Heterogeneity and Law: Pornography, Blasphemy, and the First Amendment," *California Law Review* 76 (1988): 297–335, both for his discussion of the issues and for bibliographical material. Blasphemy came only tangentially before the U.S. Supreme Court in *Burstyn v. Wilson* (1952). The Court reversed (9–0) a New York ban on showing the movie *The Miracle*.

3. A similar law has been used in France against Robert Faurisson, professor of comparative literature at Lyon. Cf. Noam Chomsky, "The Faurisson Affair: His Right to Say It," *Nation*, 28 February 1981. In 1991, Faurisson was again penalized for "contestation de crimes contre l'humanité" as a result of remarks made in a published interview. This is reportedly the first time that the Gayssot law of 13 July 1990 has been applied. It prohibits "à quiconque de mettre en doute les crimes contre l'humanité jugés par une juridiction française ou internationale." *Le Monde*, 20 April 1991, 12. See also 25 March 1991, 10.

4. The Ontario Court of Appeal [(1987) 58 OR (2nd), 129] in ruling that § 177 does not conflict with the Charter, canvassed a wide range of legal opinion, Canadian, Commonwealth, and U.S., having to do with freedom of expression. Although, as noted above, they made the common mistake of saying that "A person is not at liberty to shout 'fire!' in a crowded theater," apparently forgetting that Justice Holmes (in *Schenck* [1919]) spoke of "falsely shouting," they were satisfied that in all jurisdictions the preponderance of learned opinion is that freedom of expression is not absolute.

5. Appeals to the Ontario Court of Appeal were dismissed, 5 February 1990. *Regina v. Zündel* (No. 2), (37 OAC, 354).

6. "Zündel Appeals on New Grounds," *Canadian Jewish News*, 23 May 1991.

7. McLachlin comments later in her opinion: "One of the cases relied upon [by the dissenters] in support of the proposition that the section deals only with

statements of fact and not with expressions of opinions, *Regina v. Hoaglin* [(1907), 12 C.C.C. 226 (N.W.T.S.C.)], demonstrates just how slippery the distinction may be. If the expression in issue in that case, in which a disaffected American settler in Alberta had printed posters which stated 'Americans not wanted in Canada. Investigate before buying lands and taking homesteads in this country' is an example of a 'false statement of fact' falling within the prohibition [of this statute] one shudders to consider what other comments might be so construed" (1993) 95 DLR (4th), 272.

8. Editorial, "The Right Ruling on False News," *Globe and Mail* (Toronto), 28 August 1992.

9. Ibid., 1.

10. Patricia Chisholm's report on the decision illustrates the *Globe and Mail* editorialist's complaint. In her piece, "The Right to Lie," she writes: "Ultimately, Ottawa may have to enact new legislation to control the dissemination of some kinds of hate literature. In Toronto [Ontario Attorney General Howard] Hampton said that officials of his ministry will meet with their federal counterparts 'to discuss drafting a Charter-proof section of the Code' to deal with cases like Zundel's. Added Hampton: 'We don't yet know if that is possible.' " *Maclean's*, 7 September 1992, p. 47.

11. Editorial, "The Right to Be Wrong," *Globe and Mail*, 31 August 1992.

12. Appeals to the so-called Nürnberg defense were not notably successful in the Indo-China conflict, the activities of victors (or at least the more powerful) being, by definition, legal.

13. Noam Chomsky has often raised this question, for example, in *Reflections on Language* (New York: Pantheon, 1975), chap. 1.

14. Pierre Bayle, *Oeuvres diverses*, 4 vols. (Den Haag: Husson et al., 1727–31), vol. 2, 397.

15. A defamatory libel case, *Rex v. Wicks*, 25 Crim. App. R. 174. Also cited in *Rex v. Unwin*, Alberta Supreme Court, App. Div. 69 Cdn. Crim. Cases, 202 (1938). As noted above, the Canadian Supreme Court makes a similar point in *Zündel*.

16. Article 19 of the same *Covenant* reads: "1. Everyone shall have the right to hold opinions without interference. 2. Everyone shall have the right to freedom of expression. . . . " In § 3, however, we read that there may be certain restrictions: "but these shall only be such as are provided by law and are necessary: (a) For respect of the rights or reputations of others; (b) For the protection of national security or of public order, or of public health or morals." President Jimmy Carter signed this covenant on behalf of the United States in 1977. The vacuous quality of Article 19 constitutes the legal "theory" behind the Campaign for Human Rights that the United States has waged in the interim in, for example, El Salvador, Nicaragua, and Panama.

The European Convention on Human Rights provides a large set of constraints on freedom of expression in Article 10: "The exercise of these freedoms, since it carries with it duties and responsibilities, may be subject to such formalities, conditions, restrictions or penalties as are prescribed by law and are necessary in a democratic society, in the interests of national security, territorial integrity or public safety, for the prevention of disorder or crime, for the protection of health or morals, for the protection of the reputation or rights of others, for preventing the disclosure of information received in confidence, or for maintaining the authority and impartiality of the judiciary." So much for the ideal of freedom of expression on the European model.

17. Donald L. Niewyk, "Jews and the Courts in Weimar Germany," *Jewish Social Studies* 37 (1975): 99–113; Ambrose Doskow and Sidney B. Jacoby, "Anti-Semitism and the Law in Pre-Nazi Germany," *Contemporary Jewish Record* (1940), 498–509; but see also Karl Lowenstein, "Legislative Control of Political Extremism in European Democracies," *Columbia Law Review* 38 (1938), pt. 1, 591–622; pt. 2, 725–774. Cyril Levitt argues that matters were by no means so straightforward as Niewyk, perhaps too enamored of his quantitative methods, suggests. See Levitt, "The Prosecution of Antisemites by the Courts in the Weimar Republic: Was Justice Served?" *Leo Baeck Institute Yearbook*, vol. 35 (London: Secker and Warburg, 1990), 151–167; and idem, "Racial Incitement and the Law: The Case of the Weimar Republic," in *Freedom of Expression and the Charter*, ed. David Schneiderman (Toronto: Thomson Professional Publishing, 1991), 211–242. Levitt concludes: "If there is anything we can learn from the Weimar experience, I think it is this: The law can only be an effective instrument in containing, controlling and discouraging racist expression if it is founded upon a sound democratic political culture" (242). Prior to *1984* the assertion that only a "sound democratic culture" can provide the basis for an effective use of the law to suppress freedom of speech would have been discarded as a contradiction.

18. For an interesting study of some of the intellectual roots of the Holocaust, particularly in medieval Christianity, see Malcolm Hay, *Europe and the Jews: The Pressure of Christendom on the People of Israel for 1900 Years* (Boston: Beacon Hill, 1961).

19. "In Defence of the Truth," an interview by Karina Dahlin in the *University of Toronto Magazine*, Autumn 1991, 7–11. N.B. In Canadian universities, the chancellor, as in the British system, is generally not an academic. Like the chair of a university board of regents or trustees, it is a position of honor and prestige, with some influence over policy questions but little over day-to-day university operations.

20. § 319(2) reads: "Every one who, by communicating statements, other than in private conversation, wilfully promotes hatred against any identifiable group is guilty of . . . [etc.]"; § 319(4) adds: "In this section, 'identifiable group' means any section of the public distinguished by colour, race, religion or ethnic origin."

21. Appeals #17699 and 17701 (87 AR 200, 60 Alta LR (2nd) (CA)). It is interesting to see how differently the Alberta court understands freedom of expression in comparison with the subsequent decision of the Canadian Supreme Court in *Keegstra* (1990) 3 SCR, 697. The Alberta court, for example, emphasizes a different set of U.S. Supreme Court cases from the Ontario court and takes more seriously (although it rejects) the absolutist interpretations.

The Alberta Court of Appeal also finds the hate literature statute unconstitutional in that it requires a jury to convict even if the jury thinks that what an accused has said might be true or if the jury is convinced that not a single Canadian actually came to hate any member of any group as a result of what an accused has said. The court also objected that the statute [because of § 319 (3): "No person shall be convicted of an offense under subsection (2): (a) if he establishes that the statements communicated were true"] put the onus of proof on the accused to prove that what he or she said was probably true, rather than the crown having to prove its probable falsity.

22. Case #21118 (1990) 3 SCR, 697. In this connection, see *Regina v. Andrews* (65 OR (2nd) 161) in which the Ontario Court of Appeal (1988) rejects an appeal against a hate literature conviction. The multicultural nature of Canada, as specified in the Charter, plays an important role in evaluating the priority to be accorded the Charter's protection for freedom of expression. At the time the Supreme Court of Canada (SCC) handed down its decision in *Regina v. Keegstra* (1990), it also ruled against the appeal from 65 O.R. (2nd) 161 in *Regina v. Donald Clarke Andrews and Robert Wayne Smith*. The SCC supported § 319(2) on grounds similar to those given in *Regina v. Keegstra (1990) 3 SCR, 870*.

23. In 1990, the Supreme Court of Canada also supported the constitutionality of § 13(1) of the Canadian Human Rights Act in the case of *Regina v. John Ross Taylor and the Western Guard Party* (1990) 3 SCR, 892. The act provides: "It is a discriminatory practice for a person or a group of persons acting in concert to communicate telephonically or to cause to be so communicated, repeatedly, in whole or in part by means of the facilities of a telecommunication undertaking within the legislative authority of Parliament, any matter that is likely to expose a person or persons to hatred or contempt by reason of the fact that that person or those persons are identifiable on the basis of a prohibited ground of discrimination." The accused allegedly made prerecorded hate messages available on a call-in telephone system in Toronto.

24. Recalling the vast police and military force arrayed against the native Indians near Oka, Quebec, and Montreal during the summer of 1990, one may wonder what multiculturalism really amounts to.

25. Contemporary philosophers have, especially since Martin Heidegger and Wittgenstein, devoted much effort to arguing for the socially determined role of language. In general, such philosophers (for example, see Michael Dummett, "Language and Communication," in *Reflections on Chomsky*, ed. Alexander George [Oxford: Blackwell, 1989], 192–212) see the primary role of language to be communication. From this, certain things are said to follow about the social dimension of language, about speaker/hearer intentions, about rule following, about the acquisition of a "form of life," and so on. This is usually put in opposition to Descartes's view, and Chomsky's, that language is for the expression of thought. The additional claim (by, e.g., Chomsky) that each human develops his or her own ideolect does not sit happily with these philosophers. Chomsky writes at some length about these matters in his *Reflections on Language*, esp. chap. 2, where Grice, Searle, and Kripke are critically discussed. See also Chomsky's two papers in Asa Kasher, ed., *The Chomskian Turn* (Oxford: Blackwell, 1991), esp. the second.

26. The doctrine that individual rights must be subordinated to group rights is found in many countries, for example, in Indonesia, where it is a direct consequence of the *pancasila* state ideology. All critics of the government may be penalized, but since March 1992, even Indonesians who criticize it while outside their country run the risk of not being allowed to return. The government is especially sensitive to criticism of its invasion of East Timor and its policy of genocide there. See N. G. Schulte Nordholt, "In Indonesisch besluit ligt een ultimatum besloten," *NRC Handelsblad* (Rotterdam), 31 March 1992, 11.

27. A variant of this theme is discussed in Richard Greeman, "The French Republic and the Holocaust: French Anti-Semitism, Ethnic Cleansing, and the Nation-State," *Z Magazine*, January 1993, 43–45. Greeman notes: "[P]ost-Solidarity Poland deserves some sort of special prize for promoting 'anti-Semitism without Jews,' . . . The *reductio ad absurdum* of the Polish example seems to indicate that racism and xenophobia, like war, are the necessary features of the nation-state, arising independent of any actually existing internal or external 'enemy' " (43).

28. Quoted in Claude-Armand Sheppard, "La tolérance et les législations linguistiques: Le modèle canadien," in *The Notion of Tolerance and Human Rights*, ed. Ethel Groffier and Michel Paradis (Ottawa: Carleton University Press, 1991), 59. The Charte de la langue francaise (Bill 101) was introduced after the promulgation of the Canadian Charter (1982); several sections were later found unconstitutional by the courts but were nevertheless enacted by means of the Canadian Charter's "not withstanding" clause whereby a province can legislatively overrule a Supreme Court decision with which it disagrees. See also the essay "Les aspects juridiques de la tolérance: Essai de terminolgie" by Ethel Groffier in the same volume.

29. In James Crawford, ed., *Language Loyalties: A Source Book on the Official English Controversy* (Chicago: University of Chicago Press, 1992), 288. The case is *Yniguez v. Mofford*, 730 F. Supp. 309 (D. Ariz. 1990).

30. *Language Loyalties* presents the several state constitutional amendments, statutes, and ordinances requiring English at 132–135. The Arizona amendment is given on 132–133.

31. *Daily News Tribune* (Tempe, Ariz.), 4 November 1992. (AP story)

32. In this general connection, see the work of Shirley Brice Heath, esp. "A National Language Academy? Debate in the New Nation," *International Journal of the Sociology of Language* 9 (1976), 9–43; idem (with Frederick Mandaback), "Language Status Decisions and the Law in the United States," in *Progress in Language Planning*, ed. Juan Cobarrubias and Joshua A. Fishman (Berlin: Mouton, 1983). See also the focus article by David F. Marshall, "The Question of an Official Language: Language Rights and the English Language Amendment," *International Journal of the Sociology of Language*, 60 (1986), 7–75. There are comments by eighteen commentators including Shirley Brice Heath and Lawrence Krasner (157–162) and Marshall's "Rebuttal Essay," (201–211). And see Joshua A. Fishman, *Language and Ethnicity in Minority Sociolinguistic Perspective* (Philadelphia: Multilingual Matters, 1989).

33. Quoted in Mordecai Richler, "A Reporter at Large: Inside/Outside," *New Yorker*, 23 September 1991, 40–92. The "Inside/Outside" in his title refers to the incredible (and to an outsider, hilarious) rules whereby the government proposed to allow English signs *inside* stores, and so on, but not outside, provided the English was smaller, less visually contrastive, and the like. The article greatly offended Québécois politicians and journalists. They attacked Richler for suggesting that anti-Semitism has on more than one occasion been a part of Quebec intellectual life, and several took the opposite tack: for example, "Richler is a disaffected, English-speaking, Jewish writer, outside the mainstream" and that he only wrote such disgusting stuff because he could make money with it. See "Mordecai Richler Pens His Reply," *Gazette* (Montreal), 28 September 1991. Full page, A10.

34. Mordecai Richler, *Oh Canada! Oh Quebec! Requiem for a Divided Country* (Toronto: Penguin, 1992). While Richler skewers many of Quebec's culture heroes and their present-day defenders, he briefly does the same for the Alliance for the Preservation of English in Canada (APEC) and for U.S. English (founded by McGill graduate and former U.S. senator, the late S. I. Hayakawa).

35. All quotations in this paragraph are from the article by Patricia Poirier in the *Globe and Mail* (Toronto), 20 March 1992, A4.

36. Richler, *Oh Canada!* 95. The quote is from Claude Ryan, one-time distinguished intellectual and editor of *Le Devoir* (Montreal), metamorphosed into a hack politician. Richler also cites the work of Esther Delisle. See her *The Traitor and the Jew* (Montreal: Robert Davies, 1993) for evidence of *Le Devoir*'s anti-Semitism in the 1930s.

37. Quoted in Mordecai Richler, "Special Report: In the Eye of the Storm," *Maclean's*, 13 April 1992, 28–30. Richler notes: "So much for the PQ fiction that anybody who lives in Quebec is a Québécois. In *La belle province* [Quebec], as on Animal Farm, some voters will be more equal than others come October [scheduled voting date], and if the referendum [on independence] result is close, as I anticipate, say only 52 or 53 percent opting to stay in Canada, things could get hot for Quebecers named Kelly, Lin, Bercovitch or MacNeil. Anybody who suggests otherwise is either a fool or a liar" (30).

38. See the article by Tom Fennell, "Going Down the Road: Toronto Is a Magnet for Montreal Jews," *Maclean's*, 13 April 1992, 39. It is reported that since the 1960s, 300,000 more Anglophones have left the province than have moved to Quebec. There has been a 57 percent decline in the province's English-school enrollment. The exodus is expected to accelerate. Montreal is not likely to become another Beirut because the tensions between the two major colonial groups (the English and the French) are not of that order and because residents can move to other parts of Canada (albeit at an economic price) without needing visas.

39. Richler, *Oh Canada!* 51. (The address was made in March 1989.)

40. See, for example, Joseph M. Weiler and Robin M. Elliot, eds., *Litigating the Values of a Nation: The Canadian Charter of Rights and Freedoms* (Toronto: Carswell, 1986). See the three essays in pt. 4, "The Regulation of Pornography: A Case Study in Freedom of Expression," by Kathleen A. Lahey, Louise Arbour, and Robin Elliot.

41. That is, in *Brown v. Board of Education of Topeka* (1954).

42. Sallie Tisdale, "Talk Dirty to Me: A Woman's Taste for Pornography," *Harper's*, February 1992, 37. Quoted passage is at 45 (author's emphasis). In her reply to several critics, Tisdale writes: "The most effective way to stop violence against women is to empower women and remake the roles that have harmed them. The world of pornography is a male world, as are the spheres of medicine, industry, law, and government. Why should we applaud women entering these worlds but not the world of pornography? Why should we think the one occupation will damage women more than, say, practicing corporate law?" *Harper's*, May 1992, 78.

43. Editorial, *Globe and Mail*, 29 February 1992.

44. *Globe and Mail*, 29 February 1992, A4. MacKinnon is cited in the article as having assisted in the preparation of one of the briefs presented to the Supreme Court of Canada.

45. *Report of the Special Committee on Hate Propaganda in Canada*, 1966, 8. Cited in the *Canadian Bar Association Report of the Special Committee on Racial and Religious Hatred*; Ken Norman, chair, 1984.

46. Interview by Kees Verteegh, *NRC Handelsblad*, 11 May 1992, 2. Lijphart (University of California–San Diego) was in the Netherlands to receive an award for his work in "comparative political science."

6

The Curriculum, Deconstructionism, and Freedom of Speech

One place where a convergence is emerging between American and Canadian jurisprudence is on American university campuses. There is much increased support for the introduction of group libel legislation. Free speech on campus has long been a concern of the AAUP and especially of the ACLU. Believing that the values embodied in the U.S. Constitution ought to find unfettered expression within universities, these organizations have sought to guarantee that the academic freedom of students and faculty be at least as broad as the First Amendment guarantees.

In the larger context in which universities exist, over and above the inhibitions on ideas generated by oaths, witch-hunting investigations, and the like, there is always the risk that subtle, and sometimes not-so-subtle, concern for orthodoxy, discipline by discipline, will be expressed in hiring policies. These latter practices are seldom enshrined in law, and they should be recognized as having been a part of the academic scene since the Middle Ages, if not since Aristotle was prevented from succeeding Plato as head of the Academy.[1] Blacklisting and other forms of nongovernmental censorship have long been accepted features of cultural and educational policies in America. Current efforts by neoconservative academic elements to arouse concern over such new censors in the Academy as the deconstructionists (whose efforts at censorship *are* reprehensible) might be more persuasive were they not themselves dedicated to the continued imposition of the old censorship. According to the neoconservatives, there are two very different diseases plaguing American universities. One is affirmative action; the other, shifts in *the* curriculum. The first touches on racist aspects of the society at large and the introduction of legal palliative measures.

Hence, this also affects the university. The second is seen as a response to ideological pressures purely within the university and without legislative sanction. Both are seen as core principles of "Political Correctness." Political Correctness is little more than a label for a cluster of ideas and attitudes that the neoconservatives do not like, with affirmative action perhaps the most offensive and feminism and Marxism added ideological irritants.

Various sorts of affirmative action programs have been on the American scene for at least three decades. They are an attempt primarily to redress the three centuries of inequitable and discriminatory treatment accorded African-Americans by requiring that employers hire qualified minority workers until the numbers show that race is no longer being used as a barrier to employment. The step from laws that simply prohibit discrimination to the creation of such affirmative action acts as Equal Opportunity Employment legislation has angered some (many?) whites because they believe that they are being deprived of such benefits as their employment, promotion, and seniority rights in order that such benefits might be allotted to minority group members. The Reagan and Bush administrations sought, as part of their general opposition to civil rights legislation, to persuade the courts to restrict the impact of affirmative action programs.[2] Such programs provided a focus for the racist rhetoric that George Bush first used so successfully in his 1988 presidential campaign by fostering a sense of grievance between blacks and whites at the lower end of the economic spectrum.

It is because affirmative action programs bear on university staff hiring and student admission policies that campus conservatives, the old censors, are distressed by affirmative action. With respect to students, it is objected that African-Americans are admitted with much lower qualifications than whites, who "must" be turned away. This, it is argued, is not only unfair to those whites, but it is reducing the intellectual level of the students in American universities. Given the small numbers involved in most universities, it is hard to take seriously the proclamations about falling standards being a consequence of affirmative action. But at the faculty level, many other considerations are involved. Affirmative action is a threat to that "old boys' network" that has been so successful in making it difficult for African-Americans, other minority groups, and especially women to break into faculties. Moreover, faculty members who gain access to academia with the assistance of affirmative action may be inclined to hold political views out of phase with those of the old censors.

Affirmative action policies are sometimes said to be a form of "reparation" for past sins of commission and omission. It is hard to argue that such sins do not besmirch American and European (if not *all*) history. Nevertheless, it is problematic whether by according benefits in terms of one's membership in a particular group we can somehow create a society in which each citizen, regardless of group membership, is equitably treated before the law. These issues have been discussed for many years, and only one aspect is of immediate relevance to my own thesis. The university forms used to monitor institutional compliance use five classifications (over and above male/female): (1) American Indian or Alaskan native; (2) Asian or Pacific Islander—glossed as "persons having origins in any of the original people of the Far East"; (3) black—not of Hispanic origin—glossed as "persons having origins in any of the black racial groups of Africa"; (4) Hispanic—glossed as "persons of Mexican, Puerto Rican, Cuban, Central or South American, or other Spanish culture or origin regardless of race"; and (5) white—not of Hispanic origin—glossed as "persons having origins in any of the original people of Europe, North Africa, or the Middle East." That an Argentinean can count as Hispanic and a Berber as white for the purposes of affirmative action policy may seem perverse, but that is just one of the peculiarities that arises once one classifies persons into *five* groups and presses for some sort of "racial" balance in appointments (and admissions) among these five.[3] It is puzzling that barely a generation after trying to prevent further unfortunate consequences of policies based on racial ranking, one can again accept a central element of Nazi theory by checking for *limpieza de sangre*.

That may seem an offensive way to characterize a policy that aims at equity and fairness. Indeed, no one who has spent much time in the academic world is under any illusions about the difficulties of persuading colleagues to take, say, women candidates seriously so long as men, often less qualified, are available. "Voluntary" or "good-faith" efforts tend to come to naught. All too often, private prejudice constitutes public policy. That is why legal coercive measures have been resorted to. The aspect of affirmative action that bears directly on my thesis, however, is that this legislation accords rights to *groups* because it is said that it is simply by virtue of being a member of a group that one was (is) discriminated against. An individual acquires rights superior to those granted others simply by being a member of a specified group—and not because said individual has a discrimination grievance against the university. It is thus paradoxical that a member of a minority group who may never have been subjected to discriminatory practices can take precedence over a member of a majority group who has never discriminated against a member of a minority group. As I shall show, the creation of group rights is crucially important in certain sorts of restrictions on freedom of speech.

Conservatives may object to affirmative action as "reverse discrimination," but they are sometimes willing to admit that certain minority groups have historically either been underrepresented in both student bodies and faculties or systematically excluded. Until long after World War II, African-Americans were victimized by legally enforced segregated and/or inferior education in many parts of the United States, and they often, "informally," still are. Jews were discriminated against in admissions to most universities and colleges prior to World War II, and they were not welcomed into faculties.[4] Professional and economic opportunities for women being restricted everywhere, they are restricted both in the United States and in Canada. Although women constitute a majority, they are still often discriminated against in law and practice.

Oberlin College was coeducational from its inception in 1832 and open to students of all races from 1835. Most state universities west of the Mississippi River were coeducational from their date of founding (e.g., Iowa, 1847). But it was not until the Nineteenth Amendment to the U.S. Constitution in 1920 that women, in principle, got the right to vote. A majority of Canadian provinces gave women the vote at the time of World War I, although Quebec waited until 1940. In 1930, the English Privy Council overruled the Canadian Supreme Court and declared women to be persons in law. That did not seem to help the case of Annie Macdonald Langstaff. She was graduated from McGill University's Faculty of Law in 1914, was refused admission to the bar, and was subsequently defeated in her court challenge. No woman was admitted to the bar of Quebec until 1941. Annette Baier, president of the Eastern Division of the American Philosophical Association, notes in her Presidential Address that in 1895 the division's first woman president, Mary Whiton Calkins (1918), after unofficially meeting the requirements and being examined for a Ph.D., was informed: "The Harvard Corporation is not prepared to give any Harvard degree to any woman, no matter how exceptional the circumstances."[5]

As the defenders of Political Correctness have correctly pointed out, the traditional curriculum has apparently not been very effective at communicating the recent, no less the older, facts about the patterns of discrimination endemic in our societies, patterns that are much more complex than the five racial groupings given metaphysical status by the U.S. equal opportunity laws. Or perhaps it has just been very easy to forget how recently the ways to higher education and to jobs were blocked for members of many of the groups whose access is now being slightly facilitated by affirmative action. It is true that so-called substandard students enter universities. More than a few students from white upper-middle-class "European" families now arrive at universities all but functionally illiterate. It has apparently also been forgotten in the concern for higher standards that universities—anxious to recruit star athletes—have been known to turn a blind eye toward the fabrication of phony high school transcripts. Not long ago universities routinely advertised that they reserved blocks of admission places for the children of their alumni or for those from distant states and foreign lands. As the critics of affirmative action should be willing to grant, almost no universities ever admitted all their students purely on grounds of some uniform standard of merit.

The second disease that troubles the old censors is curriculum revision. It is alleged that curricula, especially in the humanities, are being rewritten to highlight feminism, Third Worldism, racism, phallo-logico-centrism,[6] and so on. Shakespeare, or so the complaint goes, is being replaced by Alice Walker. Generally, what one discovers is that more options are being made available, rather than that the classics (i.e., those stipulated a decade ago) are being excluded. The depth of the traditionalists' commitment to the classical tradition can often be gauged when budget crunches hit universities, and appointments or even entire departments are eliminated. If, by sacrificing, say, a Latin Department (are there any left to sacrifice?), their own salaries can be protected, traditionalists tend to accord priority to salaries over Latin.

When it comes to teaching in any of the older domains, new material often does filter in, and that can also cause offense to neoconservatives. Thus, to take examples from philosophy, students may discover that Locke defended slavery in both theory and practice, that Hume was a dedicated white supremacist,[7] that the philosophies of Aristotle and Thomas Aquinas are sexist, or that Frege and Heidegger were anti-Semites. It is not obvious that "European civilization and culture" must be transmitted without critical information, comment, or insight.

Robert Hutchins, onetime president of the University of Chicago, must be laughing in his grave at all the praise the curriculum defenders are heaping on the Great Books. When the Great Books movement exploded on the academic scene in the 1930s, it was ritually denounced for its distortions of our educational traditions. The chronologically ordered careful reading of the 100 Great Books—very few of which are, in the ordinary sense, works of literature—was not the sort of thing that went under the label *liberal education* anywhere. Not only were at least half the books not in most curricula, but the systematic avoidance of secondary sources in the interest of confronting the original texts was an offense to most educators. Worst of all, unlike most of those working in the liberal arts, Hutchins & Co. had a clear idea of what constituted a liberal education and what it was to be a liberated person. In the end, the main impact on curricula of the movement was at the University of Chicago and St. John's College, Annapolis. Those who challenged Hutchins knew there was nothing new either in challenging *the* curriculum or in defending it. And all parties to the present curriculum disputes should know that for as far back as we have histories of universities, academic programs have *always* been under examination and review.

Although questions about the nature of a liberal education are omnipresent in discussions about curricula, university reform, the literary canon, and the like, one seldom comes upon a sensible doctrine. One exception is the historically based theory of Scottish education that George Davie presents.[8] He discusses the special role of philosophy in the Scottish universities and the very different theories that guided English educational planning from the eighteenth century onward. Roughly speaking, the Scots believed that a democratic society requires that all of its citizens study some of the general problems and concerns that we have simply by virtue of being humans and members of a society, rather than to have an educational system geared to producing small numbers of specialists (in the English style). Democracy, the Scots argued, requires that everyone have an edu-cated sense for individual, social, and political matters, lest we be easy targets for tyranny. That is why philosophy, taken broadly, is assigned the task of cultivating our human nature in the furtherance of the *democratic intellect* we can all possess. An educational system that ignores that respon-sibility by providing us only with particular skills will fail to sustain democratic values. Davie's historically informed and philosophically sen-sitive books should be required reading not only for anyone who is inter-ested in the sorts of issues that have pervaded curriculum planning for centuries but, more important, for those who find themselves enmeshed in debates over liberal education but who are so confused about what it is that they are unable to articulate its goals with clarity and conviction.

Today's discussions, however, contain an ideological component that is more explicit than it was in the eighteenth century and even than in the 1930s. According to some neoconservatives, the villain of the piece is *deconstructionism* because it provides a methodology within which, espe-cially in literary subjects, the old curriculum can be conceptually dismem-bered. Indeed, insofar as Political Correctness is coherent enough to have a theoretical core, that core is deconstructionism.

The roots of deconstructionism go, via de Man and Derrida, to Heideg-ger and Wittgenstein. Newton Garver, for example, discusses not only the primacy of rhetoric over logic for Derrida and Wittgenstein but also a number of other affinities and parallels between them.[9] Wittgenstein him-self briefly comments on Heidegger, as Michael Murray points out.[10] Moreover, there is considerable evidence that the scientific-technological worldview that is so anathematized by Heidegger is also an object of fear and contempt for Wittgenstein. Ray Monk, author of the recent excellent biography of Wittgenstein, says: "In a curious sense [Wittgenstein] even welcomed the [atomic] bomb, if only the fear of it could do something to diminish the reverence with which society regarded scientific progress." He quotes Wittgenstein: "It isn't absurd, e.g., to believe that the age of science and technology is the beginning of the end for humanity; that the idea of great progress is a delusion, along with the idea that the truth will ultimately be known; that there is nothing good or desirable about scientific knowledge and that mankind, in seeking it, is falling into a trap. It is by no means obvious that this is not how things are."[11]

Wherever one locates the roots of deconstructionism, deconstructionist practice employs moves that superficially resemble those of Pyrrho and the Greek sceptics, objectivity is systematically undermined, and the subject or ego is dissolved. Everything is a text, everyone is a reader, there is no independent text, and there is no independent reader. It is heady stuff and fun as far as it goes. However, the ancient sceptics, anxious that they not fall into the trap of being dogmatic about their own scepticism, were much more sensitive to the self-referring quality of their own apparent "argu-ments," profoundly concerned with whether they were even entitled to use the notion of an argument, and ever alert to the conundrum of whether their talk about "proof" did or did not constitute a proof. Such subtlety is absent from the deconstructionists. They are dogmatists; they seem to be following in the footsteps of the so-called academic Sceptics (rather than the Pyrrhonians) and, for example, *asserting* that it is true that nothing can be known.

One may even see in the Greek sceptics an appeal, via the arguments from relativity, support for the now-popular talk about "diversity." But the Pyrrhonian sceptics offer challenges on at least two levels: the level of theory, which we might take to be ideology, and the level of logic. Our contemporary proponents of diversity seem to employ their deconstructionist weapons to attack some, but not all, ideological positions. Were there modern Pyrrhonians, they could, in the quest for diversity, question any and all ideological claims, for example, feminism, Marxism, or capitalism. As for logic, and the framework within which they formulate their criticisms, the Pyrrhonians, as just noted, remain ever sensitive to the status of their proofs and would not claim priority for any one diversity that their framework logic of the moment might seem to support or undermine.

In the 1990s, behind the surprisingly dogmatic talk about the destruction of all standards, the rendering impotent of logic and morality, the clearing, so to speak, of the mental state, there is, at least for some, a Politically Correct agenda. There was also a political agenda when sceptical argumentation flourished in the sixteenth and seventeenth centuries.[12] Scepticism was first used as a strategy to defeat the Protestants by showing that they had no rational grounds for their position, no way to establish the text of the Bible, no procedures for interpreting the text, and that hence they should retreat into the authority of the Catholic church. As Popkin has shown, scepticism and learning to live with scepticism were major issues in religion and science well into the eighteenth century. To judge from the history of such movements as the Church's use of Pyrrhonism in the sixteenth and seventeenth centuries, and deconstructionism, they seem intended to leave us defenseless in the face of irrational and overwhelming political force, although that force need not be Nazi, as it was in the cases of both de Man[13] and Heidegger.[14]

Philosophical support for deconstructionism, or at least some features of it, may be found among philosophers other than Derrida. Thus, Richard Rorty, perhaps America's most widely known contemporary philosopher, after citing a passage from Sartre, writes: "This hard saying brings out what ties Dewey and Foucault, James and Nietzsche, together—the sense that there is nothing deep down inside us except what we have put there ourselves, no criterion that we have not created in the course of creating a practice, no standard of rationality that is not an appeal to such a criterion, no rigorous argumentation that is not obedience to our own conventions."[15]

McGill professor Charles Taylor, Canada's foremost philosopher, in his contribution ("Overcoming Epistemology") to the same collection of essays, takes a position somewhat like Rorty's in opposition to foundationalism in epistemology. But Taylor goes on to explore what he considers a more fundamental issue, representationalism, that is, the thesis "that knowledge is to be seen as correct representation of an independent reality. In its original form [Descartes] it saw knowledge as the inner depiction of an outer reality" (466). Both philosophers, but especially Taylor, are concerned with working out moral and political analyses compatible with, indeed enriched by, their rejection of the epistemological tradition of objectivity. Deconstructionists may not be interested in pursuing all of Taylor's ideas about intentionality, but his attitude toward objectivity and his claim that "the roots of our identity [are] in community" (481) are welcome.

Deconstructionism has also caught on in some of America's better law schools. This is hardly surprising given that in the seventeenth century dogmatic scepticism was employed in the courts. Ordinary bits of evidence, rules of evidence, and legal principles generally are no match for the systematic demands the sceptics could make by appealing to any of their favorite weapons. Thus, they could discredit a witness by challenging evidence based on sense data by means of the infamous "arguments from sense variations," that is, by citing such things as the variations that can occur in perception reports. Given these varying sense reports, they then employ the criterion argument: They demand a criterion whereby we can distinguish the real from the apparent, the true from the false, and so on. They then demand a criterion of that criterion, ad infinitum. The rich catalogue of sceptical arguments that Sextus Empiricus compiled provide theologians, philosophers, and lawyers with a truly marvelous arsenal for the unraveling of texts. Legal reasoning, despite the fact that it had not been claimed to produce mathematically necessary truths, was an easy target. Courts and, we might say, philosophers of law found a solution: reasonable doubt.[16] Guilt must be proved, but the insistence that convictions are warranted only when absolute certainty is established is to play no role in the law. The only doubts to be entertained in determining guilt must be reasonable.

Arguments to the effect that a text does not mean what it says, that there are entire frameworks of interpretation that affect the drafting of laws, that these frameworks are really idiosyncratic, remind one of the appeals to the infinite regresses that were the stock in trade of the seventeenth century Pyrrhonian practitioners of these rhetorical arts. Appeals to "reasonable" can be dismissed as just phallo-logico-centric thinking. But once again, the difficulty is that our modern dogmatic sceptics insist on *dismissing* and *refuting* arguments. Unlike the Pyrrhonists and even the "mitigated sceptics" of the seventeenth century, they insist on defeating their opponents. The dogmatic scepticism that generates such attack weapons as the theses that "Everything is relative" and "There are no absolutes" is grist for the

Pyrrhonist mill. Once the dogmatic sceptic draws a distinction between, say, what is probable and improbable, between light and dark grays, or between appropriate and inappropriate speech, the Pyrrhonist can apply a revised version of the criterion argument and thereby undermine whatever distinctions the dogmatic sceptic would like to preserve in order to disarm, say, the absolutists. The ancient Pyrrhonians were content to suggest the difficulties into which their opponents *seemed* to be plunged, but modern dogmatic sceptics are not seeking to achieve the mental quietude sought by the Pyrrhonians. Instead, in seeking the destruction of their enemies, they are hoist with their own petard.

Returning to the question of the ideological commitments of the new reformers of the university curriculum, the defenders of the old curriculum try to disguise the fact that they, too, have an ideological stake. Rather than mounting defenses of the status quo, the temptation has been to hold that what is now misleadingly called the traditional curriculum is value free and ideologically entirely neutral. This has sometimes proven to be a clever dialectical move (and is often employed in the social sciences), because the innovators are forced to start out trying to avoid the charge that *their* novelties are simply part of *their* ideology. Thus, the defenders of the traditional curriculum are "one up" on their critics.

In the present disputes, the defenders no longer hold that advantage. By insisting from the very outset that the traditional liberal arts curriculum is totally immersed in ideology, and by the clever use of antiracist, profeminist, and the like, rhetoric, they have put the traditionalists very much on the defensive. As a consequence, the traditionalists are exposed as advancing, now and in the past, their own political agenda. I think that they had and have such an agenda, but I also think that they should be able to mount rational defenses of their positions. Instead, now as in the past, they prefer to appeal to their alumni, legislators, and the media to make war against this new subversive, if not Red, menace in our midst. While most defenses in the real academic world are basically turf-preservation/-expansion moves, the traditionalists should in principle be able to mount a defense in a more direct sense than the deconstructionists can. That is, having "dissolved" the structure of arguments on the way to the total extirpation of phallo-logico-centric thinking, the deconstructionists have paradoxically disarmed themselves. That is why, like Wittgenstein, they are obliged to retreat to rhetoric. At a more mundane level, the traditionalists should be historically informed enough to know that curricula were already the ever-changing products of ideological disputes in the medieval universities. I discovered, as an undergraduate shortly after World War II, that my school's language requirement for the B.A. degree could not be met with a modern language. During the intervening years, the barbarians have triumphed, and even French is now acceptable.

In any event, being unwilling or unable to muster cogent defense arguments, traditionalists have responded to the threats of the new censors by resorting to their traditional methods. They counter the new rhetoric with the old, they try to block appointments and promotions, and they appeal to outside forces to come to the defense of the American values that they claim find expression in the old curriculum.

Although one might think that the old censors would enjoy intellectually jousting with the new, that is not what has happened. In the 1960s, the old censors generally met the challenge of the civil rights movement, and later the antiwar movement, by restricting the discussion in university senates; by dismissing, wherever possible, "activist" faculty members; and by doing their best to preserve their control of course content, research domains, and most important, maintaining the barricades. The "barricades" were (and are) the limits within which what is euphemistically called "rational discourse" takes place. Thus, for example, discussion that systematically questions the basic assumptions and motives of American policy is "off limits." A straightforward, and by now neutral, example of how these constraints work is to be found in Conor Cruise O'Brien's discussion of the counterrevolutionary subordination of scholarship.[17]

The current curriculum debate within historical disciplines often takes the form of challenging whether the priorities of the curriculum reflect primarily male, white, or European interests and values. It also takes the form of questioning the actual "doing" of history, that is, historiography à la Foucault, the *mentalité* school, deconstructionism, positivism, and so on. In literature, in addition to the straightforward ideological battles, is the collateral issue of the literary canon. Berkeley philosopher John Searle[18] puts the position of the new censors this way:

The history of "Western Civilization" is in large part a history of oppression. Internally, Western civilization oppressed women, various slave and serf populations, and ethnic and cultural minorities generally. . . . The so-called canon of Western civilization consists in the official publications of this system of oppression, and it is no accident that the authors of the "canon" are almost exclusively Western white males, because the civilization itself is ruled by a caste consisting almost entirely of Western white males. So you cannot reform education by admitting new members to the club, by opening up the canon; the whole idea of "the canon" has to be abolished. It has to be abolished in favor of something that is "multicultural" and "nonhierarchical."

Searle adds: "Unless you accept two assumptions, that the Western tradition is oppressive, and that the main purpose of teaching the humanities is political transformation, the explicit arguments given against the canon will seem weak: that the canon is unrepresentative, inherently elitist, and, in a disguised form, political. Indeed if these arguments were strong ones, you could apply them against physics, chemistry, or mathematics."

Searle clearly thinks that important features of American culture have been omitted from the core general education courses. He thinks that this can be rectified, as it has so often in the past, by doing exactly what the opponents of the so-called current curriculum reject, namely, "by opening up the canon" to the newly appreciated material. That option is rejected because one stated goal of the new censors is to "turn the curriculum into an instrument of social transformation." As he also correctly notes, the liberal arts, as represented in any sort of fixed portion of the curriculum, is by now down to at most one or two courses. Hence, it seems strange that so much heat has been generated in the debate. But of course that is not the point. Searle holds that the denials of objectivity, which are so much a part of the deconstructionist claims, cannot, given the antilogic of deconstructionist theory, be supported by logical argument. He is also less frightened about the efforts at so-called reform by the advocates of Political Correctness. Whereas the reformers assume that their students will accept the new gospel with the same uncritical air with which it is being dispensed, Searle, on the contrary, seems to believe (on the basis of the history of universities rather than because of any theory) that although the reformers may make the notion of any sort of "tradition" harder to articulate and defend, some students will still manage, despite the best efforts of the reformers, to find dissident mentors and texts and hence will develop their own critical skills and ideas.

There are at least two other dimensions to the controversy over the curriculum. First, all sides recognize that voracious readers are few and far between. No one who has taught at the university level in recent years is under any illusions about either the willingness or the ability of many students to read the bare minimum that may be required in a course. That is what adds urgency to the matter. It is believed to be of great importance that the "right" books get into the canon, lest they slip off into anonymity and the students slide into political sin. Second, as Katha Pollitt[19] writes:

The culture debaters turn out to share a secret suspicion of culture itself, as well as the antipornographer's belief that there is a simple, one-to-one correlation between books and behavior. . . . [B]ooks are not pills that produce health when ingested in measured doses. . . . Books cannot mold a common national purpose when in fact, people are honestly divided about what kind of country they want—and are divided, moreover, for very good and practical reasons, as they always have been. . . . The way books affect us is an altogether more subtle, delicate, wayward and individual, not to say private, affair. (331–332)

The discussions on the state of universities, on the curriculum canon, on Political Correctness, and on various related issues do not always bear on free speech and academic freedom. However, even when neither free speech nor academic freedom is an explicit issue, one can often detect signs of what I consider deeper questions. That is why I cite Pollitt. I believe she is correct in suggesting that the various parties to the recent debates share, as she puts it, the antipornographer's belief. If one examines the controversies from that standpoint and asks what the presuppositions of the antipornographer's belief are, then, as I have been suggesting all along, we find (even without reference to free speech) theories of human nature. That is, all parties share similar beliefs both about how our minds are furnished and about how those who claim to possess the authority should set about the furnishing—with the intent of imprinting the right political values.

We are once again back to the behaviorist-empiricist picture. When we start with that picture, then the debates make some sense. As Pollitt points out, literate people who reflect on their own lives with books, and with the influences that have shaped their lives, should, on good empirical grounds, be among the first to reject any one-to-one correlation between what we read and what we do. Alas, all that seems to be forgotten when it comes to force-feeding *any* ideological position. In such instances, empiricist-behaviorist theories tend to be presupposed by both sides. Moreover, each side seeks to constrain freedom of speech and academic freedom, albeit the speech of their opponents. The old censors dislike an environment in which criticism might threaten the status quo, *their* status quo. The new censors want limits set on freedom of speech because they share Marcuse's view about how freedom of speech functions in a capitalist system, or they seek legal sanctions on pornography and various other forms of offensive (e.g., racist) speech.

The late Allan Bloom's *The Closing of the American Mind: How Higher Education Has Failed Democracy and Impoverished the Souls of Today's Students*[20] is a diagnosis of what ails universities. His analysis is driven by his conviction that it is cultural relativism that has undone the traditional curriculum. This has, in turn, significantly contributed to the weakening and progressive undermining of the values that have bound the American culture into a unitary whole. American values and American culture are being replaced by the so-called cultures of the much-heralded and propagandistically defended "diversities." The strength of America is thus being sapped by cultural relativism. It receives an additional major blow from rock music. Bloom's comments on this "gutter phenomenon" (79) apparently depend on the "music theory," which first seems to have surfaced among members of the John Birch Society in the 1960s. The various corroding influences he detects must be countered with a rejection of feminism, plus a return to the " 'ole time" curriculum, and something akin to the " 'ole time religion."

I am not saying anything so trite as that life is fuller when people have myths to live by. I mean rather that a life based on the Book is closer to the truth, that it provides the material for deeper research in and access to the real nature of things. Without the great revelations, epics and philosophies as part of our natural vision, there is nothing to see out there, and eventually little left inside. The Bible is not the only means to furnish a mind, but without a book of similar gravity, read with the gravity of the potential believer, it will remain unfinished. (60)

By expressing opinions so much in tune with the views of the moral majority, it is not hard to understand why Bloom's book became a best-seller.

NOTES

1. "It is often suggested that pique made Aristotle leave Athens. If we are thus to speculate, we might guess that Aristotle's marked lack of homosexuality (as evident in his writings as homosexuality is in Plato's) prevented him from being in every way a success in the Academy." G.E.M. Anscombe (with P. T. Geach) in *Three Philosophers* (Oxford: Blackwell, 1961), 3.

2. The effort to ensure that a small percentage of contracts be awarded to minority-owned contractors was annulled by the Supreme Court in *City of Richmond v. J. A. Cresson* (1988). See the opinion by Reagan appointee Antonin Scalia. On the thesis that a race-free legal system is virtually impossible, see Neil Gotanda, "A Critique of 'Our Constitution Is Color-Blind,' " *Stanford Law Review* 44 (November 1991): 1–68. In a complex decision (*Bakke v. University of California* (1978)), the U.S. Supreme Court rejected the use of quotas to achieve racial balance in admissions (the case involved a white petitioner at the University of California–Davis medical school) but allowed granting certain advantages to minority applicants.

3. Those who drafted this classification scheme probably do not realize that the first use of race as a classification tool at the dawn of racial theorizing in the seventeenth century also used five not dissimilar categories. See my *Mind and Language, Essays on Descartes and Chomsky* (Dordrecht: Foris, 1984), chap. 2.

4. For example, see Marcia Graham Synnott, "Anti-Semitism and American Universities: Did Quotas Follow the Jews?" in *Anti-Semitism in American History*, ed. David A. Gerber (Urbana: University of Illinois Press, 1987), 233–271. In his Introduction (15), Gerber mentions that Jews were often denied the vote and the right to hold office. Thus, while Rhode Island lifted its ban only in 1842, New Hampshire waited until 1877. Recall that the First Amendment was not held to be binding on the states until 1925.

5. Annette Baier, "A Naturalist View of Persons," *Proceedings and Addresses of the American Philosophical Association* 65, no. 3 (November 1991): 5–17. The data on Calkins appear in Baier's n. 1. Hugo Munsterberg, Josiah Royce, G. H. Palmer, William James, George Santayana, and Paul H. Harris unsuccessfully petitioned on Calkins's behalf. "In 1902," Baier adds, "when Radcliffe College was permitted to grant women degrees, she was begged to have a Ph.D. retrospectively conferred. Splendid woman that she was, she refused. My information comes from Bruce Kuklick, *The Rise of American Philosophy* (Yale, 1977) Appendix 4, and Otto Strunk, ' The Self-Psychology of Mary Whiton Calkins,' *Journal of the History of the Behavioral Sciences* 8 (1972) pp. 196–203." Baier is the fifth woman elected president of the division. Terms are for one year.

6. I prefer this term to *phallogocentric* so as to emphasize the hostility to logic.

7. See "Essence, Accident and Race" and "Philosophy and Racism" (chaps. 2 and 3, respectively) in my *Mind and Language.*

8. George E. Davie, *The Democratic Intellect: Scotland and Her Universities in the Nineteenth Century,* 2nd ed. (Edinburgh: University Press, 1964); idem, *The Crisis of the Democratic Intellect: The Problem of Generalism and Specialisation in Twentieth-Century Scotland* (Edinburgh: Polygon, 1986). His insightful "The Social Significance of the Scottish Philosophy of Common Sense" (The Dow Lecture, University of Dundee, 1973) is extremely relevant to this theme.

9. See the Preface, by Newton Garver, to Jacques Derrida, *Speech and Phenomena,* trans. David Allison (Evanston: Northwestern University Press, 1973).

10. Ludwig Wittgenstein, "On Heidegger on Being and Dread," ed. with commentary by Michael Murray, in *Heidegger and Modern Philosophy: Critical Essays,* ed. Michael Murray (New Haven: Yale, 1973), 83.

11. Ray Monk, *Ludwig Wittgenstein: The Duty of Genius* (New York: Free Press, 1990), 485. Wittgenstein was clearly no Nazi, but he retained a lifelong admiration for Otto Weininger and his misogynist and anti-Semitic writings. Monk writes that "many of Hitler's most outrageous suggestions—his characterization of the Jew as a parasite [etc.] . . . find a parallel in Wittgenstein's remarks of 1931. Were they not written by Wittgenstein, many of his pronouncements on the nature of Jews would be understood as nothing more than the rantings of a fascist anti-Semite" (314). Wittgenstein came slowly to a recognition of Nazi goals, but despite the apparently principled opposition of his brother Paul he worked diligently in 1939 (in Berlin, Vienna, and New York) to assist in the financial machinations required for a vast transfer of family wealth from America and Switzerland to the Nazi government (400). In return, the Nazi authorities declared that the regulations governing those of "mixed Jewish blood" (under the Nürnberg laws) would not apply to them, and so Wittgenstein's sisters, although three-quarters Jewish, were able to remain in Vienna through the war. In 1938, Paul left for Switzerland alone.

12. See the classic study of this material by Richard H. Popkin, *The History of Scepticism from Erasmus to Spinoza,* rev. ed. (Berkeley: University of California Press, 1979).

13. Cf. David Lehman, *Signs of the Times: Deconstruction and the Fall of Paul de Man* (London: André Deutsch, 1991). Lehman gives a good survey of the movement and considerable biographical material on de Man. He also includes his English translation of de Man's "The Jews in Contemporary Literature," from *Le Soir,* 4 March 1941. It seems that de Man published no fewer than 170 articles in *Le Soir* and 10 others (in Flemish) in another Nazi collaborationist paper, *Het Vlaamsche Land.* There is one aspect of deconstruction's usefulness that Lehman seems not to have noticed. A university committee, charged with vetting staff members for promotion or review, is in an awkward position when it comes to dealing with deconstructionists. They claim that since all standards are indefensible, and doubly so when an appeal is made to discredited phallo-logico-centric thinking, there can be no barriers to the promoting of such candidates. If a committee is composed of people from a variety of departments, they may very well decide that the challenged talk about academic standards is just a game the people in humanities departments play, and that there are really no standards in the humanities. As I have had occasion to observe, stranger things have happened on the way to tenure.

14. Thomas Sheehan provides a useful introduction to the literature on Heidegger's Nazism in his "A Normal Nazi," *New York Review of Books* (*NYRB*), 14 January 1993, a review of Richard Wolin, ed. *The Heidegger Controversy: A Critical Reader* (MIT Press), and of Ernst Nolte, *Martin Heidegger: Politik und Geschichte im Leben und Denken* (Propyläen). Wolin, believing that he had authorization, included in his book an interview with Derrida that had already been published in *Le Nouvel Observateur*. This upset Derrida, and he, through his lawyer, threatened legal action and successfully banned a second edition of the book containing the offending interview. But Derrida was presumably more upset with Wolin's charges that, as Sheehan puts it, he seeks to "salvage Heidegger's philosophy from the charge of Nazism" and that his "strategy is motivated by a desire to immunize his own philosophy of deconstruction against infection by the Heidegger affair." The controversy continues in the pages of the *NYRB*, for example, in "L'Affaire Derrida: Another Exchange," 25 March 1993, which contains lengthy letters by Derrida, Wolin, and Sheehan. To judge from this correspondence, Derrida clearly takes the stakes in the matter of whether Heidegger's philosophy, and hence perhaps his own, is itself Nazi to be high; otherwise, he would not seem so crudely to have falsified the record of his book dealings with Wolin. A letter signed by a group of distinguished scholars (*NYRB*, 22 April 1993, pp. 68–69) seeks to defend Derrida by the traditional ploy of ignoring the issues, that is, of book suppression and the question of the taint of Nazi thinking in Heidegger and hence in deconstructionism, in favor of mounting an obfuscating attack on Sheehan's competence as a translator. Sheehan replies in the same issue. See also my "Some Reflections on Our Sceptical Crisis," in *Knowledge and Language. Volume I. From Orwell's Problem to Plato's Problem*, eds. Eric Reuland and Werner Abraham (Dordrecht: Kluwer, 1993), 59–70.

15. Richard Rorty, "Pragmatism and Philosophy," in *After Philosophy: End or Transformation*, ed. Kenneth Baynes, James Bohman, and Thomas McCarthy (Cambridge: MIT Press, 1987), 60. Also see Charles Taylor's chapter, "Overcoming Epistemology," in idem, 464–488. There are also essays by Lyotard, Foucault, Derrida, Davidson, Dummett, Putnam, Apel, Habermas, Gadamer, Ricoeur, MacIntyre, and Blumenberg.

16. See Theodore Waldman, "The Origin of the Concept of 'Reasonable Doubt,' " *Journal of the History of Ideas* 20 (1959): 299–316. See also Popkin, *History of Scepticism*, chap. 7, "Constructive or Mitigated Scepticism."

17. Conor Cruise O'Brien, "Politics and the Morality of Scholarship," in *The Morality of Scholarship*, ed. Max Black (Ithaca: Cornell University Press, 1967), 59–88. O'Brien discusses American social science research on Venezuela. His point is that the decisive control exercised by American oil companies over that nation's economy did not find its way into such studies.

18. John Searle, "The Storm over the University," *New York Review of Books*, 6 December 1990, 34. This is in part a review of material from a conference that Richard Rorty (a participant) describes as a "rally of the cultural left." Three letters from infuriated academics (criticized by Searle) appear in reply in the 14 February 1991 *NYRB*. There is something charming about those who are committed to the university being antielitist and nonhierarchical signing their names as holders of prestigious "name" chairs. Or perhaps we have the *NYRB* to thank for that contribution of a bit of irony. In any case, Searle does an excellent job of puncturing the

pompousities of the "canon revisers," and that perhaps explains why those he has squashed claim he distorts their positions. They complain: Searle says we said so and so, whereas what we said was so and so. In his reply, in which he otherwise offers no balm for their bruised egos, Searle admits that the traditional curriculum was politicized. He says that "the university, like all human institutions and activities, has all sorts of political effects and consequences. . . . [But] it is a fallacy to conclude, that the only or the primary criteria for assessment of its activities are political or that its objective should be political. Universities at their best often achieve social transformations because knowledge can transform people and institutions. But the aim should always be knowledge, not transformation." From the *NYRB*, 14 February 1991, 49. Searle is giving nothing away by making this admission because, as he knows, his opponents not only consider the curriculum and the university politicized, they also consider such notions as objectivity, knowledge, and metaphysical realism to be political. Which is why he introduces a defense of these notions and an attack on *their* politicization.

19. Katha Pollitt, "Canon to the Right of Me . . . ," *Nation*, 23 September 1991, 328.

20. Allan Bloom, *The Closing of the American Mind* (New York: Simon & Schuster, 1987). Bloom reviews two books on University of Chicago president Robert Hutchins in the *TLS*, 7 February 1992, 4. His 1987 book reveals no signs that he was acquainted with Hutchins's educational ideas at that time.

7

Political Correctness

To judge by the quantity of discussion it has generated, the most devastating attack on Political Correctness comes from Dinesh D'Souza's book *Illiberal Education: The Politics of Race and Sex on Campus*[1] and his March 1991 article "Illiberal Education" in the *Atlantic*. D'Souza, whose own commitment to cultural freedom is attested by his service as editor[2] of the notorious (because blatantly racist, antifeminist, and homophobic) *Dartmouth Review*, tells us about the current campus pressures for political conformity, the need to toe the new Politically Correct party line with respect to anything that might be interpreted as threatening "cultural diversity." His stories are vividly written, and although many have been challenged, the overall impression he seems only too happy to create is that academic freedom has been sacrificed at the six universities he surveys (Harvard, Howard, Duke, Michigan, Berkeley, and Stanford), and that diversity in practice means the institutionalizing of the various separatist movements that have enough clout to be represented on the American campus. D'Souza's enemies also take cultural relativism a step beyond what distresses Bloom and try (not easy, given that they "reject" logic and argument) to establish, as noted in the passage from Searle cited above, that white-male Western culture is not just one among others but is actually worse than the others.

Playing on the title of Sidney Hook's book, Eugene D. Genovese entitles his review of D'Souza "Heresy, Yes—Sensitivity, No."[3] Genovese, a self-styled, onetime "pro-Communist Marxist," believes that D'Souza's indictment of American higher education and the "atrocities" of academic repression that are chronicled deserve a wide audience and careful analysis. Reviewing D'Souza gives Genovese the opportunity to mount an attack on the intellectual corruption that he sees corroding the values of our educational institutions. For example, he is appalled that in the name of fighting racial discrimination Berkeley discriminates against Asians. He writes:

But Asian students, as is well known, offend the sensibilities of true egalitarians and democrats by displaying a passion for hard work, and by having strong and supportive families. Could America have been built if it had relied on such perverse people? Or more precisely, it must have relied on such people, which would explain its emergence as a racist, sexist, homophobic, imperialist country. Either way, a sensitive person must see that the fight against racism demands the exclusion of Asians in favor of people with safer credentials. How could we demonstrate that Asians are not better motivated and self-disciplined than the rest of us if we let them demonstrate that they are? And if we let them demonstrate that they are better motivated, how could we ever be sure that they are not also smarter? (31)

Genovese holds that "any professor who, subject to the restraints of common sense and common decency, does not seize every opportunity to offend the sensibilities of his students is insulting and cheating them, and is no college professor at all" (33). He also correctly reminds us that the demand for separate programs, for example, "area studies, religious studies, Jewish studies, or film studies, some of which also arose in response to political pressures" (33), came about because the traditional departments refused to include the teaching of, and research on, such material. He holds that the mere existence of separate programs need not be damaging to academic standards. (One might hope that universities would try to ensure that the curricula are so structured that such programs stand a chance of being integrated into the entire program and not cast into outer academic darkness by curriculum committees.) Even in the case of one of D'Souza's favorite targets, women's studies, Genovese notes exceptions, although he is dismayed by the extent to which universities now tolerate, and often justify, the application of political and ideological criteria in hiring and promotions in women's studies as well as history. As befits someone whose work has largely been on American slavery and African-Americans, Genovese argues persuasively (1) that affirmative action is not the cause in the decline in American educational standards (in fact, he thinks that "affirmative action properly implemented ought to replace mediocre professors with superior ones" [32]) and (2) that *all* Americans should have a deeper understanding of black history and that black studies, like women's studies, Jewish studies, and so on, *should* provide "a legitimate means of promoting scholarship about valuable subjects long and stupidly ignored" (33).

D'Souza is thus seen as formulating with style and grace many of the problems in American universities, but for Genovese, he is not nearly tough enough on the real villains of the piece: the gutless administrators and senior faculty members without whose complicity academic freedom would not have come under such threat. D'Souza's remarks on Harvard's handling of racial insensitivity charges directed against historian Stephen Thernstrom prompt Genovese to say that President Derek Bok and most of his deans "are merely doing their best to create an atmosphere in which professors who value their reputations and their perquisites learn to censor themselves."[4] But his harshest remarks are reserved for Stanford president Donald Kennedy and his abject capitulation to student demands. (In the meantime, Kennedy has resigned because of a scandal over the misuse of National Science Foundation funds.) Finally, here is Genovese's hardly novel recommendation for saving universities: "The hard truth is that academic freedom—the real work of scholarship—requires a willingness to set limits to the claims of democracy. It requires a strong dose of hierarchical authority within institutions that must be able to defy a democratic consensus. Sooner or later we shall have to face this fact, or be defeated by those who seek the total politicization of our campuses" (34).

It is another "hard truth" that it was the "hierarchical authority" of the universities of thirty years ago that had until then successfully blocked the creation of those very academic programs Genovese now welcomes, for example, black studies, Jewish studies, religious studies, women's studies, and area studies.

Yale professor C. Vann Woodward has also reviewed D'Souza.[5] Like some other anti–Political Correctness commentators, he apparently feels obliged to remind us of the external threats to universities posed by McCarthyism in the 1950s and the internal threats posed by students, and some faculty, in the 1960s. My own experience at Arizona State in the 1960s was very different. I was on one occasion amused to discover a right-wing intimidation squad seated at the back of a large lecture hall to hear my announced lectures on Berkeley. They were hoping to catch me commenting on Mario Savio and Berkeley's Free Speech Movement, whereas I have always hoped they learned something about Bishop Berkeley's *esse* is *percipi* principle. I later discovered that the dean of my faculty (nostalgic for the Hiss case?) had ordered without my knowledge or consent that samples be taken from my typewriter and those of my colleagues. Threats were delivered, by post and by phone, to opponents of the war, and demands for my dismissal were regularly aired in the media. I most certainly never had the impression that my opposition to the Vietnam War represented majority sentiment among students or faculty or university administrators or in the larger community or in the Pulliam press or the other media.[6]

My recollection is that the "oppressive" forces Genovese encountered at Rutgers in the 1960s were also from the Right, for example, from "patriots" in the legislature, and not the result of either Old Left or New Left student pressures. If Vann Woodward found the 1960s oppressive because *opponents* of the war were engaged in an "assault on freedom," it is hardly surprising that he is impressed by D'Souza in the 1990s.

Vann Woodward writes: "Curtailment or discouragement of free speech came [in the 1960s], as often happens, to promote worthy moral causes"

(35). Perhaps he has forgotten that the Free Speech Movement began as a free-speech movement and that Berkeley, like many other universities, had significant restrictions on freedom of speech. Even someone as conservative as John Searle could write: "To a person of traditional American political convictions, reading our old political rules is embarrassing to the point of discomfort."[7] At several universities, certain groups that administrators considered politically dissident were denied university recognition and, accordingly, were prevented from having speakers on campus or from holding meetings in university buildings, privileges routinely accorded conservative groups. Berkeley's administration and faculty, like those at most other universities, may have believed that by curtailing freedom of speech they were enhancing democratic values, or at least those values that had survived the 1950s. The U.S. Supreme Court was not always generous with respect to freedom of speech cases in the 1950s, although in *Sweezy v. New Hampshire* (1957) it ruled against the state in a case involving a legislative investigation into a lecturer and his remarks. It prompted Justice Frankfurter to say:

A university is characterized by the spirit of free inquiry, its ideal being the ideal of Socrates—to follow the argument where it leads. . . . It is the business of a university to provide that atmosphere which is most conducive to speculation, experiment and creation. It is an atmosphere in which there prevail the four essential freedoms of a university—to determine for itself on academic grounds who may teach, what may be taught, how it shall be taught, and who may be admitted to study.[8]

In *Healy v. James* (1972) the Supreme Court dealt with an attempt by a group of students at Central Connecticut State College to set up a chapter of Students for a Democratic Society. The administration of the college, fearing that the group would be "disruptive," refused recognition. Lower court decisions supporting the college administration were overturned by a unanimous Supreme Court ruling. William Van Alstyne writes: "The philosophy of the organization, even assuming it countenanced violence and disruption, 'affords no reason' [Justice Powell] for disallowing it to persuade others of the truth of its point of view, so long as it in fact operated on campus in an orderly fashion."[9]

I have no doubt that there were instances in the 1960s where opponents of the American invasion of Vietnam violated the freedom of speech rights of others and that some of the rhetoric of the day had a McCarthyite ring. As Searle once said: "To accuse a professor of conducting secret war research for the Defense Department nowadays has the same delicious impact that accusations of secret Communist Party membership did a decade ago."[10] Nevertheless, it is not as if academics have generally upheld the tradition of disinterested scholarship.[11] On the contrary, Professors Robert Scigliano and Wesley Fishel, for example, of Michigan State University, played a particularly active role in Vietnam, in the "discovery" and "creation" of Diem as a political figure, and in his subsequent installation by the United States as president of South Vietnam. In 1966, it was Vann Woodward's Yale colleague David Rowe who proposed to a House Committee that the United States buy all surplus Canadian and Australian wheat in order to generate mass starvation in China and thereby to destabilize the communist government. It was Harvard professor of government Samuel Huntington who gave currency to the idea of "forced draft urbanization" for the Vietnamese countryside, that is, by means of massive bombing to "encourage" the people to leave the rural areas and enter "villages" where they could be kept "secure" from communist influences. More generally, political science professors (e.g., Robert Scalapino at Berkeley and Ithiel de Sola Pool at MIT) were extremely active in their public support for the war, and many wore second hats as advisers to the Defense and/or State departments. Psychologists explored the uses of sensory deprivation as a torture technique.[12] A portion of the secret work done on campus in the 1950s, 1960s, and 1970s could reasonably be construed, on the analogue of research in Nazi Germany, as "criminal." The products of secret research were often so lethal, and the research so pervasive at some universities, that those who engaged in it were wryly called "Professors of Thanatology."

One can raise moral objections to such research activity, but it was perfectly "legal" under American law, however questionable its status might be under international law. I have heard colleagues say that to deny scientists the right to engage in secret research violates their academic freedom. To deny scientists the right to study and write about whatsoever they may choose would be to impinge on their free-speech rights. But it is appropriate to restrict them from engaging in certain activities that bear directly on the notion of free inquiry *within* the academy. For example, they should not be able to require that all students and faculty members, who seek access to their heavily guarded university laboratories and research facilities, or who wish to attend their "classified" seminars, must possess security clearances. This restricts, on political grounds, the class of those who have access to a given domain of knowledge, as does their publishing the results of their *university* research in inaccessible classified corporate or government publications.[13] To recommend that universities make efforts to *re*-create and keep alive a vestige of Lovejoy's notion of "open-minded inquiry and of frank and unhampered discussion" is not to recommend the violation of anyone's academic freedom.

It is not surprising that a number of student protesters in the 1960s quite rationally took the position that the fig leaf intended to protect the unspeakable parts of academia was inadequate. What is surprising is that Searle and Woodward have such selective memories about the 1960s. I agree that student protesters have no excuse for violating the free-speech rights of others; by the same token, those who engage in secret research within the confines of the university have no excuse for violating the academic freedom of others—as must happen when graduate students are required to hold security clearances. Installing sealed laboratories and erecting elaborate barriers to access are not exercises of freedom of speech. At least in the 1960s and 1970s, research in the social sciences was skewed in favor of support for the Indo-China War and American policies by restricting both the areas studied and the style and content of "responsible" criticism and analysis. In brief, the claim now often made by right-wingers that the primary violations of academic freedom and freedom of speech in the 1960s were the work of student-faculty activists while the true scholars sought to preserve the traditional integrity of universities is false. The primary violations of academic freedom and freedom of speech in the 1960s, and they were massive, were the work of the old censors. By means of the control they largely retain over appointments and promotions, the old censors continue to exercise a "rational" level of ideological purity in accordance with their definition of responsible academic freedom.

Returning to Vann Woodward's review, we find that he sees the plight of African-American students somewhat differently from Genovese. Vann Woodward is more distressed by university efforts to attract unprepared and unqualified African-Americans, whereas Genovese sees that problem against the larger background of a longer-term and more general lowering of student quality having nothing to do with affirmative action. Second, Vann Woodward makes the interesting point that with administrations giving black students separate student unions, and so on, the whole effort at affirmative action is generating a new racism that he finds to be "unrepentant and scornful of sensibility indoctrination. Tactics developed to combat the old racism don't work against the new" (36). And this new racism, he says, is especially virulent in those better schools that were once in the vanguard of the civil rights movement. Black separatism has broken the old coalitions, and white separatism is now said to be the consequence. Vann Woodward also believes that at the human level the attitudes that many whites exude that any black appointed has gotten there by "academic racial policy," and not by merit, has been very painful for those blacks. I am sure he is right about this, but the victims of such attitudes should develop some sense for the role that "pure merit" plays in appointment and promotion decisions in the "real" academic world.

One of the primary targets of D'Souza's attack on Political Correctness and deconstructionism is Duke University professor Stanley Fish. Fish has written an article that makes only too clear how at least one of the new censors looks at freedom of speech: "There's No Such Thing as Free Speech and It's a Good Thing Too."[14] He asserts that "free speech" is an abstract concept that has only such content as may have been given to it. He says that free speech "is never a value in and of itself, but is always produced within the precincts of some assumed conception of the good to which it must yield in the event of conflict" (4). Fish's discussion comes down to two points: First, although First Amendment jurisprudence is often discussed in terms of the speech/action distinction, the distinction becomes unstable as soon as speech becomes "at least potentially consequential" (23). Once speech is perceived to cross from the appropriate to the inappropriate, it is suppressed, even as we pay lip service to the free-speech principle. Applying his account to the matter of offensive speech on campus, Fish says that "given that any college or university is informed by a core rationale, an administrator faced with complaints about offensive speech should ask whether damage to the core would be greater if the speech were tolerated or regulated" (24). Hence, "the only question is the political one of which speech is going to be chilled" (25).

Fish rejects the absolutist reading of the First Amendment because, among other reasons, American courts have never accorded freedom of speech a transcendent value. It has always played its assigned role in a context wherein the domain of the "acceptable" is in fact delimited by political power. Whenever speech is significant enough to have potential consequences, it is counted as action rather than mere speech and is then often constrained. Fish appears to be following, but not citing, the arguments of Herbert Marcuse;[15] he seems to be saying that the speech we allow to be free is the speech we deem harmless. Fish holds, however, that *all* speech is action and that "everything we say impinges on the world in ways indistinguishable from the effects of physical action" (26).

Fish's second claim is more general and is logically independent of his observations on freedom of speech. Value and meaning are only created by our acts of *exclusion*. If we utter a meaningful assertion, we do so by an act in which we distinguish (i.e., exclude) our putative assertion from all other possible assertions. All meaning, all "meaningful assertion" (4), and all values are created by our acts of exclusion, by our placing our assertions within a negated background framework. Our assertions are meaningless without that excluded background. This holds for everything—hence also for freedom of speech. For it, too, "has never been general and has always been understood against the background of an original exclusion that gives it meaning" (4). That is simply a consequence of his thesis that all predication is negation. Note that we can only make true assertions when we know what we have excluded. If we are to create a meaningful assertion, we must place it, by an act of exclusion, against everything it is not. That's a Tortoise that Achilles may need a long time to catch.

Fish's first point is the familiar one that as a matter of historical fact politics determines how we employ and enforce the free-speech principle in the real world. Not satisfied with "showing" how the free-speech principle generally functions, he then seeks to establish that even if the historical evidence might seem to support a speech/action distinction and an absolutist free-speech principle, such an interpretation is rendered nonsensical by his exclusion theory of meaning. That is why he advances his second point. By means of it, he believes he has established that there *can* be no independent value, no universal principle, to which defenders of free speech can appeal. Thus, according to Fish's account, the absolutist free-speech principle not only has no valid historical credentials; it is ruled out as logically absurd.

In his introductory Editor's Note, MIT professor Joshua Cohen says that Fish's remarks are being published "not to edify but to challenge" (1). Admittedly, Fish's essay has a cutesy title. Moreover, Fish correctly observes that when courts or university administrators apply the free-speech principle, they routinely discard the speech/action distinction in favor of a balancing of their not-always-disinterested "guesstimate" of the probable good and bad consequences. But this is not news. Except for a few justices like Hugo Black, and a few scholars, the modern history of the free-speech principle has in good measure ignored the absolutist reading. Balancing, rather than absolutism, has explicitly characterized First Amendment jurisprudence at least since the introduction of the clear and present danger test. Nevertheless, one wonders why Fish feels compelled to tell us that the free-speech principle is generally abused. Whenever people stand on matters of principle, they are well aware of the fact that practice does not always accord with principle. From that, however, one ought not to conclude that the very concept of a principle is absurd.

There is little sense to be extracted from Fish's assertion that our talk "impinges on the world in ways indistinguishable from the effects of physical action" (26). Are the effects of speech and of physical action really indistinguishable? One might wish to grant that we can be hurt by certain words and that such words cause bruises, but are such psychic bruises indistinguishable from bodily ones?

Fish's claim that meaningfulness depends on exclusion, that speech "only becomes intelligible against the background of what isn't being said" (25), is contextualism with a vengeance. It is no refutation of what Fish appears to be saying that it reflects, albeit through his own poststructuralist prism, the dialectical analyses recommended by the great idealist philosophers of the nineteenth century and by Heidegger in our own. But it does seem to be a consequence of Fish's *exclusion theory of meaning* that we are unable ever to know what any given utterance means without knowing everything. He would also seem to be committed to counting "logic" and "truth" as instances of political rhetoric, although he has no hesitation in advancing a variety of "arguments" and appealing to "logic." By now the nonsensical character of his remarks should be obvious.

Fish is obviously free to advance the sorts of free-speech doctrines that Sidney Hook and Herbert Marcuse advanced before him and to maintain that we must silence "hate speech" lest we "slide down the slippery slope toward tyranny" (26). But he has a problem in explaining both the meaning and the negative force of "hate" or "tyranny" except in terms of the political clout he can muster on their behalf. But in any case, the genius of Fish's paper is that it is an omnipurpose text. The title could read: "There's No Such Thing as Truth [or Logic or . . .] and It's a Good Thing Too," and with a few substitutions of "truth" [or "logic" or . . .] for "free speech," Fish would have a new paper and another publication.

In a rejoinder[16] to Fish, Berkeley law professor Robert C. Post writes that "[w]e protect speech in order to achieve particular values, and these values in turn shape the contours and boundaries of that protection. When analyzing a right of free speech, therefore, the question is always the values we wish the right to serve. Any other account is mystification."[17]

In his Reply to his Critics, Fish retorts that his opponents take him to be making a recommendation that we abandon principle.

But in fact, I am not making a recommendation, but declaring what I take to be an unavoidable truth. That truth is not that freedom of speech should be abridged, but that freedom of speech is a conceptual impossibility because the condition of speech's being free in the first place is unrealizable. . . . My point . . . is that constraint of an ideological kind is *generative* of speech and that therefore the very intelligibility of speech (as assertion rather than noise) is radically dependent on what free-speech ideologues would push away. Absent some already-in-place and (for the time being) unquestioned ideological vision, the act of speaking would make no sense, because it would not be resonating against any background understanding of the possible courses of physical or verbal actions and their consequences. Nor is that background accessible to the speaker it constrains; it is not an object of his or her critical self-consciousness; rather, it constitutes the field in which consciousness occurs, and therefore the productions of consciousness, and specifically speech, will always be political (that is, angled) in ways the speaker cannot know.[18]

Throughout his Reply, Fish alternates between posing empirical rejoinders to his critics—namely, that the history of free-speech discussions, Supreme Court decisions, and so on, is the history of drawing lines between such speech as is classed as "free" versus that which is anathematized; and on the other hand relying on the logical claim that the *concept* of freedom of speech is incoherent, its incoherence being a function of his previously articulated exclusion theory of meaning. On this occasion, Fish emphasizes that we cannot in principle know the background that constrains, negates, excludes, and thus makes intelligible our understanding, consciousness, and speech. As I noted above in connection with Fish's earlier remarks, to know anything on his account, we need to know everything (the totality of the background). But we cannot know everything; hence, we cannot know anything.

As for Post and others who make an appeal to basic values informing the Bill of Rights, or who ask, Where do values come from? Fish answers: *political power.* "Politics," he writes, "is the *source* of principle. . . . [My critics] assume I am counseling readers to set aside principle in favor of motives that are merely political, whereas in fact I am challenging that distinction and counseling readers to act on what they believe to be true and important, and not to be stymied by a doctrine that is at once incoherent and (because incoherent) a vehicle for covert politics."[19]

In this Reply as in his earlier paper, Fish rests his case on his thesis about meaning, truth, and logic—a thesis that he seeks to bolster by appealing to a variety of empirical claims, his "facts." But, as I note above, his empirical-historical remarks are logically independent of his thesis about meaning, truth, and logic. I believe he succumbs to the temptation not to recognize them as distinct principles because he interprets them as drawing sustenance from the same source, that is, power. His dogma, which amounts to saying that "political values come out of the barrel of a gun," is neither a self-evident truth nor a particularly helpful tool in the analysis of meaning and truth, but it does have good historical credentials—from Plato's Thrasymachus to Nietzsche and their twentieth-century heirs.

NOTES

1. Cf. Dinesh D'Souza, *Illiberal Education: The Politics of Race and Sex on Campus* (New York: Free Press, 1991).

2. See, for example, the letters and material cited in the Letters columns of the *Nation*, 8 July 1991, 38.

3. Eugene D. Genovese, "Heresy, Yes—Sensitivity, No," *New Republic*, 15 April 1991, 30–35.

4. Catherine R. Stimpson reviews *Illiberal Education* in the *Nation*, 30 September 1991. Among other things, she observes, obviously correctly, that D'Souza, in his criticism of minority self-segregating societies, and the like, seems to have forgotten that for generations fraternities, sororities, eating clubs, religious propaganda centers, and so on, have enjoyed varying forms of university support—although most of them are clearly self-segregating. In the same issue of the *Nation*, Jon Wiener's "What Happened at Harvard" convincingly recounts numerous errors and distortions in D'Souza's report on the accusations of racist course content directed by black students against Thernstrom. On the basis of what Wiener reports, I think it is correct that the complainants had not intended to prompt Thernstrom to stop teaching the course in question but merely to expose the "racial insensitivity" he had exhibited in some classroom remarks on the black family and in his presenting the perspectives of slave owners via their journals but not those of the slaves, whose journals were also available. Thernstrom, in turn, seems to have been only too happy to use the occasion to attack the barbarians in the academy. However, the quotations Wiener provides from deans do not, contrary to his intentions, dispel the suspicion that Genovese's characterization of the Harvard administrators as seeking to encourage an atmosphere of self-censorship is right.

5. C. Vann Woodward, "Freedom and the Universities," *NYRB*, 18 July 1991, 32–37.

6. For detailed information and a careful and judicious study of this remarkably turbulent period, see James Franklin Vail, "Vietnam-Era Antiwar Activity and Campus Unrest at Arizona State University, 1965–68" (M.A. thesis, Arizona State University, 1989). The Pulliam Press, both in Phoenix and Indianapolis, was fiercely pro war and generally expressed the John Birch Society line in editorials. The hypocrisy of Pulliam's fierce support of the war, and vicious denunciations of

the war's opponents, in particular draft evaders, while at the same time he and his family were using their very considerable political influence to guarantee that grandson Dan Quayle could "satisfy" his military obligation with "service" in public relations with a privileged unit of the Indiana National Guard, was noted, but to no effect, when George Bush selected Quayle as his vice presidential running mate. Seattle Medal of Honor winner Richard McCool resigned from the Medal of Honor Society (an organization of those who have won the United States's highest award for valor in combat) on learning that its Patriot Award was being given to Dan Quayle. McCool said: "For an organization that is composed of people who have served in the armed forces—and served very well—to give this award to someone who did everything he could to avoid military service is inappropriate." AP, *International Herald Tribune*, 2–3 November 1991, 2.

7. John Searle, in *Revolution at Berkeley*, ed. Michael V. Miller and Susan Gilmore (New York: Dell, 1965), 94. In the context of hostility in the 1960s to the mere presence of ROTC on campus, it may also be noted that in *Hamilton v. Regents of the University of California* (1934) the Supreme Court sustained the policy of excluding as students males who would not submit to military training. Minnesota is said to have been the first land-grant university to break, in the late 1930s, with the tradition (it had apparently not been required by law) of compulsory ROTC at such institutions.

8. In this passage from *Sweezy* (1957), Frankfurter is quoting from a statement prepared by a conference of senior scholars from the South African universities of Cape Town and Witwatersrand. Quoted (at 111) in William W. Van Alstyne, "Academic Freedom and the First Amendment in the Supreme Court of the United States: An Unhurried Historical Review," *Law and Contemporary Problems* 53 (1990):79–154. Van Alstyne, past president and general counsel of the AAUP, has assembled and insightfully commented on those decisions in which the term *academic freedom* has been employed by the Court.

9. Van Alstyne, "Academic Freedom," 122.

10. John Searle, *The Campus War: A Sympathetic Look at the University in Agony* (Harmondsworth: Penguin, 1972), 25. Searle suggests a variety of factors that contributed to the "war"—from children having been raised permissively à la Dr. Spock to affluence. He also discusses academic freedom and freedom of speech, urging that mere membership in the Communist party cannot be grounds for dismissing a professor, although "[i]t is perfectly reasonable, for example, for the university's promotion committees to inquire into whether a Communist professor is using the classroom for indoctrination and propaganda" (190). One wonders if the same holds for speech-act theorists like Searle.

11. The topic has been the subject of several studies. A slightly earlier period is discussed in Sigmund Diamond, *Compromised Campus: The Collaboration of Universities with the Intelligence Community, 1945–1955* (Oxford: University Press, 1992).

12. See John McGuffin, *The Guineapigs* (Harmondsworth: Penguin, 1974).

13. A variant of the problem is still with us. The U.S. District Court for Washington, D.C., recently ordered on First Amendment grounds the National Institutes of Health to reinstate a contract to Stanford University. Stanford had "refused to agree to a requirement that it submit results of the study to NIH for approval before publication." *Science* 254, no. 4 (October 1991): 23. One wonders if Stanford's sensitivity to First Amendment issues was as keen in the 1960s.

14. Stanley Fish, "There's No Such Thing as Free Speech and It's a Good Thing Too," *Boston Review*, February 1992, 3–26.

15. See the Marcuse references in Chapter 8, n.1.

16. Criticisms of Fish's earlier paper, together with his Reply, appear in the "Readers Forum," *Boston Review*, March/April 1992, 13, 14, and 28.

17. This contains the germ of Robert C. Post's free-speech analysis in this connection. His "Racist Speech, Democracy, and the First Amendment," *William and Mary Law Review* 32 (1991): 267–327, is discussed in Chapter 10.

18. Fish, Reply, 15.

19. Ibid., 28.

8

Sensitivity Rules and Regulations

Those academic attitudes (e.g., Political Correctness) that most worry many recent conservative commentators can hardly be said to be seriously undermining the dominant orthodoxy when universities are taken in their entireties. The *truly* closed minds that Bloom and D'Souza (like that old censor Sidney Hook before them) are intent on defending remain entirely secure. They already have the media, the state legislatures, the federal government, and the vast majority of the faculties on their side. However, my interest in this latest set of moves in the academic power game is twofold: first, the extent to which the putative defense of the so-called traditional curriculum and the attacks upon it become excuses for a new round of suppression of freedom of speech within the academy. The conservative old censors and the "radical" new censors have many things in common, except that the new censors are not likely to make significant inroads into the faculty power and privilege of the old censors. Both are, however, only too happy to suppress certain sorts of speech and to anathematize people who hold the "wrong" opinions, although of course each side's "hit list" is different. John Locke saved the principle of toleration by extending toleration only to those he considered tolerant; now one saves freedom of speech in the academy by extending it only to those who "deserve" the right to exercise it.

Second, a shared theory of human nature paradoxically undergirds these efforts at suppression both by the conservatives and by the so-called radicals. What I find new and most troubling in the present university context is that the contempt for freedom of speech already articulated by Herbert Marcuse[1] and some others on the Left in the 1960s is now taking a form that is perceived to give support to group libel legislation. It is depressing to read that at the "better" universities hate literature regulations have been drafted that would sharply restrict the free-speech rights of students and staff.[2] Remarks that can be construed as causing offense to the members of a group identified on the basis of (the list varies somewhat) their national or ethnic origin(s), race, religion, color, sexual orientation, handicap, veteran status, and so on, can result in the suspension or dismissal of a student or, in the case of a faculty member, severe disciplinary action, suspension without pay, and/or sensitivity counseling. For example, *Newsweek* begins its anti–Political Correctness horror story "Taking Offense" with a report about a woman who may have thought she was being funny when she "allegedly put up a sign on the door to her dorm room listing 'people who are to be shot on sight'—among them 'preppies,' 'bimbos,' 'men without chest hair' and 'homos.' " The gay community at the University of Connecticut brought a complaint against her for violating a portion of the university's student-behavior code, namely, for " 'making personal slurs or epithets based on race, sex, ethnic origin, disability, religion or sexual orientation.' "[3] She was ordered to move off campus and not to set foot in any university dorms or cafeterias. Under threat of a federal suit, she was allowed to move back in a subsequent year, and the student code was revised to conform with the First Amendment.

Newsweek, in its effort to show the folly of Political Correctness, talks about the threats to the First Amendment being posed by Political Correctness practitioners. Yet in the article cited, we read that Duke University professor James David Barber, a political scientist and former chair of Amnesty International U.S.A., carried his fight against Political Correctness to the campus bookstore's political science section. He "turned on its spine every volume with 'Marx' in its title—and *angrily demanded their removal*" (49, emphasis added). *Newsweek* doesn't mention this as a threat to First Amendment values.

The ideological doctrine that our identities depend on the group to which we are said to belong helps create an atmosphere in which it seems to make good sense to accord special rights to some groups. An individual's free-speech rights must be subordinated to the rights of groups. Brown University, an institution that likes to think of itself as being in the upper-middle rank, dismissed a student for shouting (while drunk) racist remarks. Brown president Vartan Gregorian, in upholding the expulsion, commented: "The University's most compelling challenge is to achieve a fruitful balance between respecting the right of its individual members to operate and speak freely in pursuit of the truth and fostering a climate of mutual respect and adherence to accepted community values." More lenient sentences were reportedly given to students convicted of carrying concealed weapons.[4]

The grim history of the U.S. Supreme Court's attempts in the 1940s and 1950s to balance the First Amendment rights of individuals against what the government claimed were national security needs was surely something Gregorian was aware of when he made his "balancing" act remarks. The chances of an individual being able to "speak freely in pursuit of the truth" in opposition to community values are slim. Needless to say, Gregorian does not provide a calculus for determining when freedom of speech must be suppressed at Brown, but it is clear he will not risk defending First Amendment rights for students or staff lest "community values" be offended. Administrators at the more prestigious American institutions, such as Harvard, Michigan, Berkeley, and Stanford, have also seldom distinguished themselves in their defenses of First Amendment rights and academic freedom, but none has produced an intellectual justification whose effectiveness in denying free-speech rights has such fine historical juridical credentials as that advanced by Gregorian.

American universities would seem to have a special obligation to defend and support the free-speech principle. All universities would seem to have a special obligation to defend and support the principles of academic freedom. Presumably, that means explaining over and over again to every class and to every governing body and to every faculty member what these principles are, how they are relevant to any local crisis that may arise, and then being willing to spend time and energy in their defense. But there appears to be no rule that determines when university administrators decide to support the free-speech guarantee or the principles of academic freedom (or, for that matter, when a head of state will stand up to tyrannical pressures, as the king of Denmark did in World War II with respect to the Jews and the Dutch queen did not). Brown President Gregorian, like officials at more prestigious institutions, presumably had his reasons. Sometimes administrators, like faculty assemblies, comply with demands that threaten academic freedom because they actually agree with them, or they yield to pressures out of fear that the legislators or alumni will act on their threats to cut funds. Occasionally, it appears to be an effort to curry favor with younger faculty or with a segment of a volatile student body, in the hope that by sacrificing a principle one either will buy peace or at least will be seen in a more favorable light by the dissident group.

I am singling out for special criticism the views of what the media call Political Correctness because I am primarily concerned with the free-speech clause in the First Amendment. It is these new censors who seek to impose speech codes on the university campus and to find ways to extend the concept of group rights from university regulations to formal legislation. In other words, the advocates of Political Correctness have a positive agenda with respect to the free-speech principle. The old censors still approach both free speech and academic freedom in the spirit of Sidney Hook's "Heresy, Yes; Conspiracy, No" doctrine. Those 1950s campus political speech regulations that Searle found "embarrassing" to read (see Chapter 7) were much less the product of a theory the old censors sought to impose than a reflection of the subversion paranoia that cost Russell his job and that later helped advance the goals of the so-called cold war. In the age of McCarthy and Nixon, the old censors did not need a free-speech plank in their platform. The constraints imposed by the Supreme Court in *Dennis* (1951), the success of loyalty oaths, and the turmoil created by legislative committee investigations were not the work of the old censors, but they provided legal force and popular sentiment to bolster their preexistent attitudes. When the old censors set about scrutinizing the politics of their nontenured colleagues, they did not need to devise a new criterion to decide which views were offensive. The courts and the legislatures had already cut the First Amendment cloth to their measure. The members of the right-wing National Association of Scholars[5] can still count on a broad base of opposition to dissident ideas, one that is not restricted to their membership. The old censors' standards of academic appropriateness still hold across most faculties. On the other hand, it is precisely because, unlike the old censors, the new censors articulate and advance their own free-speech principles and group rights ideas that they warrant attention in a study of freedom of speech. By means of these principles they propose to fight for campus speech regulations and legislative proposals that sharply limit free speech.

A Canadian academic freedom case has arisen at the University of Western Ontario, London. For some time there has been a dispute over the research and writings of psychology professor Philippe Rushton. Rushton apparently defends a version of the teachings, usually interpreted as supporting white racial superiority, of Harvard professor A. R. Jensen.[6] In spring 1991, a group of students filed a complaint with the Ontario Human Rights Commission alleging that Rushton "poisons the academic learning environment." This is an attempt to expand the concept of a "poisoned work environment," which is already employed by the Human Rights Commission, to include the academic scene. The complainants want the university to fire Rushton and to create an "appropriate and enforceable race-relations policy." Canadian Human Rights commissions function as arbitration panels (in this case, resolving the issues between the student complainants and the university) rather than as proper courts. The legal consequence of this procedure is that, like Russell in the 1940 case, Rushton will not be the defendant and hence may have no legal standing before the commission. Russell, it may be recalled, never having technically been a party to the legal action that resulted in his dismissal, was never granted recourse to the courts. If Rushton is dismissed, he can try to take an action against the university in the courts, but even if he is successful in initiating such legal action, it is a very expensive affair for a plaintiff.[7] Regardless of who "wins" at Western Ontario, freedom of speech and freedom of inquiry will likely lose.

The Rushton case is a traditional academic freedom case. At issue is a scholar's freedom to seek the truth and to teach and publish his or her findings. Because Rushton is exploring a topic that many, if not most, social scientists consider to have no merit, and because there is a real risk that research on this topic not only may be used by racist groups but also may be absorbed into the "background" racism of the larger culture, the defense of his rights is often considered unjustifiable, too difficult, or even too much trouble. Nevertheless, academic communities tend to be reluctant to ban the Rushtons. First, because infallible tests for truth, especially in the so-called social sciences, are in short supply.

Commenting on the Rushton case, University of Toronto chancellor Rose Wolfe reportedly supports, "with some reservations . . . the system of peer review by which the quality and validity of academic work is judged."[8] Further, " 'I had a tough time with that case,' Wolfe says. 'I could identify with the people who were upset and said Rushton had to go, but I think the test in his case was the fact that his peers said his research was flawed. That was the most damning thing that could have been done to him and I think in a university that is probably the best way.' She pauses. 'Now if his peers hadn't judged him harshly I don't know what I would have said' " (17). Just as the chancellor is prepared to constrain the freedom of speech of a Zündel for uttering falsehoods, so presumably freedom of inquiry within a university can be constrained in the interests of, say, "social and racial harmony." Or to put her parallel reasoning more straightforwardly, just as Ontario Judge Thomas can declare a historical event to be a fact such that denying it is a crime, so peer review committees can declare what is a scientific truth such that denying it constitutes grounds for dismissal. So much for freedom of speech; so much for freedom of inquiry.

Second, once one demands that the Rushtons demonstrate that what they say is "true," the genie is out of the bottle. The genie *should* be out of the bottle. Rushton should of course be challenged, and so should his challengers. Scientific theories, philosophical and literary ideas, historical facts and methods, should routinely be subjected to serious criticism. But I have never had the impression that academics were eager to create an environment in which ideas could be routinely challenged across disciplines. The scientific foundations of, for example, economics, psychology, sociology, and anthropology are not so secure that academics would like to impose a truth test on every scholar in every such discipline whenever someone's teaching or research is challenged. Anthropology, for example, began its life in the mid-nineteenth century as a racist "science." Moreover, scientific fraud is clearly a major problem. Faking data, pursuing research topics with an eye on funding rather than on the truth, letting ideology determine one's theory, and using university political clout to silence one's critics have all contributed to the scepticism with which the claims of scientists to be truth seekers are often greeted.

Some indication of how serious these issues have become is that reports on scientific fraud appear regularly, often weekly, in *Science* as well as in *Nature*. NIH even has an Office of Scientific Integrity. One of the more spectacular cases it has had to deal with concerns charges originally brought by Dr. Margot O'Toole against the work of Thereza Imanishi-Kari, work that Nobel laureate David Baltimore vigorously defended. Recently appointed president of the Rockefeller University, Baltimore's reputation was damaged to the point that a significant number of his scientific colleagues "voted with their feet" and accepted offers at other research institutions.[9] In the autumn of 1991, Baltimore stepped down as president of the university. Another case concerns the continuing saga of who first isolated the human immunodeficiency virus (HIV) and whether chicanery was involved on the U.S. side.

As John Stuart Mill appreciated, one runs a risk in suppressing opinions. One runs the risk that true views will be denied a hearing. One also runs the risk that scientific findings will not be taken seriously once a wide segment of the informed public is inclined to think that results are routinely being fudged and that the preservation of the egos of scientists takes precedence over all other considerations. The price of suppressing the Rushtons may thus be to enhance the belief that in modern science matters of truth are increasingly being replaced by the exercise of censorship in the service of raw power. Defending the freedom of a philosophy professor who is accused of teaching that Andrew Baxter is the most important thinker of the modern era may be troublesome for the handful of people who might be involved in his or her defense. But the defense of a Russell— or for that matter, of a Rushton—means fighting for a principle against politically powerful adversaries; it means threats. It also means deciding whether one's institution is seriously committed to academic freedom.

A very different sort of freedom of speech case has emerged in Moncton, New Brunswick, Canada. High school teacher Malcolm Ross has been ordered "out of the classroom" by the New Brunswick Human Rights Commission.[10] Taking up a complaint of a parent against the local school board, the commission decided that Ross's authorship and publication of books and pamphlets, in which he claims that reports about the Holocaust are much exaggerated and that Christianity is the target of a Zionist conspiracy, contributed to the anti-Semitic flavor Jewish students felt permeated the classrooms of Moncton. There was no allegation that Ross had ever said or taught anything of an anti-Semitic nature in his mathematics classroom. The activities for which he was ordered out of the classroom (without pay unless the board finds a nonteaching post for him) took place exclusively on his own time. In this respect, his case is more like Russell's than Rushton's. Russell's offense was that he had published, some years before his appointment, material that offended various religious groups and that this made him unfit to teach. There was no claim that he planned to use his course on advanced logic as a vehicle for discussing his ethical theories. Since, rather like Russell, Ross's offense had nothing to do with his classroom role, it is hard to see how taking him out of the classroom resolves anything. Indeed, it is puzzling that he was not dismissed and deported, at least from the province of New Brunswick. If he can raise the funds, and if, unlike Russell, he is granted standing, he presumably will try to take court action against the board. Teachers unions and civil liberties groups are disturbed by this decision because three other out-of-school factors have already been mentioned as future targets: homosexuals, nuns, and single mothers.

In a Canadian Civil Liberties Association article (CCLA), A. Alan Borovoy[11] (CCLA general counsel) writes about several cases current in Canada, including the Ross case: "While professors are subject to critical scrutiny by both colleagues and mature students, high-school teachers exercise an enormous influence, and sometimes even control, over vulnerable adolescents" (1). He then adds: "This is not the place for a definitive assessment of Mr. Ross's pronouncements and activities. It is a place to acknowledge that certain expressions outside the classroom could render teachers unworthy recipients of trust for teaching, guidance and evaluation" (1). Those aforementioned future targets had better keep Borovoy's remarks in mind—and beware.

In summer 1991, Leonard Jeffries, Jr., chairperson of African-American studies at the City University of New York (CUNY), gave an address before the Empire State Black Arts and Cultural Festival dealing with, among other things, certain Jewish activities and attitudes in reference to African-Americans. His comments on Jews in the slave trade, and Jews stereotyping African-Americans while "controlling" Hollywood, were certainly put in a very offensive style and, where facts were involved, were often claimed to be in error. The summer of 1991 was not kind to racial relations in New York, as the tensions and violence in the Crown Heights section of Brooklyn showed. It was remarkable how quickly an auto accident, in which a Hasidic driver had swerved off the road and inadvertently killed an African-American child, was converted into an accusation that this was an instance of Jewish ritual slaughter of children. Several days of violence ensued. Jeffries's remarks were made prior to the Crown Heights episode, but Crown Heights did not make for an auspicious context within which to evaluate his rights. However offensive what he said was to Jews, however damaging his remarks were to the social fabric of an unhappy community, it is *extremely* unlikely that he will be removed from his professorship. Under pressure from Gov. Mario Cuomo, Senator Alfonse D'Amato, and others, the university trustees removed Jeffries from his non-tenured administrative post as chairman of black studies. A jury, however, decided that the only reason Jeffries had been removed from his chairmanship was because of the views he had expressed and that accordingly his free-speech rights were violated.[12] There is also a less-frequently mentioned philosophy professor at CUNY, Michael Levin, who espouses a "scientifically" based white-supremacist position. His free-speech rights have also been supported by the courts. Whether these matters will finally be resolved straightforwardly in terms of academic freedom or in terms of an academic version of the "balanced ticket" process much beloved by New York politicians is unclear.

In efforts to apply free-speech rights within the academic context, a perennial difficulty is the widely held notion that although everyone is entitled to free speech, so long as teachers' salaries are paid by taxpayers, the taxpayers are entitled to set limits on what their employees may say.[13] When the distress level is high, it generally proves difficult to maintain the distinction between defending a right to speak and support of the content of that speech. In each of these particular cases, at issue is the distress felt by the members of one or another so-called identifiable group and their desires to seek some form of redress on behalf of their group.

NOTES

1. Herbert Marcuse, "Repressive Tolerance," in *A Critique of Pure Tolerance,* ed. Robert Paul Wolff, Barrington Moore, Jr., and Herbert Marcuse (Boston: Beacon Press, 1965), 81–117. But see Avrum Stroll, "Censorship and Repressive Tolerance," in *Freedom and Culture: Literary Censorship in the '70s,* ed. Eleanor Widmer (Belmont: Wadsworth, 1970), 37–41.

2. "Canetta Ivy, who serves on the three-member Council of Presidents that heads the [Stanford] University student government," is quoted in the *New York Times,* 25 April 1989, A20, as saying, " 'We don't put as many restrictions on freedom of speech as we should.' "

3. "Taking Offense: Is This the New Enlightenment on Campus or the New McCarthyism?" *Newsweek,* 24 December 1990, 48. This article was an early and significant discussion in the popular media of Political Correctness. Syndicated columnist George Will, the right wing's lapdog, frequently comments on the menace Political Correctness poses.

4. See the lead article, by Steve Brown, in *Civil Liberties* (ACLU), no. 373, Spring/Summer 1991. A Brown administrator (Vice President Robert A. Reichley) complains in the Fall 1991 issue (no. 374) that Steve Brown's article distorts the case, that it was really a case of drunkenness rather than speech. As Steve Brown points out, that interpretation is not supported by what President Gregorian said, nor by the prevalence of campus drinking. Steve Brown notes: "[T]his student was the first person ever expelled from Brown University in its history." Reichley is quoted as claiming that the student was on probation "for the same sort of behavior". But the earlier offense that is said to be of the "same sort" was for "offensive speech." Hence, contrary to what the administrator says, *speech,* not drunkenness, was the violation that caused the expulsion.

5. Stanley Fish wrote to the Duke University provost suggesting that "members of the National Association of Scholars not be appointed to key university committees . . . dealing with academic priorities and evaluations." The provost rejected the suggestion. The quote is from an article on Fish by Adam Begley, "Souped-Up Scholar," *New York Times Magazine,* 3 May 1992, 50. "Prompted by D'Souza's lecture agent, Fish and D'Souza put themselves on the market—for a fee of $10,000 per debate. On five occasions in the last year the two men appeared

before packed houses on college campuses to engage in orchestrated verbal fisti-cuffs" (50).

6. Rushton has recently received an M.Sc. degree from his alma mater, the University of London, as a reward for his extraordinary scientific achievement.

7. Canadian lawyers are not allowed to operate on a contingency fee basis.

8. See "In Defence of Truth," an interview by Karina Dahlin in the *University of Toronto Magazine*, Autumn 1991, 11.

9. Anthony Cerami left, with his thirty-member laboratory team, in the summer of 1991. Two months later, Nobel laureate Gerald M. Edelman announced his departure, along with eleven scientists and the fourteen-member staff of Rockefel-ler's Neuroscience Institute. Neither said they left because of Baltimore, although both opposed Baltimore's appointment, and Edelman is reported to have been a leader in the opposition to the appointment. Cf. *Science* 254 (11 October 1991): 186.

10. Cf. *Globe and Mail* (Toronto), 31 August 1991, news story and editorial.

11. From the *Globe and Mail* (Toronto), 3 March 1989, reprinted in *CCLA News Notes*, May 1989.

12. *New York Times*, 16 May 1993.

13. An issue of *Law and Contemporary Problems* (28 [1963]) was devoted to academic freedom. The articles are historically interesting, the various definitions of academic freedom (in contrast with freedom of speech) are helpful, the argu-ments of several still hold, and the bibliographical material remains useful.

9

Group Libel Again

In the one U.S. Supreme Court decision clearly supporting group libel, Justice Felix Frankfurter argued (in affirming [5–4] *Beauharnais v. Illinois* [1952]) that if we can impose criminal sanctions on someone who directs a libel at an individual, the state can punish someone for directing a libel at a defined group. The question of the defamation of public persons is discussed in *New York Times v. Sullivan* (1964) and is considered (as is *Rosenblatt v. Baer* [1966]) to undermine the group libel position expressed in *Beauharnais*.[1] NYU and Oxford law professor Ronald Dworkin writes that Justice William Brennan, "in his opinion for the Court [in *Sullivan*], redefined the fundamental premises of the First Amendment in terms that affected not only libel but First Amendment law more generally."[2] However, in an earlier wide-ranging and unanimous opinion (*Chaplinsky v. New Hampshire* [1942]), the U.S. Supreme Court excluded lewd, obscene, profane, libelous, insulting, and "fighting words" from the protection of the First Amendment, that is, "words which by their very utterance inflict injury or tend to incite an immediate breach of the peace." One suspects the year 1942 is important, and so is the fact that Chaplinsky was a Jehovah's Witness. *Terminiello v. Chicago* (1949) marks a change in the Court's opinion. A fiercely anti-Semitic priest, Arthur Terminiello's conviction was overturned on narrow grounds by the Court. Subsequent decisions rendered after the heyday of McCarthyism have tended to extend First Amendment protection, for example, *Cohen v. California* (1971).[3]

The U.S. Supreme Court has long had difficulties with the extension of First Amendment protection to various sorts of conduct, for example, nude dancing.[4] However, perhaps best known is the bitter hate expression case generated by the attempt of a small group of American Nazis to parade in Skokie, Illinois, in 1977. A city of some 60,000 to 70,000, Skokie has a large Jewish population and many survivors of Nazi death camps. A wide variety of legal roadblocks were erected to prevent the march in Skokie (and in Marquette Park in nearby Chicago). In the end, the Nazis did not appear in Skokie, although they did hold a demonstration at Marquette Park in 1978. Although Skokie was a *conduct*, rather than a pure *speech*, case, it was the ideas of the Nazis that provoked the wrath of the community. A lawyer for the Jewish Anti-Defamation League asked a court to bar Frank Collin, leader of the Nazis, permanently, "lest he inflict 'menticide,' a form of emotional harm, on the survivors."[5] The ACLU's defense of the First Amendment rights of Nazis cost the ACLU some 15 percent of its membership nationwide and an estimated $500,000 in dues. Few First Amendment cases have aroused such passions. In the end, in 1978 the Illinois Supreme Court ruled that the Nazis could march and that the display of the swastika was protected, although U.S. Supreme Court Justice Frankfurter's opinion in support of group libel (*Beauharnais* [1952]) was cited on several occasions as the case(s) proceeded through the state courts.

The U.S. Supreme Court (*R.A.V., Petitioner v. City of St. Paul, Minnesota* [1992] has ruled on a St. Paul, Minnesota, ordinance that prohibits placing a burning cross or a swastika on private or public property. "Such an action is a crime if it 'arouses anger, alarm or resentment in others on the basis of race, color, creed, religion or gender' according to the ordinance."[6] It was ruled invalid by the trial judge (juvenile court), who noted that the city could have brought charges under a wide range of other statutes.[7] The city chose the antibias route. The Minnesota Supreme Court unanimously reversed the trial judge. The Associated Press news story also reports the Court as saying: " 'The burning cross is itself an unmistakable symbol of violence and hatred based on virulent notions of racial supremacy.' " The Minnesota Supreme Court also noted that the ordinance "can be interpreted as applying only to 'those expressions of hatred and resorts to bias-motivated personal abuse that the First Amendment does not protect.' " The U.S. Supreme Court, however, unanimously struck down the St. Paul act and noted that

[t]he ordinance, even as narrowly construed by the State Supreme Court, is facially unconstitutional because it imposes special prohibitions on those speakers who express views on the disfavored subjects of "race, color, creed, religion, or gender." At the same time it permits displays containing abusive invective if they are not addressed to those topics. Moreover, in its practical operation the ordinance goes beyond mere content, to actual viewpoint, discrimination. Displays containing "fighting words" [*Chaplinsky* (1942)] that do not invoke the disfavored subjects would seemingly be useable *ad libitum* by those arguing in favor of racial, color, etc. tolerance and equality, but not by their opponents. St. Paul's desire to communicate to minority groups that it does not condone the "group hatred" of bias-motivated speech does not justify selectively silencing speech on the basis of its content.[8]

In the majority opinion, these, among other, examples are given:

Thus, the government may proscribe libel; but it may not make the further content discrimination of proscribing *only* libel critical of the government. (4669)

One could hold up a sign saying, for example, that all "anti-Catholic bigots" are misbegotten; but not that all "papists" are, for that would insult and provoke violence "on the basis of religion." St. Paul has no such authority to license one side of a debate to fight freestyle, while requiring the other to follow Marquis of Queensbury Rules. (4671)

Four justices agree with the decision that the St. Paul act is unconstitutional but disagree with the reasons Justice Antonin Scalia provides in the majority opinion. Thus, Justice Byron White argues that under the principle articulated in this ruling (i.e., barring the selectively silencing of speech on the basis of its content), Title VII regulations governing such so-called hostile workplace claims as sexual harassment, would violate the First Amendment (4676). Indeed, it would appear that the Scalia principle would bar all selective "offensive" speech regulations and statutes. Justice White also notes: "Indeed, by characterizing fighting words as a form of 'debate' . . . the majority legitimates hate speech as a form of public discussion" (4674). His inference seems to be correct. However, it is hard to see why hate speech should not count as a form of public discussion. Perhaps there is not much public discussion in political campaigns, but hate speech is a major ingredient in most political campaigns. Justice Harry Blackmun, in turn, makes this remarkable observation: "I fear that the Court has been distracted from its proper mission by the temptation to decide the issue over 'politically correct speech' and 'cultural diversity,' neither of which is presented here. If this is the meaning of today's opinion, it is perhaps even more regrettable" (4678).

Justice John Stevens comments: "Contrary to the broad *dicta* in *Mosely* [1972] and elsewhere, our decisions demonstrate that content-based distinctions, far from being presumptively invalid, are an indispensable aspect of a coherent understanding of the First Amendment" (4679). He adds that "the central premise of the Court's ruling—that '[c]ontent-based regulations are presumptively invalid'—has simplistic appeal, but lacks support in our First Amendment jurisprudence" (4680). He adds that this "categorical approach does not take seriously the importance of *context*. The meaning of any expression and the legitimacy of its regulation can only be determined in context" (4681). That is giving short shrift to Justice Hugo Black's view that when the First Amendment says "Congress shall make no law . . . ," it means *no law*.

A defender of the free-speech principle should be pleased to see a Supreme Court decision that purports to defend the First Amendment, although given the deep differences among the justices, it is not clear how influential a precedent the case may be.[9] The Associated Press (AP) reports at the time suggest major differences in interpretation. Thus, Justice White is reported as holding that the danger "is that the ruling might let states and communities enact broader bans than the one in St. Paul."[10] The report goes on to say that nearly all states have, in recent years, passed laws "calling for special punishment for racists and bigots who commit crimes." Some communities have gone much further (like St. Paul) by making "the display of prejudice itself a crime." There is perhaps some understandable anxiety when Justice Scalia is joined by Chief Justice William Rehnquist and Justices Anthony Kennedy, David Souter, and Clarence Thomas in apparent support of the free-speech principle, although it is made very clear in their opinion that they are not calling for an absolutist interpretation. They accept a wide range of restrictions on the scope of the First Amendment. Nevertheless, it is an important decision for my purposes because it shows the extent to which several of those justices usually classed as "moderates" favor "content-based" rulings, "group rights," and a radically noncategorial reading of the First Amendment in favor of "context," flexibility, and suppleness.

In *Wisconsin v. Mitchell* (1993) the U.S. Supreme Court held Wisconsin's "penalty enhancement" statute to be constitutional. Todd Mitchell, a young black man, was initially convicted of aggravated battery, an offense that usually carries a maximum sentence of two years' imprisonment. The jury, however, found that Mitchell had intentionally selected his victim because of the victim's race (white) and so his sentence was "enhanced" to four years. The Wisconsin law under which Mitchell was convicted

is based on a model statute developed in the early 1980's by the Anti-Defamation League of B'nai B'rith, whose leaders hailed the decision today. Under this approach, the jury that has convicted a defendant of an existing crime—in this case assault—then makes a separate judgment that the crime was motivated by bias and qualified for the increased sentence. The Wisconsin law defines as bias crimes those that are committed against a person or property "because of the race, religion, color, disability, sexual orientation, national origin or ancestry of that person or the owner or occupant of that property."[11]

When Mitchell's conviction went before the Wisconsin Supreme Court the "penalty enhancement" provision was held to be unconstitutional because it was deemed overbroad and because it directly violated the free-speech clause of the First Amendment by penalizing offensive thought. The state court held that "the Wisconsin Legislature cannot criminalize bigoted thought with which it disagrees" (8). The Wisconsin Supreme Court held that a law increasing the punishment for a crime which contained a hate-speech component "had the effect of 'punishing offensive thought' and 'chilling free speech,' in violation of the First Amendment. . . . 'Without doubt the hate crimes statute punishes bigoted thought,' the [Wisconsin Supreme] court said, because application of the law requires a 'subjective examination' inquiry into the defendant's motivation in selecting a particular victim. By contrast, the state court said, conviction of the crime of assault or burglary requires only an objective determination that the act was committed by a particular defendant."[12]

But the U.S. Supreme Court apparently accepted the reasoning of the Wisconsin Attorney General that the law was "not aimed at ideas but at a particularly harmful form of criminal violence. Chief Justice William H. Rehnquist reportedly said for the Court that the [Wisconsin] law at issue does not inhibit free speech and was not unconstitutionally broad. He agreed with the arguments by the state of Wisconsin that the law was not aimed at punishing bigoted thought, but instead only punishes criminal conduct."[13]

Critics of the decision said it was a threat to freedom of expression. Martin Redish, a Northwestern University law professor who along with Prof. Alan Dershowitz of Harvard Law School and the columnist Nat Hentoff filed a brief opposing the statute, said the Court's decision was "extremely unfortunate" and a "blatant attempt at mind control. . . . In effect what the Court has done is leave as fair game all underlying political thoughts and motivations that go into committing a crime," he said. "As much as I hate bigotry, I fear much more the Court attempting to control the minds of its citizens."[14]

The aforementioned 1992 St. Paul (cross burning) decision displays ambiguities which are resolved in the *Wisconsin* case by the virtual elimination of any real distinction between thought and conduct. Although the words "thought" and "conduct" are retained in *Wisconsin v. Mitchell*, the court takes them to mean the same thing. There is thus a significant strengthening of the legal justification for supporting the restrictive speech codes now being seen on the American university campus. That is why I suggest that however much Canadian and American jurisprudence may appear to differ with respect to free speech, a process is at work that may bring them closer together—at the expense of the American First Amendment free-speech guarantee. Given the residue of decisions that supported antiadvocacy legislation at the height of the cold war plus the omnipresent conspiracy laws, elements are already in place in the United States that can be employed to show that group libel legislation on behalf of multicultural diversity does not run counter to any constitutional guarantees. In Canada, recognition of, and support for, multiculturalism is, as noted above, often given precedence over the Canadian freedom of expression principle.

Canada's respect for multicultural diversity is not, however, even-handed. Thus, unlike the United States, Canada bars the importation of, for example, anti-Semitic material.[15] The Canadian Muslim community sought to have Salman Rushdie's book *The Satanic Verses* banned from importation, under the standard hate literature regulations. Although briefly held up by Customs, that ban was lifted, and the book's importation was authorized. The Muslim community understandably felt that a double standard was being employed. Material that is offensive to the Jewish community is banned from Canada; material that is offensive to Muslims is not.

The failure of the 1990 constitutional proposals of the Mulroney government, the so-called Meech Lake (I) Accord, generated a good deal of hostility toward native Indians among those who supported the agreement. The Accord specified constitutional changes almost exclusively intended to satisfy some of Quebec's aspirations and thereby to "keep Quebec in Canada." Elijah Harper, the lone native member of the Manitoba legislature who blocked the unanimous consent required (because the provincial government had delayed acting on the measure) to take up the Meech Lake proposals, was initially perceived by many to have been responsible for exacerbating, if not creating, Canada's constitutional crisis. That episode, combined with the Canadian military actions at Oka and at Kahnawake, both near Montreal, later in the summer of 1990, fueled a great deal of harsh racist rhetoric but no action under the hate literature legislation.

In 1991, a new set of constitutional proposals was discussed across Canada. Newfoundland premier Clyde Wells "has said that he could accept individual rights being subordinate to distinct society status as long as it happened only in Quebec, by Quebeckers' choice. Mr. Mercredi [Ovide Mercredi, national chief of the Assembly of First Nations] cannot accept that situation for Quebec natives.[16] Not only are the Native Peoples demanding that their rights not be abrogated by constitutional reforms that have as their primary goal satisfying the aspirations of the Québécois for "distinct society" status, but they have also served notice, for the zillionth time, that they have treaty claims to the northern two thirds of what is now the province of Quebec. The province claims that the Native People have surrendered their rights. The federal minister responsible for constitutional affairs, Joe Clark, reacted furiously to the interventions of the Native Peoples. That land claim plus the very successful media campaigns they have waged in the United States and Europe against the expansion of Hydro-Quebec's river damming plans on their lands promises to make Native People even more unpopular than they were in 1990!

However Canada solves its perennial constitutional crisis, the fact is that the Canadian legal experience with hate literature and falsification of history has been very selective. The Supreme Court of Canada may take the Charter's affirmation of multiculturalism seriously, but the several attorneys general apparently do not. If they did, they would be spending a tremendous amount of their time applying the statutes. Canadian history of the textbook variety has long been seen very differently from the English and from the French points of view. Indeed, many Canadian histories are shot through, from the standpoints of the several groups involved, with falsification. Nor have Native Peoples (*les sauvages*) done well at the hands of many historians. In brief, the introduction of group libel and hate literature legislation and falsification of history statutes does not necessarily do much honor to a legal system that purports to be democratic, even if it brings some solace to those who feel hurt or otherwise discriminated against by what people may say. The simplest way to avoid giving citizens the impression that the scales of justice are unbalanced may be to annul all such restrictive legislation and allow free discussion to take its course rather than to try to square the circle by attempting to apply undemocratic statutes democratically.

The experience of European countries that have similar statutes reflects the same difficulty. Group libel legislation is primarily enforced when groups with political clout are offended, and contrariwise, groups with political clout can violate the statutes with impunity. In the Netherlands, for example, a pair of evangelists, the Goerees, went to prison for their biblically defended anti-Semitic and homophobic remarks. The widow of World War II Dutch Nazi leader Rost van Tonningen has been fined for her anti-Semitic remarks, and most recently, she has again been fined and threatened with jail for publishing (in Belgium) anti-Semitic remarks in her latest book, *Op zoek naar mijn huwelijksring* [In search of my wedding-band].[17] But charges against Cardinal Adrianus Simonis for his homophobic and antifeminist comments were dismissed.[18] In 1991, a right-wing member of the Amsterdam city council was fined and given a suspended sentence for publishing pamphlets with such titles as "The Netherlands for the Netherlanders" and "Immigration? No Thanks." Under Dutch law, such opinions can have no place, even in an election campaign.[19] Despite group libel legislation in most European countries and despite specific restrictions on Nazi speech, literature, and activities, neo-Nazis are active in most of the larger German cities and in a number of cities elsewhere in Europe. Early in 1992 the Austrian parliament passed legislation criminalizing neo-Nazi activities. Gerd Honsik was sentenced to a year and a half in prison for denying that hundreds of thousands of Jews were killed in Auschwitz. The court took, in effect, "judicial notice," based on historical study, of the Auschwitz facts. A court in München also ordered British historian Irving Singer to pay a fine of DM10,000 for "insulting the memory of the victims of the Holocaust."[20]

The French government has dismissed Jean-Claude Barreau, a very senior civil servant in the immigration department, for publishing a book about Islam in which he argues that it would be much easier for French Muslims to become integrated into French society if they gave up their "archaic" religious practices. In announcing the dismissal, the Social Affairs Ministry said, " 'Freedom of speech, in France, is a right that must be guaranteed, but Barreau's personal views might have appeared to express the viewpoint of a public or government office.' "[21] Barreau's *De l'islam en général et du monde moderne en particulier*, his seventeenth book, was on the best-seller list for months and earned him a literary prize, the *Prix Aujourd'hui* for 1991. He notes wryly that a civil servant could publish, without fear of repercussions, a book doubting the divinity of Christ, but one is prohibited from expressing any doubts about the Prophet Muhammad or from applying the usual critical standards intellectuals in the West employ. He reports that when the Muslim cooks at the University of Lyon said they would no longer prepare food containing pork, this was accepted, and so pork is no longer on the menu. According to the review, he said that his dismissal "proved his argument that Islam was virtually taboo as a subject for intellectual inquiry." He and his family are now under police protection.

In England, on the other hand, the efforts of Muslim communities to have Salman Rushdie's *The Satanic Verses* banned as blasphemy failed because only offensive remarks directed at Christianity count in English law as blasphemy. The Iranian Muslims have, however, pronounced a death sentence on Rushdie and offered bounty hunters a multimillion-dollar sum for his death in whatever country he is found. His Japanese translator has been murdered, and his Italian translator injured. It is interesting that a large number of distinguished writers have come, as they should, to Rushdie's defense, and he has received elaborate protection, as he should, from the British police. But those who have come forward to defend Rushdie's right to write and to publish material that has "offended" hundreds of millions of people (very few of whom have actually seen, no less read, his book) are notably silent when it comes to defending the rights of a Faurisson or other Holocaust revisionists whose writings also offend people. The lectures of Faurisson, a professor of comparative literature, have been canceled on the ground that the state could not prevent disruptions in his classes. He has been penalized by the French courts. Several of those offended by Faurisson have attacked him physically and injured him seriously. Rushdie has luckily escaped that fate, perhaps because, unlike Faurisson, he is considered worthy of police protection. Although the Rushdie case would appear to be the sort of "acceptable" free-speech/free-press case that ought to receive massive support from Western governments, there has been considerable hesitancy as well as an inclination to blame the victim, especially from the established Christian churches. In late 1992 and early 1993, Rushdie visited a number of Western capitals seeking to generate support for the cause of literary freedom. He was received at the highest level in, for example, Ottawa, given the cold shoulder by the Bush administration, told he would not be welcome in France, and invited by a parliamentary committee to visit the Netherlands.[22]

His "liberal" critics, while deploring the death sentence ordered by Iranian authorities, contend he should not have written anything that offends the Muslims. That, of course, is precisely the point that Barreau makes. Criticism of Islam, Islamic ideology, and Islamic theology are taboo subjects, although immigration restrictions are an acceptable topic. Perhaps more worrying is that John Major's Conservative government very much wants a rapprochement with Tehran, and Washington wants Iranian support against Saddam Hussein. Another indication of the validity of Barreau's complaint is that a head teacher at a Birmingham school, with a 97 percent Muslim student body, was threatened with dismissal for uttering the word "pig," a word that Muslims deem offensive.[23] Blasphemy, or its equivalent in Islamic states, is a crime in most states with an official religion (i.e., most states).

A puzzling case has been before the Dutch court system. Under the pseudonym Mohammed Rasoel, *De ondergang van Nederland* [The downfall of the Netherlands] appeared in 1990. It warns against the influence of Islam in the Netherlands. The Anne Frank Foundation sought action against the book on the ground that it encourages discrimination. Dr. T. van Dijk, University of Amsterdam professor of text-science, using computer text methodology, claimed that a certain well-known columnist for *NRC Handelsblad* and author, whom he accused of being an "elite racist,"[24] was the real author. A Pakistani Muslim and resident of Edam is now said to be the author, although he has not acknowledged authorship. He has, however, said that the Dutch are very naive and that they have stopped being a "tolerant" society because the only thing Dutch authorities now count as discrimination is when "white people criticize colored people." When Muslims appear on Dutch television and "say that Dutch women are sluts," that is acceptable.[25]

Not all nations that like to be seen as accepting so-called Western democratic values actually subscribe to them, especially where free speech is concerned, as has been noted with respect to Canada, the Netherlands, and France. Thus, Israel has repeatedly imprisoned Israeli peace activist Abie Nathan, most recently for *talking* with Palestine Liberation Organization (PLO) leaders. Israeli restrictions on Arabs are well known. After years of repression under the Soviets, Czechoslovakia may have had too much Prague Spring. Their new legislation would do honor to Stalin's culture commissar, Andrey Aleksandrovich Zhdanov. It was Zhdanov who spelled out Stalin's policies with regard to those who wrote against the proletarian revolution or who otherwise engaged in falsification of history by expressing opinions that were determined by the government to be "false." Article 260 was passed into law by the Czech parliament in December 1991: "(1) Anyone supporting or leading a movement that openly sets out to abolish human rights and citizens' freedoms, or that advocates national, racial, class or religious hatred, such as Fascism or Communism, shall be punished by one to five years in prison. (2) A three to eight year sentence will be handed down to any person found guilty of having committed the offenses mentioned in paragraph (1) through the medium of press, cinema, radio or any similar vehicle."[26]

In 1991, the two-hundredth anniversary of the U.S. Bill of Rights was celebrated. But the free-speech principle is also encountering much harder times in America. In *Rust v. Sullivan* (1991), which deals with the right of physicians in Planned Parenthood clinics to inform clients/patients about abortions, the U.S. Supreme Court has acted decisively to restrict free speech. The physicians argue that a Reagan administration administrative regulation forbidding them even to use the " 'A' word" [abortion] not only conflicts with their duties properly to explain medical options but also deprives them of their freedom of speech in the consulting room. The Court took the position that since the federal government was paying a small share of the costs of Planned Parenthood clinics, it could regulate not only what physicians *did* but also what they *said*. " 'This says he who takes the king's shilling becomes the king's mouthpiece,' said Kathleen Sullivan,"[27] Harvard Law School professor, while her Harvard colleague Laurence Tribe said, " 'The court is indirectly threatening the recipients of grants in a great many areas.' " One of President Bill Clinton's first acts on taking office in January 1993 was to cancel the regulation banning a physician from providing information on abortion in a federally supported clinic.

A very similar case went before the Irish Supreme Court. Clinics were legally constrained from informing patients about abortion options in England and on the Continent. (Abortions are prohibited under the Irish Constitution.) But on 29 October 1992 the European Court of Human Rights, sitting in Straatsburg, ruled that the Irish regulation governing the mere providing of abortion information violated the freedom of expression rights guaranteed all Europeans in Article 10 of the European Convention on Human Rights. Section 1 reads in part: "Everyone has the right to freedom of expression. This right shall include freedom to hold opinions and to receive and impart information and ideas without interference by public authority and regardless of frontiers." This is followed, as in the United Nations' Universal Declaration of Human Rights, with a large number of restrictions in the interest of state security, health and morals, and so on. However, given the indifference toward the First Amendment revealed by the U.S. Supreme Court in *Rust*, it is interesting that the European Court took the putative primacy of its "freedom of expression" article more seriously than either the Irish or U.S. Supreme Courts did. It is interesting because European nations have, at least formally, more constraints on free speech than the United States.

The implications of the *Rust* decision are far-reaching. The majorities required in each house of the U.S. Congress to reverse this sort of administrative regulation are hard to muster. Thus, there is little to prevent, for example, an antiabortion administration from imposing restrictions on the teaching of gynecology in medical schools. Or, for that matter, from drafting all sorts of regulations further restricting freedom of speech. On 4 May 1991, George Bush vigorously denounced Political Correctness in universities at the University of Michigan. He could have promulgated a regulation prohibiting all mention of any and all favorite Politically Correct topics, such as Marxism, feminism, and American racism. Administrative regulations of this type can do the work of a falsification of history statute simply by forbidding, at the risk of an institution's losing its federal funding, the discussion of certain topics. Such regulations would probably, at least in a nonelection year, generate enough opposition in the Congress to be overruled but not before a marvelous opportunity had been given to congressional committees to investigate "Political Correctness on the campus" as well as any other subversive elements that might be interpreted as constituting a threat to American life and culture. The opportunity to fabricate, expose, and suppress so-called dangerous ideas has historically proven well nigh impossible to resist.

To criticize Political Correctness is to run the risk of being considered a political ally of George Bush, Dinesh D'Souza, George Will, and their fellow travelers in the academy. But I am pessimistic enough to fear that the attacks by the advocates of Political Correctness on the First Amendment, specifically their attempts to ban "offensive" speech and to make groups the primary bearers of rights, may succeed. Hence, those, and those alone, are the only aspects of Political Correctness I am concerned with. Most of the critics of Political Correctness I mention have not in the past distinguished themselves as vigorous supporters of the principles of free speech and academic freedom. If their current attacks on Political Correctness are based on those principles, then they are indeed born-again ACLU members. Given the noncommitment of George Bush, the anti–flag-burning president whose opponent in 1988 he denounced as a "card-carrying member of the ACLU,"[28] to First Amendment values, why should he, of all people, attack Political Correctness for seeking to limit freedom of speech? Is Political Correctness really such a serious threat on so many fronts that the media are prepared to devote so much attention to chronicling its sins? It seems unlikely. But now that there is no political mileage in hunting down communists, Political Correctness is the only movement that might be worth attacking in order to protect the foundations of the cold war ideology.[29] At least it will have to do until another enemy can be found. Although I think Political Correctness does pose a threat to the free-speech principle, when something is so widely attacked outside the academy, and the inheritors of the anti–free-speech tradition of Sidney Hook organize to combat it within the academy, one knows that neither free speech nor academic freedom are the primary issues.

Finally, there are also nonlegal considerations that have been affecting the exercise of freedom of speech worldwide, for example, the tendency to treat the defenders of the rights of "offensive" speakers as subscribing to the views of those whose rights they defend. There is nothing new in this. Both Bayle and Voltaire were aware of the problem. Still, to have ACLU members denounce their organization for defending the rights of Nazis to speak in Skokie is perplexing. The ACLU is dedicated to defending First Amendment rights. Presumably the resigning members had for years been receiving, if not reading, ACLU newsletters reporting various ACLU defenses of the free-speech rights of members of the Ku Klux Klan, communists, American Nazis, and other groups. So it is difficult to understand why so many members resigned over the Skokie affair, although perhaps they felt that the history of the ACLU showed that it did not subscribe to an *absolutist* interpretation of the First Amendment, and hence that it need not have gotten involved in the Skokie affair. There is some basis for that perception.[30]

I have already mentioned the case of the Holocaust revisionist and French university professor Robert Faurisson. It is disappointing that he has found so few defenders of his free-speech rights. The most prominent name associated with the defense of those rights is Noam Chomsky. Chomsky has, for over a decade, been systematically and continuously attacked as if he were a defender of Faurisson's actual views rather than as a defender of his right to express them. To the extent that the distinction between the utterance of an unpopular opinion and the defense of the right to make such an utterance is eroded, the right to freedom of speech becomes that much more difficult to state, explain, and defend. Moreover, as the case of Chomsky attests, the very defense of someone else's free-speech rights becomes in itself an unpopular and offensive form of speech. One must then try to mount a defense of the defender's right of freedom of speech, ad infinitum.

Chomsky has consistently defended the free-speech principle from his school-day interests in anarchism and libertarian socialism to the present, and while he is not an absolutist, human freedom remains a central theme in all of Chomsky 's work, political as well as linguistic. This is already evident in the essay that first brought him to the attention of a wide segment of the American public, "The Responsibility of Intellectuals."[31] His strong opposition to the suppression of free-speech rights in the 1960s earned him the hostility of some on the Left, as did his support for the teaching rights of people he knew had abused, as theoreticians of the war in Indo-China, the freedom of others. Recently, he has cited approvingly Jeremy Bentham's view "that a free government must permit 'malcontents' to 'communicate their sentiments, concert their plans, and practice every mode of opposition short of actual revolt, before the executive power can be legally justified in disturbing them.' "[32] Chomsky appeals to what he interprets as this Bentham standard in response to an interviewer's question as to whether there is a limit to freedom of expression. The limit, he says, is that "one may not incite to criminal action."[33]

Chomsky makes his position more precise in responding to interviewer John Pilger on the BBC: "Does that right of free expression, in your view, extend to everybody?" Chomsky replies: "I mean, if we don't believe in free expression for people we despise, we don't believe in it at all." He is then asked about those Muslim extremists who are allowed to call for the death of Salman Rushdie. "Would you support their right to speak in that way?" Chomsky replies: "To speak, yes, but I think that Bentham's standard is the one that should be observed. . . . Suppose you and I walk into a store and you have a gun and I tell you to shoot the store owner. Well, that's speech but it's not protected because that's speech which is part of a violent act." Pilger then asks: "But shouldn't that be, as in the case of the racist being allowed to speak, shouldn't that be simply, and indeed it is in this country, illegal. I mean it's incitement to murder." Chomsky replies: "You have to ask whether it is incitement to imminent violent action. Now you know there's no precise litmus test that tells you where to draw the line. But freedom of speech is an important enough value so that you need an extraordinary argument to overcome it. I think there are such cases. I gave one. For example, somebody who says 'shoot' when someone else has a gun. OK. That's crossing the line. But I don't think there are many cases that cross the line."[34]

I am not convinced that the order to shoot the shopkeeper works in the intended way. Under common law systems, all parties to such a felony, even the driver of the getaway car, are guilty of robbery or murder. Speech does not enter the equation. Only the act of shooting does. Perhaps one can find another example with which to demonstrate that there are instances where the free-speech principle may deserve to be surrendered. But I think there is a more fundamental difficulty with the Bentham standard. The "incite-ment to imminent violent action" criterion (of which the *Brandenburg* rule is a variant) takes words to be deeds. And if the words are deemed violent, the line is crossed and hate speech suppression is legitimatized. Hate speech is criminalized under many legal systems precisely because it is considered profoundly hurtful to groups that are said to need and deserve protection from this form of violence.[35] Given that the words as uttered are held to be actions, the harmful effects can be as immediate as those that follow the command "Shoot." Thus, hate speech can meet the test of being incitement to imminent violent action. That is the very sort of argument that defenders of hate speech legislation advance. One can try to counter the argument by holding that psychological harms are not physical, or that the line is only clearly crossed when the words can, in some way, be construed as the immediate cause of death. How immediate is "imminent"? Can a "hit" that is ordered in writing or by telephone meet an imminence test? However reasonable it seems, appeals to the Bentham standard, like other clear and present danger clones, are fraught with difficulties. On the other hand, historically the absolutist denies that words are deeds, holds to a distinction between speech and action, and probably subscribes to the Russell dictum that "[i]n a democracy it is necessary that people should learn to endure having their sentiments outraged." In any case, if, as Chomsky says, there are so few borderline cases, why sacrifice the literal (absolutist) reading of the First Amendment free-speech clause?

As noted in Chapter 3, it is with *Brandenburg* (1969) that the Court makes more strict the clear and present danger test by requiring that the advocacy be "directed to inciting or producing imminent lawless action and [be] likely to incite or produce such action." The conclusion of the concurring opinion by Douglas and Black is worth repeating: "The line between what is permissible and not subject to control and what may be made impermis-sible and subject to regulation is the line between ideas and overt acts."[36]

As Sextus Empiricus makes plain in his *Outlines of Pyrrhonism*, it is not easy to defend a criterion of any variety, no less a criterion for distinguishing protected from unprotected speech in terms of likely effects. To the problem of the circularity or the infinite regress generated when one tries to establish by a meta criterion that the initially proffered criterion is satisfactory, there are problems of locating an impartial judge and of determining that one has applied the rule correctly.

One does not need a Sextus Empiricus to appreciate that Mill's harm principle, the Bentham standard, Holmes's clear and present danger test, the *Brandenburg* rule, and other similar candidates are one and all problematic. They are problematic because we can immediately see many ways in which such criteria can be extended far beyond their apparently intended scope. They are problematic because, fearing certain consequences that are generally unspecifiable with respect to quantity and duration, they try to find a way to protect one sort of action while imposing sanctions on another. And they are also problematic because they presuppose that we know how people will think about and act on what they hear. Such knowledge is required if we intend to criminalize what people may say. However, the First Amendment does not come with a principle of interpretation and application. Presumably, that is why the free-speech clause is stated in absolutist form. If a society aims to achieve democratic *self*-government, there is apparently no other option.

NOTES

1. On state group libel laws, see Thomas I. Emerson, *Emerson, Haber and Dorsen's Political and Civil Rights in the United States*, eds. Norman Dorsen, Paul Bender, and Burt Neuborne. 4th ed. (Boston: Little, Brown, 1976), 655.

2. Ronald Dworkin, "The Coming Battles over Free Speech," a review of Anthony Lewis's *Make No Law: The Sullivan Case and the First Amendment* in the *New York Review of Books* 39 (11 June 1992): 55. Dworkin suggests that most free-speech justifications fall into two groups: instrumental (consequentialist) defenses and a second kind for which freedom of speech is valuable

because it is an essential and "constitutive" feature of a just political society that government treat all its adult members, except those who are incompetents, as responsible moral agents. That requirement has two dimensions. First, morally responsible people insist on making up their own minds about what is good or bad in life or in politics, or what is true or false in matters of justice or faith. Government insults its citizens, and denies their moral responsibility, when it decrees that they cannot be trusted to hear opinions that might persuade them to dangerous or offensive convictions. We retain our dignity, as individuals, only by insisting that no one—no official and no majority—has the right to withhold opinion from us on the ground that we are not fit to hear and consider it. (56–57)

On neither justification is freedom of speech absolute. Although *Sullivan* made libel actions more difficult, libel law remains a significant constraint on the First Amendment. Dworkin believes the First Amendment is also threatened by a variety of groups that now favor censorship and by a Supreme Court more inclined to oblige them.

    3. Cohen was arrested in a California county courthouse for wearing a jacket on which the words "Fuck the Draft" were written. His conviction was reversed by a 5–4 decision. Justice Harlan held, among other things, that the government could not provide a clear criterion for determining which words are permissible and which are not. Justice Blackmun, with whom Justice Black concurred, considered the case was "mainly conduct and little speech." Cf. Thomas L. Tedford, *Freedom of Speech in the United States* (Carbondale: Southern Illinois University Press, 1985), 217–218.

    There are a variety of ways in which free-speech rights can be circumvented. Lawyers on occasion take civil actions in an attempt to prove damages from speech. Thus, awards have been won against the Ku Klux Klan in Alabama and the White Aryan Resistance in Oregon. In the latter case, Thomas Metzger and his son were said to have incited (mainly via cable television) followers to kill African-Americans. Civil rights lawyers took up the case when an Ethiopian student was killed. Opinions were divided: Those from the National Lawyers Guild argued for an award; lawyers from the ACLU opposed on First Amendment grounds. *New York Times*, 12 October 1990, B5.

    4. See William O'Rourke in the *Nation*, 24 June 1991. He examines several of the decisions (e.g., *Doran v. Salem Inn* [1975]) and discusses some of the distinctions often drawn between nude dancing in "lower"-class bars and modern ballet in opera houses.

    5. Aryeh Neier, *Defending My Enemy* (New York: Dutton, 1979), 49–50.

    6. Associated Press report in the *International Herald Tribune*, 11 June 1991.

    7. Some examples are arson and criminal damage to property. The teenage petitioner was also charged with a violation of a Minnesota law barring "racially motivated assaults." This count was not challenged.

    8. *United States LAW WEEK*, 23 June 1992; 60 LW 4667.

    9. A New Jersey Superior Court judge declared a section of that state's law against hate crimes unconstitutional on First Amendment grounds in the light of the *St. Paul* decision. At issue was the case of someone who had pleaded guilty to having spray painted an epithet ("Dots you smell") on the garage door of Pakistani immigrants. ("The slur is a recent one in the lexicon of bigotry, said Kenneth Goodman, the public defender who argued Mr. Mortimer's case. It refers to the caste mark, called the tilaka, or bindi, that some Hindu women paint on their foreheads.") However, the accused faces sentencing on a disorderly persons charge in connection with the same activity. An appeal to the New Jersey Supreme Court is expected. *New York Times*, 26 September 1992, 26.

    10. Associated Press report, *International Herald Tribune*, 23 June 1992, 1, 8.

    11. Page one story by Linda Greenhouse, "Justices Uphold Stiffer Sentences for Hate Crimes," *New York Times*, 12 June 1993.

    12. *New York Times*, 15 December 1992, A1, B14.

    13. Reuters/AP report, *International Herald Tribune*, 12–13 June 1993.

    14. Don Terry, "In Crackdown on Bias, a New Tool," *New York Times*, 12 June 1993, 8. Terry reports that twenty-seven states and the District of Columbia have "penalty enhancement" provisions for crimes motivated by hate or bias.

15. During the McCarthy era, the United States had an elaborate system to bar foreign subversive material as well as to discover who received it.

16. *Globe and Mail* (Toronto), 8 February 1992, 1.

17. Cf. *Trouw* (Amsterdam), 19 October 1991, 3.

18. From mid-December 1986 through February 1987, Cardinal Simonis's publicly expressed judgments are widely discussed in the Dutch press. Professor Mary Daly (see *Volkskrant* (Amsterdam), 30 January 1987) of Boston College, one of those whose articulation of feminist theology apparently upset the cardinal, was denied standing in the case. His antifeminist remarks and the homophobic comments he made in the context of claiming that a Catholic landlord who rents on a small scale had the right to refuse to rent to homosexuals *appear* to be in violation of the statutes. The court did not agree. The disparity in the treatment of the Goerees and the cardinal was noted in the press. In *NRC Handelsblad* (Rotterdam), 2 September 1989, the cardinal is also reported as speaking out in very strong terms against the "fanatic Jews" protesting the construction of a Catholic presence at Auschwitz.

19. *Trouw*, 7 May 1991.

20. Both cases reported (AP, Reuters) in *NRC Handelsblad*, 6 May 1992.

21. Associated Press report, *International Herald Tribune*, 13 November 1991. See also *NRC Handelsblad*, 13 November 1991. Almost the entire front page of the book review section of *NRC Handelsblad* for 8 February 1992 is devoted to Barreau's criticisms of Islam.

22. *Volkskrant*, 19 February 1993, 1. Although France had three times in three years refused to receive Rushdie, just prior to the March 1993 parliamentary elections Jack Lang, minister of culture, was prevailed upon to issue an invitation. *NRC Handelsblad*, 19 March 1993, 5.

23. In *Imaginary Homelands: Essays and Criticism 1981–1991* (London: Granta Books, 1991), Salman Rushdie describes his attempt to put Edward Albee's *Zoo Story* on Karachi television. Although the word *pork* occurred in the text, the television executive ruled: "The word pork may not be spoken on Pakistan television" (38).

24. See *Trouw*, 24 November 1990, and *Volkskrant*, 28 February 1992, for reports on van Dijk's charges against columnist Gerrit Komrij.

25. *NRC Handelsblad*, 29 February 1992, 3.

26. Quoted in Catherine Monroy, "Czechoslovakia Asks Whether Its Purge Has Gone Too Far," *Guardian Weekly*, 15 March 1992, 15. Václav Havel "explains" why he felt compelled to sign an earlier form of this statute in his "Paradise Lost," *New York Review of Books* 39 (9 April 1992).

27. *International Herald Tribune*, 27 May 1991. Story by Ruth Marcus, *Washington Post*.

28. In the 1950s, people were spoken of as "card-carrying members of the Communist party." Older voters understood Bush's smear. The ACLU made good use of the slogan in a membership campaign.

29. Michel J. Crozier, Samuel P. Huntington, and Joji Watanuki, eds., *The Crisis of Democracy: Report on the Governability of Democracies to the Trilateral Commission* (New York: NYU Press, 1975). It remains an interesting source of information on an influential group. Huntington writes that "some of the problems of governance in the United States today stem from an excess of democracy. . . . Needed, instead, is a greater degree of moderation in democracy" (113). He also notes: "A univer-

sity where teaching appointments are subject to approval by students may be a more democratic university but it is not likely to be a better university." Instead of telling us which universities require student approval for all their appointments, he adds: "The arenas where democratic procedures are appropriate are, in short, limited" (114). Thus, the need for encouraging "moderation" in the quest for democracy was and remains the solution for the "Crisis."

30. Norman Dorsen, writing as president of the ACLU, "Liberty or License: Can Free Speech Become Too Costly?" *Civil Liberties*, Summer/Fall 1986, answers: "The right question is, how strongly should speech be protected? The answer, under the Constitution, is to the maximum degree and not grudgingly or reluctantly." Although urging maximum support for free speech, Dorsen takes balancing to be constitutionally supported but provides no constitutional citation.

31. Noam Chomsky, "The Responsibility of Intellectuals," reprinted in Chomsky, *American Power and the New Mandarins* (New York: Pantheon, 1969); see also his Russell Lectures, *Problems of Knowledge and Freedom* (New York: Pantheon, 1971); several of the essays in *For Reasons of State* (New York: Vintage, 1973), esp. "Notes on Anarchism" and "Language and Freedom"; *Radical Priorities*, ed. Carlos P. Otero (Montreal: Black Rose, 1981); *Manufacturing Consent*, with Edward S. Herman (New York: Pantheon, 1988); *Language and Politics*, ed. Carlos P. Otero (Montreal: Black Rose, 1989); *Necessary Illusions* (Boston: South End, 1989); *Deterring Democracy* (London: Verso, 1991).

32. Chomsky, *Deterring Democracy*, 400.

33. *De Groene Amsterdammer*, 25 March 1992, 16.

34. Interview with John Pilger on "The Late Show," BBC 2 TV, 25 November 1992.

35. Here is another sort of example: In the Quebec of the late 1960s it was often said that the ruling classes used violent language in both their federalist politics and their labor negotiations. But since such speech attacks are themselves instances of violence, a physically violent response is entirely appropriate.

36. Cited in Thomas I. Emerson, *System of Freedom of Expression* (New York: Vintage, 1971), 156–157.

10

Individuals and Communities

Academics generally believe that some protection against attacks upon their research, their teaching, or their extracurricular lecturing and writing is afforded by a policy of awarding them, after a probationary period, lifetime tenure in their professorial positions. Most of the discussions over academic freedom on most university campuses are now seldom to defend a staff member or even a student for holding dissident views. Most of the energy is spent demanding that procedural due process be accorded to junior professors who are being considered for renewal or promotion. In other words, the cases that now most concern, for example, professional organizations and teachers unions are job security matters. They are generally not cases in which tenured professors are threatened with dismissal because they hold unpopular views. In the rare cases when that actually happens, professional organizations are often powerless to act against state or provincial legislatures or powerful trustees. If they are often powerless, it is in no small measure because (as at Harvard) organization leaders, university administrators, and senior professors have tended to find discretion the better part of valor and, as Genovese points out, to be more anxious to encourage an atmosphere of "sensitivity" than defend academic freedom and such unpleasantries as might be entailed.

One of the rare instances where a senior professor at a major university has run into trouble in recent times is that of Charles Curran. He lost his post as a teacher of Catholic ethics at the Catholic University of America. But even his was a special case. Father Curran was teaching Catholic ethics under papal authorization. The Vatican withdrew his license to teach on the ground that his teaching had become heterodox, with respect to the

Church's teaching on birth control and related topics, and that a Catholic institution has the right to demand that those who teach such courses under the religious rubric subordinate their own opinions to the authoritative truth promulgated by the Church. The Swiss theologian Hans Küng had his papal license lifted for holding views the Vatican deemed heterodox but was translated to a department whose members were not required to hold a papal license. Curran, unlike Russell, was, after a few bumps, able to find a professorial post at Southern Methodist [!] University. Professors at small church-supported colleges can still encounter problems when they are charged with teaching evolution. But at the more important state and private universities, the charge that someone is or was a communist is now not likely to result in dismissal. There are often squabbles internal to a department that end in blocking the appointment or renewal of a person for holding the "wrong" methodological views. The discrimination in such cases tends to be harder to document, and hence appeals are not likely to be successful. In the event an appellant's publication record is exemplary, the fact that a department still wishes to dismiss him or her becomes harder to justify.

No longer do the major free-speech problems arise from subversion or religion/irreligion debates. At present, the most sensitive area, the one that generates the most problems for those who subscribe to an absolutist reading of the free-speech clause, or indeed, for anyone who would defend a reasonably strict interpretation of the free-speech principle, is that of offensive speech. The sorts of speech that give such offense that they are banned by law or regulation fall into several categories, although the legal principle that really carries the burden is one previously discussed: group libel. Speech that is felt to be offensive to any identifiable group, such as racist or sexist speech, either is proscribed or there is political pressure to proscribe it. That is why it is important to observe how universities are handling this issue. Seventy percent of American colleges and universities are said to have introduced regulations to restrict offensive speech. Once it becomes acceptable to restrict free speech on the campus, as it did in the 1940s, it becomes much more acceptable to restrict it in the community at large. University regulations that are applicable only to the content of speech are generally found to be unacceptable to U.S. courts because they are seen to contravene First Amendment rights.[1] But mounting a court challenge consumes vast amounts of both time and money. Canadian courts, of course, follow different legal precedents.

The pressure is on to find ways to circumvent these U.S. court decisions and to find a device whereby group libel legislation can be made acceptable so that racist and sexist speech can be banned. One route always available, in principle, for Americans is to draft, and then gain approval for, a constitutional amendment. It is, however, a cumbersome process requiring two-thirds approval in each house of the Congress, plus ratification by three fourths of the state legislatures. The fact that flag burning has been given

First Amendment protection by the U.S. Supreme Court did not prevent George Bush from recommending a constitutional amendment to prohibit it. There is nothing in principle to prevent the Congress and the several states from passing an amendment authorizing group libel legislation. However, the pressure has not yet reached that point. Instead, one can expect that as cases go before the courts, the free-speech barrier to group libel will gradually be eroded, and U.S. practice will increasingly conform to Canadian and European norms.[2]

There are many signs that both philosophers and lawyers are finding in "communitarian" theory a philosophical basis for group libel legislation. An examination of recent articles in several law reviews suggests that the First Amendment is no longer even in the abstract seen as a "good thing." On the contrary, the First Amendment is seen as the legal vehicle that justifies racist speech. It is the most serious barrier to the successful introduction of legislation that would prevent the harms that racial slurs produce. These harms are perceived to be so hurtful, so damaging to members of certain communities, so self-evidently immoral, that draconian legislation is required. Some proposals are phrased so sweepingly that even talking about racism in class would constitute a violation.[3]

In an article defending First Amendment values in the context of racist speech, Robert C. Post,[4] mentioned earlier in connection with Stanley Fish's paper ("There's No Such Thing as Free Speech and It's a Good Thing Too"), discusses various harms racist speech causes to, for example, individuals and educational institutions. He offers an account of the values of the First Amendment with special emphasis on "the relationship between freedom of expression and democratic self-governance" (279) and thus with the First Amendment's role in protecting "public discourse." He comments on the tension between community and democracy: "Public discourse within a democracy is legally conceived as the communicative medium through which individuals choose the forms of their communal life; public discourse within a community is legally conceived as a medium through which the values of a particular life are displayed and enacted" (286). Finally, he explores the matter of restrictions on racist speech within universities—noting that "the regulation of racist speech within public [universities] . . . does not turn on the value of democratic self-governance and its realization in public discourse" (318), although that is how the courts have generally treated the matter. "The current controversy regarding the constitutionality of regulating racist speech on university and college campuses may most helpfully be interpreted as a debate about . . . the constitutionally permissible educational objectives of public institutions of higher learning" (318). Thus, Post evades the issue of suppressing free speech on campus by making it seem to be a question of a university's "mission." One might have thought that however one characterizes the mission of a university, the values incorporated into the First Amendment—the values of free speech and academic freedom—ought to be central to that mission. Instead, Post simply urges that we err on the side of caution in restricting speech, ever mindful of the values that undergird and inform the First Amendment. As even this thumbnail sketch of his position shows, Post intends to reject Fish's doctrine that talk about regulative ideals is empty, although Post, contrary to the argument I am advancing, takes individuals to be nonautonomous. "I define 'community' as a social formation that inculcates norms into the very identities of its members" (286). He adds: "Questions of personal identity are in fact always at stake in discussions of collective self-definition. . . . As our collective aspirations change, so will our respective personal identities" (301).

The tension Post postulates between "democracy" and "community" may, however, threaten his enterprise. Given the uses to which he puts his corelated notions of "identity" and "community," it seems to me that he effectively undermines the conceptual foundations for self-governance. Thus, those First Amendment values, for example, sustaining public political discourse, to which Post is committed have no conceptual protection against being overwhelmed by communitarian pressures and thereby becoming "flexible principles." Post of course fully appreciates that defenders of tribal considerations are often blind to the requirement that in a true democracy one must accept the need for public discourse. Nevertheless, the only foundation Post advances for public discourse *and* for democratic self-governance, his core First Amendment values, rests on communal factors. And even First Amendment values can be discarded on campus in the interests of a university's mission. Hence, I am inclined to delete the *self* from his "self-governance." Post[5] approaches the First Amendment from a very different philosophical position from the one I claim originally provided the basis for the absolutist form in which the free-speech clause appears.

Because public discourse is understood as the communicative medium through which the democratic "self" is itself constituted, public discourse must in important respects remain exempt from democratic regulation. *We use the speech/action distinction to mark the boundaries of this exemption. . . . [T]his distinction is purely pragmatic.* [Emphasis added.] We designate the communicative processes necessary to sustain the principle of collective self-determination "speech" and thus insulate it from majoritarian interference. (285)

Lest it appear that I may be taking Post's comments out of context, here is a similar passage: "Democracy necessarily presupposes some form of social institution, like community, through which the concrete identities of 'autonomous' democratic citizens can be defined and instantiated. [Note the status he accords *autonomous* by placing it in quotation marks.] The paradigmatic examples of such institutions are the family and the elementary school" (287). If the speech/action distinction is merely "pragmatic," if the autonomy of the individual is qualified by, and inferior to, the community, and if, at bottom, shifting communal forces provide the only basis for democratic (First Amendment) values, then values seem to be grounded in political muscle, and his position runs the risk of being indistinguishable from Fish's (and Thrasymachus's).

"Harms" and "communities" are also involved the case of two law professors at the District of Columbia Law School. Journalist Nat Hentoff reports that Bob Catz and Tom Mack "have become charged [by students and colleagues] at their own law school with disloyalty, insensitivity, political incorrectness, and behavior unfit for a faculty member at a public-interest school."[6] They have sinned by defending, on First Amendment grounds, a Georgetown University law student who attacked his institution's affirmative action admissions policy. He alleged that the educational achievements of black applicants were far inferior to those of whites. The accuracy of the claims was not at issue, but a student who attacks affirmative action is perceived as expressing racist views, and for law professors to defend such a student is Politically Incorrect. Dean William Robinson is quoted as saying that the two professors "are on 'a kind of probation with some segments of the student body and with some faculty.' " When Hentoff pointed out that these lawyers were defending the Georgetown student's First Amendment rights, he was told: " '[C]ivil liberties, while being within the pale, are not the focus here. Faculty members must keep in mind the hurt their actions will do to the community of the law school.' "

In articulating grounds for antiracist and antisexist legislation, philosophical theories not only of a communitarian sort but also of the self or person are often appealed to. Thus, there have been, since the decline of Cartesianism, theories of human nature that authorize the awarding of *essential* status to certain human properties that the Cartesians generally count as *accidental*, that is, as nonessential. In Descartes's radical dualism, things like skin color and sex are nonessential. His system simply does not authorize ascribing color to minds. Cartesian minds think; it is bodies that have such properties as color or sex. The Cartesian unity of the human species is broken by Locke and others. With Locke, we find that human natures can be scaled. With Hume, we find blacks classed as *essentially* inferior. It was probably the slave trade that encouraged the development of racial theorizing, and it may have been the slight increase in the economic power of women that made it more important to reinforce by means of sexist theory the status of women as chattels. Racism, unlike xenophobia, does not appear to have been an omnipresent feature, but sexism has been with us since the Garden of Eden. Philosophically, at least, the inferiority of women is "demonstrated" in the writings of Aristotle, Thomas Aquinas, and most philosophers—especially those on the empiricist side of the Western tradition.

Historically, it is with the systematic rejection of dualism that theories emerge within which the body, the cultural environment, or the impact of the religious or national or linguistic community can be interpreted as key determinants of personhood. Non-Cartesian philosophies were available to facilitate this shift. Thus, phenomenological analyses often seem to provide insightful characterizations of how we think about our bodies, how we think about other people, and how we "make" other people into objects and how we ourselves are so "made." When the antidualist theories of Sartre, Heidegger, and Merleau-Ponty are taken to illuminate the human's "objectifying" stance as something essential to our being, they can be useful to those who are seeking to understand why and how our bodies are "seen" and "treated" as *objects*.

Insofar as free-speech issues are concerned, the important step is the adoption of a doctrine of human nature within which (1) speech loses the special status it has with dualism and (2) speech becomes one more form of action. In these respects, the elaborate materialist forms of phenomenological existentialism are indistinguishable from empiricist-behaviorist doctrine. In both systems, the self is primarily, if not exclusively, a product of external forces, although in communitarian-based accounts of the self the importance of cultural factors is magnified and enhanced. Those cultural factors that are said to be based on one's sex, skin color, language first learned and still spoken, national history, and so on, are impressed on and absorbed by each person. Proponents of the communitarian model would deny that it resembles stimulus-response behaviorism, but it does possess an analogous circularity in that the cultural patterns "inform" each self, and when we probe a given self, it is said to be primarily a product of those cultural patterns. (Just as within behaviorist theory, a stimulus is located by its response, and vice versa.) Within both the behaviorist and the communitarian systems, speech is a form of action. One thus has a means of taking any and all forms of offensive speech as instances of violence and, for example, sexist speech as coercive. With speech as action, one has a basis for using the criminal code to proscribe *talk* that sexually demeans and, more generally, talk that demeans people on the basis of any identifiable characteristic.

However, it is behavior rather than talk that creates most of the problems for people who suffer discrimination. The women's movement has been obliged to remind men that in Canada and the United States women earn roughly one third less than men. They often earn less when doing the same job. Their promotion rate is slower, and they are often restrained by the "glass ceiling" from reaching the highest levels in business, government, or academia. An interesting indication of how men have structured social institutions and legal systems to create and preserve their hegemony over women is found in the question of rape within marriage. In 1991, the English High Court ruled unanimously against the traditional view, long embedded in English law and social custom, that a husband can do what he wants with his own chattels, including his wife. The court now holds that a husband can be tried for raping his wife.

Women in the workplace and in universities object to being subjected to sexual demands and sexual threats by men who have supervisory power over them or who stand in a teacher–student (power) relation to them. In both Canada and the United States, regulations now seek to penalize objectionable behavior and to hold employers, companies, and institutions liable for the untoward acts of their employees toward women. In the United States, sexual harassment falls under Title VII of the Civil Rights Act of 1964,[7] although the agency charged with its enforcement, the Equal Employment Opportunity Commission, has not built a record of vigorous prosecution of those whose discriminatory actions fall under its responsibility.[8]

In *Meritor Savings Bank v. Vinson* (1986) the U.S. Supreme Court distinguishes quid pro quo sexual harassment cases from those involving a "hostile work environment." An employer or supervisor may single out a person and demand sexual favors in return for, say, a promotion or a wage increase. Or an employer may tolerate a situation in which a class of employees—almost always women—must work in an environment in which they are subjected to remarks of a sexual nature, pornographic pictures on the walls, or behavior that demeans and degrades them. In the quid quo pro cases, more than speech is clearly involved. If the sexually harassed person says no and is discharged or not promoted, evidence of discrimination of a nonverbal sort is available. Catherine MacKinnon discusses some ways in which sexual harassment was handled under assault laws in several turn-of-the-century decisions. In some of the cases she cites, "talk" (propositioning) is distinguished from touching.[9] The talk does not constitute an offense; the touching is held to constitute an assault. However unsatisfactory this may now appear, it is a way in which a free-speech absolutist can restrict the application of sexual harassment regulations to actions while leaving speech alone.

When universities decide that they must draft regulations to ban sexual harassment, often under pressure from governments, difficulties seem to arise. The categories "sexual harassment" and "hostile work [or study] environment" are accordion concepts. In quid pro quo cases, there may be unfairly graded papers or other records of actions. However, as Genovese points out in his review of D'Souza, in attempts to guarantee that verbal harassment of a racial or sexual sort does not occur on the campus, academic freedom immediately suffers. Only one generation ago, American universities, fearful of one or another pressure group, sought to demonstrate that the halls of ivy were free of subversives. In the present environment, academic freedom will again be damaged. Last time around, the professors of treason had to be removed. This time it is the professors of indecency.

At McGill University, officials in the higher administration have fallen over themselves to show they know what is Politically Correct. "Sexual harassment," according to the regulations, "is defined as a display, by word or deed, of sexual attention towards another individual or group of individuals of a nature which may reasonably be considered to be vexatious or abusive." Nothing in the regulations prevents a lecturer from being accused of sexual harassment for talking about, or assigning readings in, material that an individual (or individuals) finds offensive or otherwise "vexatious." Thus, certain religious views can be understood as sexually offensive to both women and men. A discussion of legal efforts to distinguish the erotic from the pornographic in a course on freedom of speech could easily create problems for a teacher. In the filigree detail of the regulations, one finds that vexatious behavior can be *indirect*. Moreover, third-party complaints are encouraged. Hardly a happy state of affairs when an accusation is all that is needed to destroy a career.

There is no hint that the drafters and implementers of these regulations appreciate that in their zeal to minimize sexual harassment, like their equivalents at Toronto[10] and like those who prepared Harvard's "Sexism in the Classroom" guidelines, they have drafted rules that directly conflict with the most basic principles of academic freedom. McGill faculty members are reminded that the word *reasonably* is in the primary definition of the offense. But the procedure for establishing reasonableness is not given. Faculty members are also assured that the rules will not be applied "literally." The Harvard administrators failed the cause of academic freedom by promulgating rules in direct conflict with it. They then compounded the problem by apparently evading the issue of academic freedom in a concrete case (i.e., Thernstrom). Genovese maintains that this "create[s] an atmosphere in which professors who value their reputations and their perquisites learn to censor themselves."[11] McGill has succeeded in doing the same thing. Nothing is more likely to induce caution in a lecturer than the suggestion that the rules circumscribing what can legally be said will not be applied *literally*.

There is also a pragmatic difficulty in finding a line between a lecturer's acceptable speech in the classroom and the speech one would prohibit. That line is often in the eyes and ears of the beholder who finds an expression vexatious. In academic social contexts, an invitation for a cup of coffee in a university facility may be appropriate. A request for a date is likely to be considered inappropriate in a context where one has, or is likely to have, some measure of power over another, for example, a teacher over a student. A teacher who compliments a student on his new suit or her new glasses is employing language that, having no content relevant to course material, could constitute grounds for a charge of sexual harassment, a charge that can be filed either by the student or a third party. A word of admiration to a student who has just acquired a new Porsche might be less risky. In that case, one might argue that remarking on a person's car is different from commenting on something like clothing, a car being, at least on some interpretations, less closely related to the body. Whatever "confidential" may have meant in pre-Xerox days, it now means no more in university contexts than it does in congressional or parliamentary committees. Reports made to university sexual harassment officers have a way of becoming public charges. And charges easily become convictions when due process, opportunities to confront witnesses, and the like, are ignored in recognition of the sensitivity of such cases. The consequence is a variation of Genovese's charge: These regulations promise to have a chilling effect on academic freedom. Wise teachers avoid discussing whatever might appear to be potentially sensitive topics, minimize contacts with students, and despite passageway noise, keep their office doors open and do their research at home.

From the absolutist standpoint, sexual harassment and antiracist regulations that refer *only* to talk are illegitimate constraints because they violate the category distinction between talking and doing, the distinction that I believe sustains the absolutist free-speech principle. In this respect, they may be interpreted as creating a problem for the absolutist not unlike that posed by libel, slander, hate literature, disseminating false news, or incitement laws. These and similar regulations are aimed at improving the level of civility we display in our verbal intercourse with our friends and enemies. From the standpoint of the absolutist, problems arise once one moves from restraining actions to restricting conversations.

Threats, name-calling, flirting, propositioning, character assassination, ethnic and sexist jokes, demeaning any and all identifiable groups, and many sorts of uncivil talk have always been a part of family life, school life, church life, office life, political life, factory life, and university life and are the stuff of much of our literature and virtually all of our television soap operas. Accusations of lying, dishonesty, and incompetence are so common in public life that little notice is taken of them. Not for nothing do the members of some monastic orders take vows of silence.

American jurisprudence has often been uncomfortable with restrictive legislation, primarily because a democracy is a self-governing society, and if self-governing, then the members must be free to discuss all aspects of *their* government's policy; and second, I suspect, because of practical considerations, it has always been recognized that people are very ingenious at finding euphemisms and forms of innuendo that allow them to transmit offensive messages in legally acceptable ways. The issue of racist speech is often handled in this fashion. George Bush routinely employed "code words" to get across the same racist message a David Duke presents straightforwardly. Teachers who are known to misuse the teacher–student relationship by using vexatious speech can be confronted in class or in the teacher's office by a group of offended students or even made the targets of student protests. In a context in which the university faculties and administrations have reminded themselves and their students about the nature of and the need for academic freedom (reminders that are seldom provided), there is at least a chance that opportunities may be created for the use of argument and persuasion, something that is foreclosed once an adversarial legalistic administrative court procedure is introduced. After all, students also have both academic freedom and free-speech rights.

I do not doubt that a real psychological hurt is felt by Native Americans when they read in the U.S. Declaration of Independence about the "merciless Indian Savages, whose known Rule of Warfare, is an undistinguished Destruction, of all Ages, Sexes and Conditions" and when they reflect on the treatment later accorded their ancestors in reality as well as in histories. American and Canadian citizens of Japanese origin know that racist hatred was behind their being transported to concentration camps during World War II, just as it drives the more recent wave of "Japan bashing." Jews, many of whose families were decimated in concentration camps, are surely pained when they hear a historian assert that the Holocaust never occurred, as are African-Americans when they hear a scientist claiming to prove their intellectual inferiority. This holds also for women when they are made to understand that they are only sex objects, or Italians when they are characterized as mafiosos. So it is with any of the literally hundreds of stereotypes with which we have enriched our cultures and our legal systems. There is no denying that they all produce real psychological hurts. What is at issue is whether speech suppression as a "cure" is compatible with democracy.

Many of the relevant Canadian, European, and United Nations restrictions on freedom of expression were drafted after World War II, and these restrictions are becoming more and more acceptable among those Americans who have input into the workings of the legal system. And yet if all talk offensive to anyone is proscribed, if *offensive* is made the threshold for censorship, and universities become centers of "sensitivity to diversity," then we cannot hope that universities might provide an improved context in which ideas can be explored and opinions more freely discussed. De Tocqueville would not be surprised to discover that the pressures for political conformity and methodological purity continue to be in place in American universities. Admittedly, if all offensive talk is proscribed by legislative action in the larger community, then freedom of speech can no longer be appealed to when attempting to counter campus speech code restrictions.

The U.S. Senate Judiciary Committee hearings on the confirmation of Clarence Thomas to be an associate justice of the Supreme Court aroused great anger and frustration among many women because they believed the all-male committee was not taking the concerns of women seriously. They found proof of this in the committee's original effort to avoid taking up Oklahoma law professor Anita Hill's complaints of sexual harassment against Thomas. After they had confirmed Thomas, various senators sought to demonstrate their sensitivity to the plight of harassed women by introducing bills further to penalize sexual harassment. I would guess that the Thomas confirmation debacle will make legislatures, courts, and university administrators anxious to be exceedingly chivalrous in drafting new laws, deciding cases, and accepting new regulations. Various kinds of what in fact will be group libel proposals, bearing on sexual harassment, will find their way into law.

The risk posed by the New Brunswick (Canada) type cases must be taken seriously. A law drafted to protect women or a minority can be used in other ways. The trouble is that once it is granted that speech is action, and that by means of group libel communitarian principles offensive *speech* can then be criminalized, there is no logical hindrance to prevent an identifiable group from demanding the extension of *offensive* to cover certain actions, social practices, and life-styles of other members of the society. Group libel communitarian interests then come to the fore. Such advocates of Political Correctness as Stanley Fish seem to have forgotten that the world is full of identifiable communities, many of which would be only too willing to defend their own communitarian interests by means of group libel legislation. If, as Fish maintains, only political force counts, it might be wise to ask, as Stalin did, "how many divisions the Pope [and his allies in these matters among the moral majority] can muster" before committing his troops to battle.

In the last part of the seventeenth century, John Locke argues that it is not the responsibility of a government to impose religious conformity on its citizens. The task of a government is to protect and preserve the lives and property of the people. Locke, the enemy of Catholics, and no friend to Jews,[12] is not an absolutist about either religious toleration or free speech. But he does think that as a practical matter a government that strives to control religious beliefs, presumably with the goal of enhancing its political power, will in fact end by destabilizing the society. Although Locke's views about toleration may strike us as strangely limited, his sensitivity to the limits of governmental power in the religious domain and to the risk of the "tumults" that may ensue if we seek to violate human privacy has a distinctly modern air. His reflections on the history of attempts to guarantee the religious salvation of political communities were well known to Thomas Jefferson and James Madison. Locke had no similar interest in freedom of speech. Rather, the history of freedom of speech is largely the history of the American experience. Nevertheless, efforts to undermine it have often, like legalizing religious intolerance, proven to be imprudent for nonprincipled reasons similar to those Locke feared in the religious domain. It is paradoxical that in contemporary American politics so many elements on the Left agree *in matters of principle* with much of the Right. The disagreement between the old censors and the new is over questions of detail: which books are to be banned, which groups are to be given enhanced status, and which activist professors are to be promoted/fired. The decision power, however, especially with reference to the last point, rests almost entirely with the old censors.

We seem to be given three choices: a decision that all groups have equal rights to claim to be offended and that all offenders must be prosecuted; a decision that all groups have a theoretical entitlement but that some groups (e.g., African-Americans or women) are "more equal" than others; a decision that this is not a promising way to achieve a just society and that an absolutist reading of the First Amendment's free-speech clause, with all its difficulties, is preferable to the social discord that the Canadian experience suggests group libel law can generate. However we choose, Martin Luther King's admonition might be kept in mind: "An eye for an eye will leave us all blind."

NOTES

1. The University of Michigan's regulations were struck down in U.S. District Court on First Amendment grounds (721 F. Supp. 852 [Eastern Dist. Mich. 1989]).

2. For a sketch of some of the philosophical arguments, with references to, for example, A. MacIntyre and M. Sandel and with considerable bibliographical detail favoring a contextual analysis of First Amendment issues whereby the "harm" generated by racial slurs, and the like, can be penalized, see the Note: "A Communitarian Defense of Group Libel Laws," *Harvard Law Review* 101 (1988): 682–701. It is contended that within traditional ("categorical" analysis) First Amendment interpretation theory there is no legal remedy readily at hand to counter the harm caused to communities by racial, ethnic, and sexist remarks. That is why they propose to change the law by the simple expedient of changing what the free-speech clause says by modifying the theory of interpreting the text. The future of deconstructionism in literature may lie behind it, but it offers infinite possibilities for understanding law and other disciplines perceived as being infested with phallo-logico-centric thinking.

3. See David F. McGowan and Ragesh K. Tangri, "A Libertarian Critique of University Restrictions of Offensive Speech," *California Law Review* 79 (1991): 825–918. A good introduction to the voluminous literature on regulations meant to bar racist and sexist speech is given in fn. 21. Relevant portions of the quite remarkable University of Michigan code (held by a federal court to be in violation of the First Amendment—see above) are given in their fn. 29.

See also, in the same issue of the *California Law Review* (919–970), Sean M. SeLegue, "Campus Anti-Slur Regulations: Speakers, Victims, and the First Amendment," for a strong position on the harm question. In most discussions *Beauharnais* and *Chaplinsky*, despite having been overruled in whole or in part by later decisions, are frequently cited in support of suppressing offensive speech directed at identifiable groups.

4. Robert C. Post, "Racist Speech, Democracy, and the First Amendment," *William and Mary Law Review* 32 (1991): 267–327. Post has written frequently on First Amendment themes.

5. Although I am not convinced that a communitarian philosophy can provide an adequate basis, or even make intelligible the literal words of the free-speech clause, I find Post's paper the most important treatment of this material that I have encountered. The breadth of Post's analysis of harms and his discussion of such philosophically concerned First Amendment theorists as Schauer, Kelsen, and Meiklejohn, as well as such philosophers as Wittgenstein, Habermas, G. H. Mead, and Dewey, is extremely helpful. See also his "The Constitutional Concept of Political Discourse: Outrageous Opinion, Democratic Deliberation, and *Hustler Magazine v. Falwell*," *Harvard Law Review* 103 (1989): 603–686; idem, "The Social Foundations of Privacy: Community and Self in the Common Law Tort," *California Law Review* 89 (1989): 957–1010.

6. Nat Hentoff, "Hurt Feelings and Free Speech," *Progressive*, February 1992, 16–17. Timothy Maguire, the Georgetown University law student Hentoff refers to, presents his own case in "My Bout with Affirmative Action," *Commentary* 93 (April 1992): 50–52. Some of Hentoff's other writings on the First Amendment appear in his *Freedom of Speech: For Me But Not for Thee* (New York: HarperCollins, 1992).

7. The relevant portion of Title VII reads: "It shall be an unlawful employment practice for an employer—(1) to fail or refuse to hire or to discharge any individual, or otherwise discriminate against any individual with respect to his compensation, terms, conditions, or privileges of employment, because of such individual's race, color, religion, sex, or national origin."

8. Sexual harassment in the academic context is spelled out in detail in Title IX of the Education Amendments of 1972 and various Education Department regulations.

9. Catherine A. MacKinnon, *Sexual Harassment of Working Women* (New Haven: Yale University Press, 1979), 284–285. Emerson has a Foreword to the volume and is clearly supportive of MacKinnon's effort to "bring the force of law to bear upon an uncivilized practice that has long been silently sanctioned" (viii). He makes no mention of any First Amendment aspects of the issue. Neither does MacKinnon, but then she has never said (e.g., in discussing pornography) she accepted Emerson's theory of the First Amendment as guaranteeing freedom of expression.

10. In March 1989, a sixty-year-old University of Toronto professor was convicted before a sexual harassment panel of "lewd staring" while swimming in a university pool. On appeal before a five-person board including a former Supreme Court justice, the board voted three women to two men not to grant a new hearing on the original charge. Punishment included a ban on his use of the pool and a directive to seek counseling. The charge, the initial hearing, and the appeal were reported in detail in newspapers across Canada. The professor reportedly complained that he was a victim of harassment because graffiti appeared on campus walls saying "Drown him" and "Poke his eyes out." (Cf. *Gazette* [Montreal], 9 December 1989, A12.) Subsequent efforts to strengthen the university's sexual harassment code have generated complaints that tougher regulations will have a chilling effect on academic freedom. Sexual harassment officers say that the rules will be applied "reasonably." (Cf. *Globe and Mail* [Toronto], 1 May 1991, A10.)

11. Eugene D. Genovese, "Heresy, Yes—Sensitivity, No," *New Republic*, 15 April 1991, 30.

12. See Murray Smith, "John Locke and the Jews" (M.A. thesis, McGill University, 1988).

11

Conclusion

The absolutist doctrine of free speech that appears in the First Amendment does not come with an obvious historical pedigree. For those raised on such texts as Mill's *On Liberty*, there is simply no rationale for an absolutist version. By examining certain philosophical doctrines that are influential in the seventeenth and eighteenth centuries, I provide a rationale for the formulation of the First Amendment's free-speech clause and for its later interpretation (and misinterpretation). That is why I begin with Bayle's theory of conscience in relation to his views on religious toleration. I also show how important the dualisms of mind/body and talk/action coupled with the doctrine of mental privacy are to both toleration and freedom of speech theories. I contend that Bayle's Cartesian dualist framework provides a categorial distinction between talk and action. That distinction, in turn, gives a plausible basis for an absolutist doctrine of freedom of speech. Bayle does not advance arguments for freedom of speech per se; rather, it is a natural consequence of a doctrine of human nature that he *does* argue for. In the eighteenth and nineteenth centuries, Cartesian philosophy comes under sustained attack. As the dualist philosophical foundations for the talk/action distinction and hence for absolute freedom of speech were undermined, direct defenses—such as that presented by John Stuart Mill— had to be mounted. But the freedom defended is not the absolutist one incorporated in the First Amendment.

The rejection of dualism provides as a fringe benefit a basis for rejecting the talk/action distinction. In the citation from Conor Cruise O'Brien (Chapter 2), we see the distinction explicitly collapsed and censorship defended. Our legal systems are primarily geared to penalize untoward actions. Once speech counts as action, there is no longer any principled impediment to legislating against offensive speech, exactly Cruise O'Brien's proposal. In facilitating these moves, Bayle's Cartesian dualism is replaced with a behaviorist account of human nature. The historical lesson is that a robust doctrine of freedom of speech cannot be rigorously defended once we decide that speech is a form of action.[1]

The differences between Bayle and Locke with regard to religious toleration have a direct parallel in one aspect of modern discussions of freedom of speech. Bayle grounds his absolutist doctrine of religious toleration (1) on a Cartesian theory of the self in order to make intelligible his account of the privacy of conscience and (2) on Cartesian clear and distinct moral principles. Locke does the opposite: He rejects the Cartesian self and the Cartesian mind; he rejects even the term *principle* for its innatist associations; he rejects the appeal to conscience as a basis for toleration. Instead, Locke recommends that we pursue a policy of religious toleration simply for prudential reasons on behalf of stable government. He insists that religious toleration be accorded only to those loyal religious groups that themselves favor toleration.

Bayle articulates an absolutist theory of religious toleration. It is in the course of working out this absolutist theory that Bayle offers his account of freedom of speech. Over the course of the centuries, Bayle's absolutist position regarding freedom of speech has found much less favor than has the extension of Locke's "reciprocity" thesis: Religious toleration should be extended only to those who are themselves committed to toleration. The extension of Locke's sort of reciprocity thesis to freedom of speech is seen in the insistence, for example, by Hook and Lovejoy, that the right to freedom of speech (particularly, academic freedom) should be extended only to those who are committed to it.

Finally, I think it is useful to recall Emerson's *expression/action* distinction. His is a serious effort to make sense of the absolutist quality in the First Amendment's free-speech clause. Despite his admiration for Justice Black, Emerson may have given up on the *ipsissima verba* of the First Amendment, and any attempt to employ a *speech*/action distinction, because he wants to give First Amendment protection to nonverbal "symbolic speech." He wants to give, for example, draft card burning a privileged position as an expressive act. But *expression* and *speech* are not synonyms, and there is no literal constitutional warrant for interpreting *speech* as expression. The net effect of such a translation is to weaken the free-speech principle by erasing the once-clear ontologically grounded distinction between *speech* and *action*. By yielding that point, Emerson is forced to accept Mill's harm principle and the balancing act that goes with it. A variety of other forces in contemporary culture contribute to making Emerson's expression/action distinction increasingly difficult to draw. In popular, legal, and scholarly circles, it is often said that all expression should count as conduct and all conduct as expression. More philosophically put, it is said that any and all human activity, all human conduct, is *intentional* and hence at once expression. That Plato's *Protagoras* is a homily about the dangers of exalting rhetoric and style over substance seems to be forgotten.

With the breakdown in the acceptance of that dualism within which the absolutist free-speech principle was first articulated came the introduction of empiricist theories of the self wherein the speech/action distinction is much more difficult to maintain. Finally, we now see the development of "communitarian" philosophical theories. These theories help provide a philosophical basis for group libel legislation, legislation that promises severe restrictions on freedom of speech. "Communities" help create a framework for a more effective application of Mill's harm principle than his own vague comments could sustain. As I show, these theories find expression in Canadian hate literature legislation and American university offensive speech regulations. A major addition to the portrayal of the growth of the self, provided by these theories, is the crucial role attributed to the community forces that form and structure it. These are much enriched by a variety of intellectual forces, from Freud and Marx to Heidegger, Wittgenstein, and Merleau-Ponty and among contemporary philosophers such as Richard Rorty and Charles Taylor.

In our concern to strengthen, as bearers of rights, those communities from which it is said our identities derive, it should be noted that Pierre Bayle, although a defender of the French Protestant cause, was also interested in the human tendency to proliferate communities. Here is a recent Canadian unofficial set of "cultural communities" suggested by Amnesty International (English Section): "Language; religion; economic status; ethnic background; sexual identity; physical ability; educational attainment; historical experience; national origin; gender; geographic location (urban/rural); age group; length of time in Canada; literacy; colour; parenthood (single vs. family)."

Bayle would be delighted with such a range of cultural diversities because he knew that Christians had also always divided themselves and then further subdivided their sects into sects. In one of the more satirical articles ["Mammillaires"] in his *Dictionnaire*,[2] Bayle discusses how a sect of Anabaptists split over the matter of a young man who put his hand on the breast of the young woman he loved and whom he planned to marry. Bayle writes that one group wanted the man excommunicated; the other favored being indulgent toward him. This latter group, Bayle tells us, became known as the Mammillarians. As the list above reminds us, we can already observe the process of division at work in generating additional communities. Hence, we can expect that the same splitting process that in more recent times has afflicted political parties will radically increase the number of communities. As Bayle probably appreciated, and may have hoped for, the logic of the schismatic process implicit in communitarian thought is such that divisions will continue until at last each community is a minority of one. At that point, thanks to that fatal conceptual flaw within the notion of group rights, individuals become the sole bearers of rights and each person's "identity" is unique.

I have made much of the role of what I characterize as the empiricist-behaviorist doctrine of human nature as a major factor in depriving speech of the special position it held within Cartesian-style systems. Doctrines of human nature are largely, but not exclusively, ideological constructs. They are major elements in our accounts of human identity and of community. It is because the empiricist-behaviorist picture has facilitated making conceptually plausible such notions as identity and community that this picture proves its worth. Once upon a time it was the dominant model in psychology. It was the received wisdom as to how we learn and how we teach, as well as how we acquire concepts and language. The model has a scientific core that seems to make it intellectually respectable. And since humans are the building blocks upon which political science, sociology, and the other social sciences must build, that scientific core is thought to help ground those disciplines, too. We are told that learning takes place in accordance with stimulus-response principles, and so far as possible, nothing is attributed to the human organism.[3] It seems an unlikely hypothesis, one that is falsified by examples of growth and development elsewhere in the animal kingdom. But however perverse it may now seem to be, it has, as I have noted on occasion, one tremendous advantage: It contributes to the notion that we are plastic, malleable creatures and are totally the products of external environmental forces. As *blank tablets* we are the perfect subjects to receive direction and control from those who possess the requisite skills and power. Hence, such a theory of human nature remains a valuable ally for those who have, seek, or serve power.

The scientific core of this doctrine of human nature has largely unraveled, and the exponents of identity and community talk no longer have any grounding for their doctrines. The unraveling has been caused by psychological research in very different directions. In modern linguistics, it is claimed that there is a species-wide and innate foundation, namely, universal grammar, that makes the acquisition of language possible. And cognitive science, with its emphases on the structure of the mind and neural science, also contributes to a radical change in the direction of psychological research. The effect of these developments is to make communitarian positions more straightforwardly ideological.

This may be observed among those philosophers who try to ground their communitarian structures on social practices generally and language in particular. A primary contributor to these ways of thinking is Wittgenstein. Because his central dogmas—for example, the impossibility of a "private language," "meaning is use," "words are deeds," and the learning of pain behavior—seem so behaviorist in both method and outlook, and because he also seems to use the child's learning environment as the ultimate foundation without which one is unable to get the grammar of one's concepts clear and one's philosophical puzzles dissolved, he has often (like his contemporary Gilbert Ryle) been understood to be a behaviorist. The assumption that language and its structure are taught in accordance with behaviorist methods stands as the cornerstone of this position, even as that piece of blank tablet empiricist psychology has been effectively challenged by work in cognitive science.[4] The distinction between words and actions that I have located in Bayle and the Cartesian tradition is, by Wittgenstein and Ryle, the greatest of philosophical errors. Not surprisingly, they take Descartes to be the greatest of philosophical error makers.

I have only alluded to an important subject that is often an ingredient in attacks on the absolutist doctrine of freedom of speech, and that is the role of propaganda. It was, after all, what was judged to be the success of Nazi propaganda that prompted Canada's Cohen Commission to propose restricting free speech through hate literature legislation. In the socially overriding interest of blocking propaganda, the dissemination of falsehoods, and language that causes hurts, free speech must be sacrificed. As Chomsky, who is at once a defender of free speech and a student of propaganda, has insisted, it is only in a society that supports the free-speech principle that one can study, explore, analyze, and denounce propaganda. If, as Chomsky claimed in his famous 1967 essay, it is the "responsibility of intellectuals to speak the truth and to expose lies,"[5] then, regardless of the successes of the propagandists, in order to be able to speak the truth and to expose lies one must have freedom of speech.

Chomsky has explained why he considers propaganda to be crucially important in a democratic society. In an article in *Index on Censorship*, he writes: "From a comparative perspective, the United States is unusual if not unique in the lack of restraints on freedom of expression. It is also unusual in the range and effectiveness of the methods employed to restrain freedom of thought." He goes on to say: "Liberal democratic theorists have long noted that in a society where the voice of the people is heard, elite groups must ensure that the voice says the right things. The less the state is able to employ violence in defence of the interests of elite groups that effectively dominate it, the more it becomes necessary to devise techniques of 'manufacture of consent,' in the words of Walter Lippmann, over 60 years ago."[6]

The particular case Chomsky then analyzes is the "thought control" role played by the American media in discussions of Middle East policy. It is interesting that Chomsky's remarks were solicited by the editor of a periodical devoted to exposing and discussing instances of censorship. He discusses how Middle East issues are presented in the U.S. media "as an example," he wrote later, "of the shaping of opinion in a society free from censorship."

Chomsky's piece elicited fierce responses. Oxford's distinguished political philosopher Sir Isaiah Berlin, who once wrote a sensitive analysis of John Stuart Mill,[7] complained anonymously (through Nora Beloff) that Chomsky's revelation about media suppression and distortion "is not an exposure of censorship and hence is beyond the purview of *Index*."[8] He canceled his subscription. Perhaps more significant is the letter from Elliott

Abrams, then U.S. assistant secretary of state. He describes Chomsky as a "fanatical defender of the PLO who has set new standards for intellectual dishonesty and personal vindictiveness in his writings about the Middle East."[9] Abrams's letter was written as a government official on official State Department stationery. At the time, Abrams was responsible for providing means, clandestine wherever possible, for the slaughter of Nicaraguans. He subsequently pleaded guilty to a federal charge of lying to Congress about supplying the Contra forces.[10] Along with other criminals, he was pardoned by President Bush just before Bush's term expired.

If it is true that propaganda plays an essential role in a society in which the "people are sovereign" so that the real exercise of power by the select few is successfully shielded from the general population, then it may seem that freedom of speech provides no protection. The danger of propaganda, as we know, is that it seeks to control our *minds* by employing dishonest means to persuade us of something. Usually this is done with some subtlety and generally by using distortion or "creating" the domains within which discourse is to occur. Even when the approach is crude, the American media tend to be tolerant, as they were during the years Elliott Abrams lied to the public about Central America. Or to take an older example, Arthur Schlesinger, who when "asked by the *New York Times*, in November 1965, to explain the contradiction between his published account of the [Cuban] Bay of Pigs incident and the story he had given the press at the time of the attack, he simply remarked that he had lied; and a few days later, he went on to compliment the *Times* for also having suppressed information on the planned invasion."[11] Neither his admission nor his compliment to the *Times* apparently caused any embarrassment. He was subsequently named a distinguished professor of the humanities at a major university.

There is no way, other than struggling to discover the truth of the matter, to detect and expose propaganda. That is why the too-ready acceptance of propaganda as true is, from the standpoint at least of a Cartesian-type theory of human nature, an instance of Sartrian bad faith. One has, as Descartes argued, a moral obligation to examine the reasons with which one is presented before judging that they are true and acting on them. There is no shortcut for members of a self-governing society.

Because of the gradual rejection of dualism, beginning already in the seventeenth century, the historical case I have made for free-speech absolutism cannot easily be reconstituted. Historians of philosophy should be cautious in advancing a priori claims, so I will not assert that free-speech absolutism logically requires dualism for its support, even though the historical evidence may suggest that is the case. It is possible to defend freedom of speech by means of a distinction between speech and action that is not based on dualism. Emerson makes a noble effort to do just that. But I assume that because his system lacks something like the category distinction that dualism makes available, not only is he unable to take his speech/action distinction as absolute; his distinction collapses in the end.

Paradoxically, with the demise of behaviorism and the developments in physics, on the one side, and in neural science and linguistics, on the other, the mind and the mental still stand in need of explanation. Although in most of the recent philosophy of mind literature dualism is not an option, minds still bedevil us. Traditional attempts to find ways to treat mental terms and theories as reducible to physical ones have not proven satisfactory. We are still faced with something that, despite the best efforts of the monist philosophers who are the inheritors of the old materialist tradition, has not been adequately explained. The phenomena Descartes's physics could not handle are, as a practical matter, still with us. We are not, however, likely to return to a two-substance doctrine not only because we do not have the clear notion of body required for dualism but also because *substance* is itself not a widely and well-understood philosophical notion.

Accordingly, it is most unlikely that dualism, the original absolutist talk/action distinction, and radical free will can be reassembled even in an updated form. Humpty-Dumpty didn't fall; he was pushed! However, several of the ingredients needed for giving speech the special status, on the side of the mind that it received in Bayle and the Cartesians, and that historically provided the conceptual basis for free-speech absolutism, are possibly still available in a radically revised form. But if they are, I doubt whether they will be utilized for that purpose. As I have shown, the political pressures against reestablishing the absolutist position are real and getting stronger, pressures that are also directed at any account of human nature that might interfere with the articulation of group and community rights. To the extent that happens, freedom of speech itself runs the real risk of being a historical curiosity.

Although I personally take freedom of speech to be the core value of a democracy that aspires to be self-governing, this is primarily a historical study. My efforts should be understood as being largely restricted to explaining where those startling absolutist words in the First Amendment to the U.S. Constitution come from and how and why they have been trivialized and their impact weakened. On occasion, I have also tried to put the absolutist's case, although I realize that such attempts are viewed as quixotic. In any event, I begin with the Philosopher of Rotterdam, because he finds in Cartesian philosophy not only a theory of human nature that serves as a foundation upon which he constructs his theory of religious toleration, and of free speech, but also one that helps to provide a conceptual bulwark against exterior control of the mind—or at least against the many so-called theories that are intended both to persuade us to think of our minds as accessible to control and to convince us to yield our autonomy to our "betters." This doctrine of human nature is important to Bayle because he takes it as grounding the ultimate choice a human makes: that between the *way of examination* and the *way of authority*. It also historically provided a foundation for another sort of ultimate choice: that between freedom of speech and censorship.

NOTES

1. I believe that speech act theories, in part because they are rooted in Austin's doctrines, are the latest version of behaviorism. See the discussion of behaviorism in this context in Noam Chomsky, *Reflections on Language* (New York: Pantheon, 1975), chap. 1; and the Chomsky–Searle discussion in "Rules and Representations: Discussion," *Behavioral and Brain Sciences* 3 (1980): 1–61, where Searle's behaviorism appears.

2. Much of the article is also included in Pierre Bayle, *Pierre Bayle: Historical and Critical Dictionary, Selections*, trans. and ed. Richard H. Popkin (Indianapolis: Hackett, 1991).

3. See Noam Chomsky, "A Review of B. F. Skinner's *Verbal Behavior*," *Language* 35 (1959): 26–58; reprinted in Jerry Fodor and Jerrold Katz, eds., *The Structure of Language: Readings in the Philosophy of Language* (Englewood Cliffs, N.J.: Prentice-Hall, 1964).

4. See Norbert Hornstein and David Lightfoot, eds., *Explanation in Linguistics: The Logical Problem of Language Acquisition* (London: Longman, 1981), chap. 1.

5. Noam Chomsky, "The Responsibility of Intellectuals," reprinted in Chomsky, *American Power and the New Mandarins* (New York: Pantheon, 1969), 325.

6. Noam Chomsky, "Thought Control in the USA: The Case of the Middle East," *Index on Censorship*, July 1986. The correspondence generated runs into 1987.

7. See Sir Isaiah Berlin, *Four Essays on Liberty* (Oxford: University Press, 1969).

8. Paraphrased by Alexander Cockburn in his column, "Beat the Devil," *Nation*, 22 November 1986, 540–541. See also George Glass, "Senseless Censors," *Spectator*, 21 March 1987, 12–14.

9. Quoted by Cockburn, "Beat the Devil."

10. Chomsky's analyses are, however, by no means restricted to Israel. He has discussed propaganda in the context of, for example, coverage of the war in Cambodia and, earlier, in Laos and Vietnam; the (until recently) virtually ignored slaughter by Indonesia of up to 300,000 people in East Timor, a former Portuguese colony that Indonesia, with American and Canadian complicity, brutally annexed rather than permitting it to achieve the independence its people desired; and of course the American barbarism in Central America and the Caribbean. His views on the media are discussed in, for example, his *Intellectuals and the State* (Baarn: Het Wereldvenster, 1978); with Edward S. Herman, *The Political Economy of Human Rights*, 2 vols. (Boston: South End Press, 1979); *Towards a New Cold War: Essays on the Current Crisis and How We Got There* (New York: Pantheon, 1982); *The Fateful Triangle* (Boston: South End Press, 1983); *Pirates and Emperors: International Terrorism in the Real World* (New York: Claremont Research and Publications, 1986); *On Power and Ideology* (Boston: South End Press, 1988); and with Edward S. Herman, *Manufacturing Consent* (New York: Pantheon, 1988). See also Alex Carey, "Reshaping the Truth: Pragmatists and Propagandists in America," *Meanjin* 35 (1976): 370–378, on the role pragmatism has played in constructing a framework for developing the American propaganda machine. Perhaps this should be kept in mind now that Rorty and others, following Quine, are "rehabilitating" pragmatism.

11. Chomsky, "The Responsibility of Intellectuals," 325.

Selected Bibliography

Bayle, Pierre. *Dictionnaire historique et critique*. 4 vols. Rotterdam: Michel Bohm, 1720.

———. *Oeuvres diverses*. 4 vols. Den Haag: Husson et al., 1727–31.

———. *Pierre Bayle: Historical and Critical Dictionary, Selections*, trans. and ed. Richard H. Popkin. Indianapolis: Hackett, 1991.

Baynes, Kenneth; Bohman, James; and McCarthy, Thomas, eds. *After Philosophy: End or Transformation*. Cambridge: MIT Press, 1987.

Black, Hugo. *One Man's Stand for Freedom*, ed. Irving Dilliard. New York: Knopf, 1963.

Blackstock, Nelson. *COINTELPRO: The FBI's Secret War on Political Freedom*. New York: Vintage, 1976.

Bloom, Allan. *The Closing of the American Mind*. New York: Simon & Schuster, 1987.

Bracken, Harry M. *Berkeley*. London: Macmillan, 1974.

———. *Mind and Language: Essays on Descartes and Chomsky*. Dordrecht: Foris, 1984.

———. "Toleration Theories: Bayle vs. Locke." In *The Notion of Tolerance and Human Rights: Essays in Honour of Raymond Klibansky*, ed. Ethel Groffier and Michel Paradis. Ottawa: Carleton University Press, 1991.

Carey, Alex. "Reshaping the Truth: Pragmatists and Propagandists in America." *Meanjin* 35 (1976): 370–378.

Chisholm, Patricia. "The Right to Lie." *Maclean's*, 7 September 1992, 47.

Chomsky, Noam. *Cartesian Linguistics*. New York: Harper & Row, 1966.

———. *Language and Mind*. New York: Harcourt, Brace & World, 1968.

———. *American Power and the New Mandarins*. New York: Pantheon, 1969.

———. *Reflections on Language*. New York: Pantheon, 1975.

———. "The Faurisson Affair: His Right to Say It." *Nation*, 28 February 1981.

———. *Knowledge of Language: Its Nature, Origin, and Use*. New York: Praeger, 1986.

————. *Deterring Democracy*. London: Verso, 1991.

————. Interview with John Pilger on "The Late Show," BBC 2, 25 November 1992.

Connell, Desmond. *The Vision in God: Malebranche's Scholastic Sources*. Louvain: Éditions Nauwelaerts, 1967.

Cook, Fred J. *The FBI Nobody Knows*. New York: Macmillan, 1964.

Cordemoy, Gerard de. *Oeuvres philosophiques*, ed. Pierre Clair and François Girbal. Paris: PUF, 1968.

Crawford, James, ed. *Language Loyalties: A Source Book on the Official English Controversy*. Chicago: University of Chicago Press, 1992.

Crozier, Michel J.; Huntington, Samuel P.; and Watanuki, Joji, eds. *The Crisis of Democracy: Report on the Governability of Democracies to the Trilateral Commission*. New York: NYU Press, 1975.

Davie, George E. *The Democratic Intellect: Scotland and Her Universities in the Nineteenth Century*. 2nd ed. Edinburgh: University Press, 1964.

————. "The Social Significance of the Scottish Philosophy of Common Sense." The Dow Lecture, University of Dundee, 1973.

————. *The Crisis of the Democratic Intellect: The Problem of Generalism and Specialisation in Twentieth-Century Scotland*. Edinburgh: Polygon, 1986.

Descartes, René. *Meditationes* (1641) in *Oeuvres philosophiques*, ed. Ferdinand Alquié. 3 vols. Paris: Garnier, 1963–73.

Dewey, John, and Kallen, Horace M., eds. *The Bertrand Russell Case*. 1941. Reprint. New York: Da Capo Press, 1972.

Doskow, Ambrose, and Jacoby, Sidney B. "Anti-Semitism and the Law in Pre-Nazi Germany." *Contemporary Jewish Record* (1940): 498–509.

D'Souza, Dinesh. *Illiberal Education: The Politics of Race and Sex on Campus*. New York: Free Press, 1991.

Dworkin, Ronald. "The Coming Battles over Free Speech." *New York Review of Books* 39 (11 June 1992): 55.

Editorial. "The Right to Be Wrong." *Globe and Mail* (Toronto), 31 August 1992.

Emerson, Thomas I. *The System of Freedom of Expression*. New York: Vintage, 1971.

————. *Emerson, Haber and Dorsen's Political and Civil Rights in the United States*. ed. Norman Dorsen, Paul Bender, and Burt Neuborne. 4th ed. Boston: Little, Brown, 1976.

Fish, Stanley. "There's No Such Thing as Free Speech and It's a Good Thing Too." *Boston Review*, February 1992, 3–26.

Genovese, Eugene D. "Heresy, Yes—Sensitivity, No." *New Republic*, 15 April 1991, 30.

Hiss, Alger. *In the Court of Public Opinion*. New York: Knopf, 1957.

Hook, Sidney. *Heresy, Yes; Conspiracy, No*. New York: John Day, 1953.

Hornstein, Norbert, and Lightfoot, David, eds. *Explanation in Linguistics: The Logical Problem of Language Acquisition*. London: Longman, 1981.

Hoult, Thomas Ford. *The March to the Right: A Case Study in Political Repression*. Cambridge, Mass.: Schenkman, 1972.

Hyman, Harold M. *To Try Men's Souls*. Berkeley: University of California Press, 1960.

Jurieu, Pierre. *Histoire du Calvinisme*. Rotterdam: Reinier Leers, 1683.

Knetsch, F.R.J. *Pierre Jurieu: Theoloog en Politkus der Refuge.* Kampen: J. H. Kok, 1967.

Labrousse, Elisabeth. *Pierre Bayle.* 2 vols. Den Haag: Nijhoff, 1963–64.

———. *"Une foi, une loi, un roi?" La Révocation de l'édit de Nantes.* Geneva: Labor et Fides, 1985.

La Forge, Louis de. *Traitté de l'esprit de l'homme* (1666). In his *Oeuvres philosophiques,* ed. Pierre Clair. Paris: PUF, 1974.

Lang, Helen S. "Bodies and Angels: The Occupants of Place for Aristotle and Duns Scotus." *Viator* 14 (1983): 245–266.

Langendoen, D. Terence. "Freedom of Speech in America: How Free?" City University of New York, CUNYForum No. 2, 1977.

Lattimore, Owen. *Ordeal by Slander.* New York: Bantam, 1951.

Lehman, David. *Signs of the Times: Deconstruction and the Fall of Paul de Man.* London: André Deutsch, 1991.

Levy, Leonard W. *Emergence of a Free Press.* New York: Oxford, 1985.

Liebling, A. J. *The Press.* 2nd rev. ed. New York: Ballantine, 1975.

Locke, John. *Epistola de Tolerantia: A Letter on Toleration,* ed. with a Preface by Raymond Klibansky, trans., Introduction, and Notes by J. W. Gough. Oxford: Clarendon, 1968.

———. *An Essay Concerning Human Understanding* (1690), ed. Peter H. Nidditch. Oxford: Clarendon, 1975.

Luce, A. A. *The Dialectic of Immaterialism.* London: Hodder and Stoughton, 1963.

McGowan, David F., and Tangri, Ragesh K. "A Libertarian Critique of University Restrictions of Offensive Speech." *California Law Review* 79 (1991): 825–918.

MacKinnon, Catherine A. *Sexual Harassment of Working Women.* New Haven: Yale University Press, 1979.

Meiklejohn, Alexander. *Political Freedom.* New York: Harper & Row, 1960.

Mill, John Stuart. *On Liberty,* ed. Currin V. Shields. Indianapolis: Bobbs-Merrill, 1956.

Monk, Ray. *Ludwig Wittgenstein: The Duty of Genius.* New York: Free Press, 1990.

Navasky, Victor S. *Naming Names.* New York: Viking, 1980.

Niewyk, Donald L. "Jews and the Courts in Weimar Germany." *Jewish Social Studies* 37 (1975): 99–113.

Paganini, Gianni. *Analisi della fede e critica della ragione nella filosofia di Pierre Bayle.* Firenze: La Nuova Italia, 1980.

———. *Scepsi moderna: Interpretazioni dello scetticismo da Charron a Hume.* Cosenza: Busento, 1991.

Pollitt, Katha. "Canon to the Right of Me . . ," *Nation.* 23 September 1991, 328–332.

Popkin, Richard H. *The History of Scepticism from Erasmus to Spinoza.* Rev. ed. Berkeley: University of California Press, 1979.

———. *The High Road to Pyrrhonism,* ed. Richard A. Watson and James E. Force. San Diego: Austin Hill, 1980.

Post, Robert C. "Racist Speech, Democracy, and the First Amendment." *William and Mary Law Review* 32 (1991): 267–327.

Rabban, David M. "The First Amendment in Its Forgotten Years." *Yale Law Journal* 90 (1981): 514–595.

Rawls, John. "The Basic Liberties and Their Priority." *Tanner Lectures on Human Values* 3 (1982): 1–87.

Richler, Mordecai. *Oh Canada! Oh Quebec! Requiem for a Divided Country.* Toronto: Penguin, 1992.

Rorty, Richard. "Wittgenstein, Privileged Access, and Incommunicability." *American Philosophical Quarterly* 7 (1970): 192–205.

———. "Pragmatism and Philosophy." In *After Philosophy: End or Transformation,* ed. Kenneth Baynes, James Bohman, and Thomas McCarthy. Cambridge: MIT Press, 1987.

Russell, Bertrand. *Why I Am Not a Christian and Other Essays on Religion and Related Subjects,* ed. Paul Edwards. New York: Simon & Schuster, 1957.

Scanlon, T. M., Jr. "A Theory of Freedom of Expression." *Philosophy and Public Affairs* 1 (1972): 204–226.

———. "Freedom of Expression and Categories of Expression." *University of Pittsburgh Law Review* 40 (1979): 519–550.

Schlossberg, Herbert. "Pierre Bayle and the Politics of the Huguenot Diaspora." Ph.D. dissertation, University of Minnesota, 1965.

Searle, John. *The Campus War: A Sympathetic Look at the University in Agony.* Harmondsworth: Penguin, 1972.

———. "The Storm over the University." *New York Review of Books,* 6 December 1990, 34.

Skinner, Quentin. "A Reply to My Critics." In *Meaning and Context: Quentin Skinner and His Critics,* ed. James Tully. Cambridge: Polity Press, 1988.

Taylor, Charles. "Overcoming Epistemology." In *After Philosophy: End or Transformation,* ed. Kenneth Baynes, James Bohman, and Thomas McCarthy. Cambridge: MIT Press, 1987.

Tedford, Thomas L. *Freedom of Speech in the United States.* Carbondale: Southern Illinois University Press, 1985.

Tully, James, ed. *Meaning and Context: Quentin Skinner and His Critics.* Cambridge: Polity Press, 1988.

———. "Toleration, Scepticism and Rights: John Locke and Religious Toleration." In *Truth and Tolerance,* ed. E. J. Furcha. Montreal: ARC Supplement #4, Faculty of Religious Studies, McGill University, 1990, 13–27.

Vail, James Franklin. "Vietnam-Era Antiwar Activity and Campus Unrest at Arizona State University, 1965–68." M.A. thesis, Arizona State University, 1989.

Van Alstyne, William W. "Academic Freedom and the First Amendment in the Supreme Court of the United States: An Unhurried Historical Review." *Law and Contemporary Problems* 80 (1990): 79–154.

Weiler, Joseph M., and Elliot, Robin M., eds. *Litigating the Values of a Nation: The Canadian Charter of Rights and Freedoms.* Toronto: Carswell, 1986.

Index

About the Author

HARRY M. BRACKEN is affiliated with the University of Groningen in the Netherlands. He has taught philosophy at the Universities of Iowa, Minnesota, and California (San Diego), and at Arizona State University and McGill University. He is the author of *The Early Reception of Berkeley's Immaterialism, Berkeley,* and *Mind and Language: Essays on Descartes and Chomsky.*